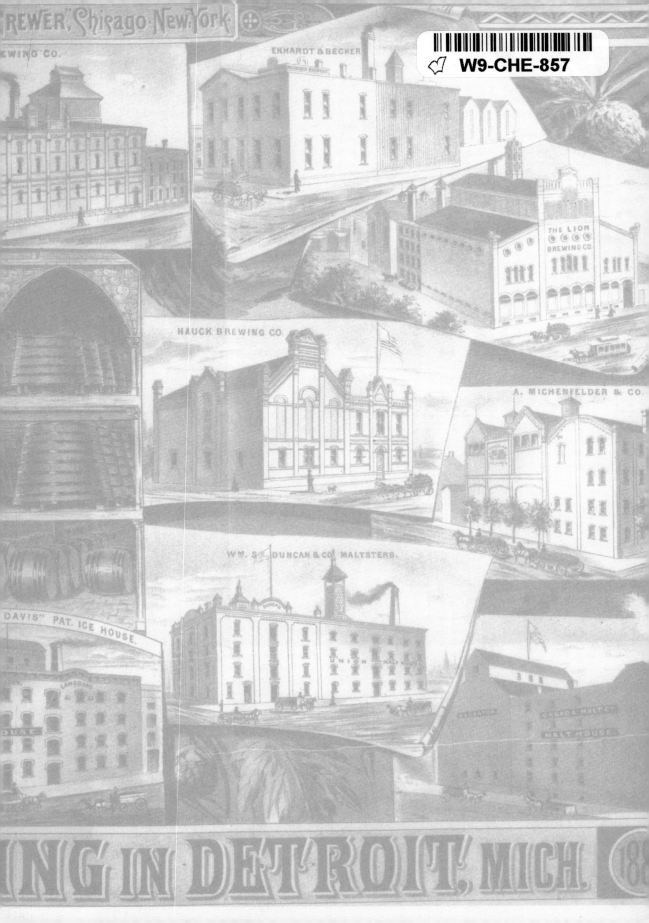

BREWED
IN
DETROIT

PREFACE

The brewing of ale and beer in Detroit started in the 1830s, and large-scale operations ended when the Stroh Brewery closed in 1985. During these 150 years, dozens of breweries opened. Some lasted only a few years, while others prospered for several generations. The style and size of breweries changed greatly during this span. Buildings with fancy brickwork and crenellated rooflines replaced more modest structures of simpler design, and were in turn replaced by tall structures with strong vertical lines.

There was a Stroh Brewery on Gratiot Avenue for 120 years. Time, however, does not stand still. The large urban brewery, erected when horses or the earliest trucks were the mode of delivery, is almost extinct in this country. Since the 1960s, new impressive breweries have been built on very large suburban tracts convenient to major interstates and railroads. They can produce a wide range of beers efficiently and uniformly on a very large scale. But one's romantic streak—not to mention a sense of history—has to be satisfied elsewhere.

It was my privilege to have worked in a great historic brewery during its finest years. I am pleased to share its history with you, as well as that of other Detroit-area breweries.

In recent years, brewing in the Detroit area has resumed as it began—in the home, in pubs where food is served, and on a very small scale. The beers, mostly ales, often imitate those brewed a century ago. If the past is prelude, large breweries will be operating again in the tri-county region in years to come.

A great many persons have helped me by lending photographs or opening their collections, or by contributing anecdotes passed down through a family. This helped greatly to bring the history of local brewing alive. I particularly wish to thank the following: William A. Barber, a grandson of Fred Goettman of Koppitz; Rex Halfpenny, editor of the *Michigan Beer Guide* and source for information on microbreweries and brewpubs; Mary Hunt of the *Ann Arbor Observer;* James Jozwiak, collector of Pfeiffer items; James Kaiser for photographs of his collection; Charles and James Koerber, retired brewmasters and grandsons of John Koerber; collector Don Limpert; Norman O. Lorway (deceased) and Betty Lou Morris, both of Mount Clemens; William Marentette of Windsor; Ernie Oest; Herman K. Rosenbusch, a descendant of Konrad Koppitz and third-generation Stroh brewmaster; Gertrude Rickabus of Mio, a daughter of John Walker; Paul Rothrock, formerly of Pontiac; Paula and Kathy Sarvis, descendants of Philip Kling and enthusiastic collectors of Kling memorabilia and preservers of Kling history; Frank X. Schachner (deceased) of Port Sanilac, who brewed with his father at Mundus; Terry Warrick, the most knowledgeable of the Detroit collectors; and Frank Zynda, a great-grandson of John Zynda and collector of family memorabilia.

Detroit is fortunate to have unique resources in the extensive Burton Historical Collection and the Automotive History Collection, both at the Detroit Public Library. Other institutions that provided important material were the Bentley Library in Ann Arbor, the Oakland County Pioneer and Historical Society, the Public Library of Mount Clemens, the Macomb County Historical Society, the Public Library of Windsor, the Wyandotte Museum, and the Ypsilanti Historical Museum. Student research papers on area businesses prepared for the anthropology department at Wayne State University were made available by Prof. Gordon Grosskop. The research on the early brewing trade journals by Carlson's Brewery Research of Walker, Minnesota, added greatly to individual corporate histories.

Many of the historic photographs were obtained through the courtesy of Bud Manning, a third-generation photographer, and the Manning Historic Photographic Collection. The generous support of the Stroh Brewery Company is gratefully acknowledged, particularly for the color reproductions. About sixty photographs have been included courtesy of the Stroh Brewery Company. The illustration used on the endpapers was published in the journal *Western Brewer,* and reproductions were made available by Anheuser-Busch archivist William Vollmer of St. Louis.

Finally, the patience and support of my wife, Nona, were much appreciated.

The Stroh Extra poster was lithographed by Louis Prang of Boston in 1890. Prang was well known as a skilled printer, and is credited with developing holiday greeting cards.

FROM THE STROH BREWERY COMPANY ARCHIVE

Children were often used in poster art at the turn of the century, when this ten-color lithograph was printed. The Bohemian beer bottle has a special blue ribbon label HIGHEST AWARD and MEDAL/WORLD'S FAIR 1893. FROM THE STROH BREWERY COMPANY ARCHIVE.

One hundred years ago nothing objectionable was seen in a child drinking some Stroh's Brown Stout, a rich malty brew, which was sweet and low in alcohol.

The Stroh mascot, a boy in the habit of a brewer's monk similar to the emblem of Munich, is carrying a giant bottle of Bohemian beer and large radishes. These were peeled, spirally sliced, and salted, and were a traditional German snack with beer.

FROM THE STROH BREWERY COMPANY ARCHIVE.

A dozen dwarves had lined up with tankards for some Stroh's, but half were knocked over or drenched during tapping of the vat in this great calendar lithograph. The theme of dwarves working in a brewery originated in medieval German folklore and was used by brewers in many cities, including Koppitz-Melchers in Detroit.

FROM THE STROH BREWERY COMPANY ARCHIVE.

Stroh's boy mascot is shown in four seasonal scenes depicting Easter, Independence Day, Thanksgiving, and Christmas. The artwork originated before the turn of the century, when bottles were sealed with a cork and wires, like champagne. The two vignettes at the bottom indicate that the oval label with the characteristic "cracked" design was developed by the Cleveland branch, which distributed Detroit-brewed Stroh beer to homes in its own bottles.

FROM THE STROH BREWERY COMPANY ARCHIVE.

This ultra-rare Voigt lithograph shows several scenes in which men are enjoying Rheingold beer, as well as illustrations of the brewery and a bottle. The label on the bottle has the frequently seen pre-Prohibition text declaring the product free of drugs or poisons and mentions the Food Laws, e.g., the Pure Food and Drug Act of 1906.   COLLECTION OF TERRY WARRICK.

Top to bottom: Koppitz-Melchers invoked German folklore by having dwarves boil a brew of Pale Select in an open kettle outdoors. The Detroit Brewing Company knew exactly how the man of the house should be served his beer. The most dramatic design of any tray was commissioned by Kling, showing only the essentials against a deep blue background. Patriarch John Zynda lent his personal authority and corpulent presence to his Crystal Pale lager. Conrad Pfeiffer chose University of Michigan colors for his Famous brand in an early "pieplate" shape. The siren Lorelei is playing the harp as the sun sets behind the hills along the Rhein in the most attractive Detroit tray, commissioned for Voigt's Rheingold beer. The small Union Brewing Company used its patriotic trade mark with good graphics for the Gilt Edge brand.

    From the collections of James Kaiser, The Stroh Brewery Company, and Frank Zynda.

Two small colorful folders carried endorsements on the inside. Above: The lady of the house opening the door to a home delivery before a party dates from the 1890s. The Stroh boy mascot in a monk's habit and leather apron seemed to have no trouble carrying a wooden case filled with two dozen heavy bottles. Below: The waiter ready to serve Stroh's in a fine restaurant was issued a decade later. The design of both folders permitted the front and back to be viewed as separate scenes.   FROM THE STROH BREWERY COMPANY ARCHIVE.

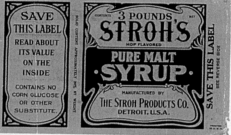

Top row: A folder promoting Stroh's malt syrup for food and beverage use, without mentioning beer. **Second row:** a blotter listing Stroh's Prohibition products and a label from a malt syrup can. **Third row:** An advertisement for ginger ale by The Stroh Products Company and a pint carton for Alaska brand ice cream. **Bottom:** Artwork for an outdoor ice cream poster. Only the ice cream was kept after the repeal of Prohibition.

FROM THE STROH BREWERY COMPANY ARCHIVE.

Top row: Pfeiffer's 1939 fiftieth anniversary reverse-on-glass (R-O-G) sign, and an E&B ale tin-on-cardboard (T-O-C). **Second row:** Tivoli Pilsner was packaged in a clear bottle when this 1930s sign was produced; the Goebel T-O-C sign has the German eagle emblem and the cypress cask slogan of pre–World War II years. **Third row:** A 1930s Schmidt R-O-G saloon sign and a large metal outdoor sign for Stroh's malt syrup, 1920s. **Bottom row:** A fine Auto City R-O-G; one of the first outdoor signs used by Stroh shows the bottle still with the Stroh Products Company label; and a rare black Stroh T-O-C.

Labels used by the Stroh Brewery Company. The rectangular label dates from the 1890s.

Labels used by Detroit breweries other than Stroh.

Labels used by breweries in surrounding cities.

PART

I

BACKGROUND

1

Beer:
Culture and Craft

Beer, that pleasant and sociable beverage, has been part of human life for at least as long as history has been recorded. Beer was already important when the oldest Babylonian tablets were written about 4000 B.C. While not the clear, carbonated, and chilled beverage we expect today, it was beer—brewed from grain and fermented with yeast, and no doubt expected to make life a little more enjoyable.

Early History

The brewing of beer grew with the growing of grain, notably barley. It has even been suggested that civilization began when the desire for beer caused people to exchange their nomadic existence for life in agricultural settlements. It must have been one of the great accidental discoveries of all time to find that sprouted grain would yield alcohol after being mixed with water, heated, and left to ferment. Yeast for fermentation is widely distributed in nature. Difficult as it is to turn dry grain into foamy beer, people along the Nile and the rivers of the Near East, in China, Russia, Scandinavia, Africa, and South America, found ways to brew it with local grains.

Baking or brewing require that grain, whether wheat, barley, rye, rice, corn, or millet, must first be ground, moistened, and mixed. And in the case of beer, the grain has to be sprouted first, or at least chewed, as was done in some primitive societies. The Egyptians baked a barley

Barley plant, in *Cruyd-Boek* (Book of Plants) by Rembertus Dodonaeus, Leiden, 1601.
COURTESY GEORGE VAN GHELUWE.

bread from sprouted barley. They mixed it with water, warmed it, and permitted it to ferment. The fermented mash was then strained to yield a beverage. The usual way to obtain yeast for both brewing and baking was to add dough or beer from the previous batch. The brewing of beer developed into a major industry in Egypt.

Some of the ancient beer types have survived on a small scale in the Russian kvass and a beverage brewed in parts of the Sudan. In South Africa, the traditional Bantu beer is still brewed from millet for native consumers, but now on a large scale in modern facilities. European beers may have been developed independently by several societies, but there is strong evidence for a Scandinavian origin. Our word *beer* came from the Norse *pior,* later *bior,* via the German *Bier.* The Romans preferred wine but knew about beer as well. The Latin *cervesia* survived in the early medieval French *cervoise,* a beer brewed by women in the home.

There was a time, roughly from A.D. 800 to 1000, when women both baked bread and brewed beer. Gradually, a class of itinerant brewers developed, men who went from household to household to help with the brewing. This was the origin of the Brewers Guild. It did not take long for the ruling powers to discover that granting licenses to brew beer was a source of income. With time, the preparation of beer moved from the homestead to a licensed brewhouse, a monastery, or an estate. As the power of the guilds grew, women were largely excluded from making beer, and by 1700, many brewers considered their presence in breweries an undesirable influence on the sensitive and mysterious process of fermentation.

Brewing became a craft to be learned through a lengthy apprenticeship, and, after Pasteur, it was increasingly a science. Simple thermometers and hydrometers were already used in the seventeenth century to measure the temperature of the mashing process and the strength of the resulting wort.

BEER IN NORTH AMERICA

Beer arrived in North America with the earliest settlers. *Mayflower* records show that the supply of beer was factored into deciding how much time could be spent looking for sites to stay ashore. Prominent Virginia planters like George Washington and Thomas Jefferson had breweries on their estates, for ale was a part of civilized life.

Nor were the northern states of the new republic without breweries. A wealthy New England brewer who had a bright daughter but could not find a good college for her decided to finance a women's school himself; it is too bad that Vassar's Ale is no longer available.

Later immigrants from northern Europe, notably Germans but also Slavs, brought their beer types and brewing skills with them.

Hop plant, in *Cruyd-Boek* (Book of Plants) by Rembertus Dodonaeus, Leiden, 1601.
COURTESY GEORGE VAN GHELUWE.

Today, after a century of biochemistry and instrumentation, it might seem that not much remains to be learned about the brewing process. But modern consumption habits and long-distance distribution have generated difficult problems, particularly in the areas of clarity and flavor stability. The early brewers did not have to worry about beer becoming hazy at low temperatures or about the formation of stale flavors. Beer was a robust beverage with a strong bitterness from hops. If it needed to be shipped far, as for instance the India Pale Ale which traveled by sail for months, it was hopped enough to retain a characteristic hop flavor.

With all the modern equipment, large-scale operation, sophisticated quality techniques, and business trappings, the brewing process remains essentially unchanged. Competition and marketing have brought new variations such as light, dry, or ice beer. But barley is still malted, wort is still boiled with hops, and yeast is still used to form alcohol. It is also possible to learn from the past. Many of the formulas of a century ago are being revived as brewers offer a wider flavor spectrum. This is evident from the recent increase in the number of microbreweries and brewpubs. And because the process is complicated, relying on experience and judgment, brewing has remained a craft as well as a science.

HOW BEER IS BREWED

FROM BARLEY TO MALT

Malting and brewing have been separate industries since before Prohibition, but at one time many breweries had their own malthouses, and workers were busy there during the cold months when beer demand was lowest. Men with malt shovels are often seen in group photos of

Tightly compressed hops were shipped in 200-pound bales, wrapped in a coarsely woven fabric which gave "hop sack" its name. The hops were stored cold to preserve their aroma, and they needed to be broken up and weighed into containers for addition to the boiling kettles. Automated addition of pelletized hops has largely replaced manual handling of compressed hops.

FROM THE STROH BREWERY COMPANY ARCHIVE.

brewery workers before Prohibition. But quite early—certainly by the 1860s—some brewers either preferred to deal with grain or saw better opportunities in supplying brewers, and independent maltsters became an allied industry.

Malting is essentially the sprouting of barley and its subsequent drying. Barley is soaked in cold water (steeped) for one and a half to two days and then germinated until small rootlets are formed, which takes from four to six days. At this stage, enzymes in the seedling are activated and begin to digest the starch stored in each barley kernel as nutrient for the young seedling.

The sprouting of steeped barley was originally done in shallow layers on a hard surface, and the germinating grain was turned by hand with flat wooden shovels. Such floor malting was slowly replaced by mechanical means beginning in the 1870s. One method used a large rotating drum, which revolved slowly to prevent the roots from matting. Large fans moved air past water sprays, and the moist air was blown through the grain during germination. Drums built for batches of 300 to 750 bushels (a barley bushel is equivalent to 48 pounds) became quite popular in this country.

As the batch size for malting increased, drums proved to be too expensive. An early competing method of germinating was the "compartment," consisting of a perforated metal floor and concrete side walls 6 to 8 feet high. The steeped barley was pumped into these compartments to a depth of about 4 to 5 feet. Moist cooled air was blown through the grain, and a turning machine crawled on rails along the top of the walls, extending rotating corkscrew blades into the grain.

The sprouted barley, called green malt, was then dried or kilned. This preserved most of the enzymes for the brewing process, formed malt flavors, and permitted safe storage of the malted grain. The use of higher kilning temperatures produced caramel flavors and yielded beers of a darker color.

CEREAL ADJUNCTS

Most beer brewed in the Americas uses both malt and unmalted cereal, called adjunct. In this country, the predominant adjunct grain is corn. Brewers also used rice, but by the end of World War II, a reliable supply became a problem, and almost all brewers shifted to the use of corn. The traditional method of using corn was in the form of ground and sifted granules called grits, which are mostly starch as the germ has been removed. In recent decades, corn processors have provided the adjunct in the more convenient form of syrup.

Microbrewers, who elect to follow the German Reinheitsgebot—the Purity Law of 1516, which limits brewing ingredients to water, malt, hops, and yeast—at times criticize the use of adjunct because it is less expensive than malted barley. But adjuncts are very suitable for North American barleys, which have a much higher protein content than those

The traditional open fermenting vessels, made out of cypress, were replaced by closed horizontal tanks in the 1930s, and in recent decades by very tall vertical stainless steel tanks with conical bottoms. These wooden fermenters were still used by Stroh well into the 1970s.

grown in Europe, and adjuncts provide greater stability for clarity and flavor. This is of little consequence to a brewpub or a brewer with a local clientele but an important factor for major shipping brewers.

FROM MALT TO BEER

The actual brewing process takes place in two distinct phases, going first from warm to hot and then from cool to cold. The brewhouse operations yield a fermentable liquid called wort. This takes most of a working day. After being boiled and cooled, the wort is fermented into beer, which takes approximately a week. The young beer is chilled, aged, filtered, and carbonated. It is then ready to be packaged into kegs, bottles, or cans.

Phase 1: From Malt to Wort

To begin a brew, malt is ground and mixed with warm water, a step called doughing in—a reminder of the common history of baking

Only the ends, or "heads," of glass-lined tanks were visible in a 1960s addition to the Stroh stock building block on Gratiot Avenue.   From The Stroh Brewery Company Archive.

and brewing. The resulting mash is heated according to a closely controlled cycle. This is called mashing. In medieval times, the mash had to be stirred by hand, and a special long-handled stirrer or rake evolved for this purpose. The mash rake became part of the design of the brewers' crest and has been incorporated into current master brewer emblems.

During mashing, the enzymes in the ground malt kernels change the starch to sugars. The amount of fermentable sugars and therefore the alcohol content can be varied according to the temperature to which the mash is raised and how long it is held there. Then the mash is pumped to a very large round vessel called the lauter tun, where the sweet wort is separated from the grain residue. This process is called lautering. Lauter tuns have a false slotted bottom a short distance above the actual bottom of the vessel. Grain particles stay above the slots as the wort flows through to the brewkettle. The shallow grain bed is kept from packing by rakes that rotate slowly about the center. As the liquid is withdrawn, hot water is sprayed over the grain bed to replace wort held within the grain mash, an operation called sparging.

Cooper shop, about 1890. The man the in foreground is shaping a top with a draw knife while sitting on a *Schnitzelbank* (carving bench).   FROM THE STROH BREWERY COMPANY ARCHIVE.

Historic mashing equipment consisted of a combination mash and lauter tun. Because the grain bed was deep, it took four to six hours for the wort to run off. Modern lauter tuns are 30 or more feet in diameter, and the entire operation—including filling, first wort runoff, sparging, and emptying—is done within two hours.

In brewhouses built before 1940, pipes from different sections of the lauter tun bottom led the wort to a central valve and collecting station called the grant. These were of copper with fancy brass endplates, and the worker in charge of the valves, or "taps," had a prestigious job. A clear and timely lautering required attention and experience. Modern lauter vessels are of stainless steel, and the multiple drawoff taps have been replaced by a single large pipe. As the operation is now controlled from a central station, prestige has shifted to the control room.

The boiling of wort has not changed in principle. It still takes place in large vessels called kettles, now usually 600 to 1000 barrels in size and fabricated from stainless steel (one beer barrel is equal to 31 gallons, the historic unit still very much in use). Copper was the traditional material, which could be shaped easily and did not rust, and was used until World War II. Stroh's 250-barrel fire-kettles had to be of copper because heat-conducting ability was critical. Brewkettles represent the very heart of a brewery, and owners of breweries built before Prohibition often had their kettle floors extensively decorated.

Hops are added during wort boiling, and their bitter compounds are extracted, in very much the way tea is prepared from leaves that are then strained out. A vine with inconspicuous tiny flowers hidden in small leaves that form a green cone, hops contain a strong aromatic fragrance and impart a clean, bitter flavor to an otherwise bland beverage. Cultivated varieties have been grown commercially for a very long time, notably in the English county of Kent, the Hallertau region in Bavaria, and the Saaz region in Bohemia. Hops were cultivated early in New York State and, since the turn of the century, in the U.S. Northwest, particularly Washington's Yakima Valley. Hop vines with cones and barley sheaves have long been a common decoration on brewery trademarks and labels.

The traditional method of preserving hops after picking is to dry them and press the dried cones into bales. Cool storage is important, as the flavor deteriorates with time and warm temperature. In recent decades, such "leaf" hops have largely been replaced by hop pellets, which can be stored more conveniently and with less flavor loss. Most brewers consider the details of their hop addition—number of times, varieties, and amounts—to be confidential.

The hot wort is held for an hour to permit particles to settle, forming the so-called trub. The historic way to accomplish this was in a very large shallow pan called coolship, a translation from the German term *Kuehlschiff.* The last process step in the brewhouse is the cooling of the hot wort, from about 190 to 200 degrees Fahrenheit to 50 to 60 degrees. The technology of modern heat exchangers is far more efficient than the primitive open coolers used early in this century, where hot wort ran over the outside of horizontal pipes filled with flowing cold water or ammonia solution.

Phase 2: From Wort to Beer

Cooled wort is a solution of sugars and a very good medium for all kinds of bacteria. It is therefore important to add yeast without delay, a process called pitching. Yeasts are large single-cell organisms, and those of the species *Saccharomyces* have the ability to feed on a variety of sugars, producing alcohol and carbon dioxide and small amounts of aromatic byproducts. During baking, the alcohol is driven off by heat, and the carbon dioxide gas raises the dough. It was Louis Pasteur who taught brewers to examine yeast under the microscope and monitor its condition to avoid contamination with bacteria. Modern breweries have developed this into a special field of microbiology.

The historic fermenting vessel was made out of wood slats and had a flat bottom, not unlike a giant old-fashioned wash bucket. Wooden fermenters of 200 to 600 barrels in size were a common new installation when breweries opened after Prohibition. A Detroit slogan from the 1940s and early 1950s was "Right from the cypress casks of Goebel,"

Bottling operations in the 1930s at Detroit's Schmidt brewery. Clean bottles are emerging from the "soaker" in center background. The bottles are then filled on a rotating filler at left, capped by an eight-place crowner in the center foreground, and loaded by hand on the pasteurizer at right. The same operations are still performed in modern bottling but at vastly greater scale and speed.   FROM THE MANNING BROTHERS HISTORIC PHOTOGRAPHIC COLLECTION.

and Stroh maintained some beautiful cedar fermenters well into the 1970s. Most fermenters are closed tanks, now made of stainless steel. Open fermenters also find use. The yeast available in historic and medieval times floated to the top at the end of fermentation, where it was skimmed off. This top-fermenting type is still used for traditional ale. Another characteristic of ale production is a warmer fermentation temperature, which results in a faster process and more fermentation byproducts, producing a more aromatic flavor. In the 1820s, Danish brewers isolated yeast strains that settled out, and in the 1880s, Danish brewing scientists developed techniques for propagating pure yeast cultures. These bottom-fermenting strains permitted a simpler way to remove beer from yeast. Their use spread slowly throughout Europe, and then to the United States, until now most domestic beer is bottom-fermented.

In the post–World War II era, brewing plants became very large, turning out batches every few hours around the clock, instead of just a few times a day. Investment could be reduced by fermenting two or three batches in one large tank. This led to the design of tall, round, vertical vessels with conical bottoms. Rows of such cylindro-conical tanks are now a standard sight at many modern breweries throughout the world.

After fermentation is completed, the yeast still in suspension is removed. The "green" beer is chilled to near freezing and placed in a storage tank in the stock cellar or in a large vertical outdoor tank. There have not been real cellars for a very long time, but the historic term is still used for what are now tall buildings, also called stock houses. At one time, beer was held for months in huge barrels underground. It is now known that very cold temperature is much better for a clean beer flavor than a long storage time, and rarely is beer held for more than four weeks.

At the end of the storage period, the aged beer receives a final filtration and usually a treatment with an adsorbent to prevent a haze from forming when the final product is chilled in a home refrigerator. This is called chill-proofing and, of course, was not necessary a century ago when beer was not expected to be brilliantly clear. The beer is carbonated and is ready for packaging. The historic way of providing additional carbon dioxide was to add some fermenting wort, a process called kraeusening. While this has the romance from the era of wooden kegs, the vast majority of brewers opt for injection equipment capable of superior control. The carbonated beer is then pumped through a meter to measure volume on which excise tax will be paid, and into a tank in the "government cellar." After a final quality check, the beer is now ready to be packaged into bottles or cans, or to be racked into barrels.

THE BREWMASTER

Given the complexity of mashing, fermenting, and finishing, it is no surprise that the person in charge of brewing the beer had to serve a long apprenticeship and work his way up to this responsible position. By the 1870s, the German tradition of apprenticing boys in their early teens to learn the trade, the German language, and the camaraderie of the brewery was in full swing. The work was hard, the hours were long, the foremen could shout and even cuff, but the young apprentices took pride in their product, and drinking beer was part of life in a brewery and part of being a working man.

Brewery owners were VIPs, and the brewmaster was king of the hill inside the plant. The Michigan Brewers' and Maltsters' Association held its first convention in Detroit in 1887, and then the men and their wives boarded the Star Island ship for an excursion to the Star Island House. The following year, the brewmasters organized nationally as the Master Brewers Association of America and formed districts in major

Excursion of the Michigan Brewers' and Maltsters' Association to the Star Island House after its first convention, July 15, 1887. Corpulent E. W. Voigt is sitting in the second row center.

<small>From The Stroh Brewery Company Archive.</small>

cities. The founding members were German to the core, and in the bonhomie of the occasion, they sent a telegram to the Kaiser wishing him the best on his birthday. In 1897, the ninth annual convention of this group was held in Detroit. Local brewmasters could show off their breweries, discuss problems, eat heartily, and sample beers day and night.

Needless to say, the war with Germany was a most unwelcome development. Before the United States entered the war on the Allied side, brewers from a German background were sympathetic to their ancestral homeland. They fully supported the war effort after 1917, but prohibitionists used the "German connection" to place beer in an unpatriotic light and to push the use of grain for food instead of beer. This led to peacetime Prohibition (1918–1933), and, for all but a few, the years of training and tradition had to be shelved.

The pattern of monthly meetings, seasonal dances, summer outings, and festive Christmas banquets was resumed in the 1930s, always with the traditional hospitality and good food. Annual conventions again included technical sessions, brewery visits, and formal functions. Detroit

Acceptance to full membership in 1897 in the United States Brewmaster Society was recognized with an ornate diploma in German. Illustrations include angels toasting beer over the brewer's German motto (freely translated: "Hops and Malt—God Uphold!"), the emblem of the brewers guild, a Pasteur flask, a thermometer, and a hydrometer. Peter Clemens was brewmaster of the East Side Brewery and later in Pontiac.

breweries hosted conventions in 1951 and 1968, when Stroh brewmasters Herman A. Rosenbusch and his son Herman K., respectively, were presidents of the Master Brewers Association. To be a master brewer of a large brewery was a respected and honored position.

As breweries became larger, the function of the brewmaster within the firm changed to that of a technical director, with a staff of one or more assistants and a chemist. The industry had supported consulting firms with laboratories and courses in brewing technology since the 1880s. After repeal of Prohibition, the larger breweries also started their own labs. The art of brewing received a sounder scientific foundation, and beer became a more uniform product as analytical methods and specifications were developed.

Even a technical director with brewing background was no longer sufficient for the very large breweries of the post–World War II era. It

Detroit area master brewers pose after a luncheon hosted by the Rickel Malting Company, about 1950. *Seated, from left:* Frank Bauer, Goebel; Oscar Teeg, Altes; unidentified; Armin Rickel; unidentified; John Merkt, Goebel; Herman Zerweck, Goebel; Max Walsdorf, Schmidt; unidentified. *Standing:* Rickel staff member; unidentified; Robert Pflugfelder, Goebel; unidentified; John Geyer, Goebel; James Koerber, Friars Ale; Herman A. Rosenbusch, Stroh; unidentified; Conrad Freimann, Stroh; unidentified; Herman K. Rosenbusch, Stroh; unidentified; John Newell, E&B; unidentified; Mel Maegerlein, Detroit; John Rickel; John F. Longe, Rickel.

FROM THE COLLECTION OF JAMES KOERBER.

now required managerial expertise to coordinate brewing, packaging, engineering, laboratory, and industrial relations with product demand and corporate objectives. A century ago, a brewmaster could supervise a small brewery himself; now he is likely to supervise a staff of assistants and foremen and report to a plant general manager.

2

DETROIT
BREWING HISTORY

W hen Alexis de Tocqueville visited Detroit in 1830–31 in his
search for the American frontier, he found a village that
seemed to grow before his eyes. Ships with settlers were
arriving steadily. De Tocqueville found the frontier thirty miles to the
northwest, in the woods of the Pontiac settlement. After spending a mis-
erable night being bitten by mosquitoes, he returned to Detroit, tired but
satisfied that he finally had reached the very edge of settling in the
wilderness.

Brewing in Detroit seems to have started about the time of de Tocqueville's visit. He may even have refreshed himself with ale by Detroit's
first brewer. There is a short paragraph in an 1829 issue of the Cleveland
Herald about a shipment of Detroit beer having arrived, and in 1831, the
Farmer's Brewery of Owen & Scott advertised in the weekly Detroit
newspaper "that they constantly have on hand Porter, Beer and Table Ale
in barrels, half barrels and kegs," and offered to pay "the highest cash
price for Barley." When the first city directory appeared in 1837, it listed
two breweries: the City Brewery at Congress and First, and the brewery
of Emerson Davis & Aaron Moore on Woodbridge.

These brewers appeared at the beginning of the first of six periods
of brewery development in the Midwest: (1) the early British ale brewers were supplanted by (2) German lager brewers, which gave rise to (3)
brewing dynasties; 1917 marked the start of (4) the Prohibition period in
Michigan, until (5) the competition following its repeal in 1933; the final
development period was (6) the postwar shakeout. The pattern was the

same from Cleveland to Kansas City, from St. Paul to St. Louis. With minor variations and different dates, it held true for most of the country.

THE EARLY ALE BREWERS

During the 1830s and 1840s, the settlers were mostly of English, Irish, or Scottish origin. The early Detroit brewers had Anglo-Saxon names and brewed primarily a variety of ales, with some porter and stout. Ale had practical advantages in addition to being a familiar product. Ales required little aging. In fact, they were better when fresh, and their darker color and stronger flavor could hide any number of minor defects in taste. Ale brewing was thus very suitable to primitive conditions in frontier towns. This advantage would be rediscovered by microbrewers and brewpubs in the 1980s and 1990s.

In an 1861 issue of the *Detroit Daily Advertiser,* an early Detroit newspaper, there appeared a review of the brewing history of Detroit. It looked back to 1836, when there was just a single brewery. This was located on River Road, now Atwater or Fort Street. It was almost cer-

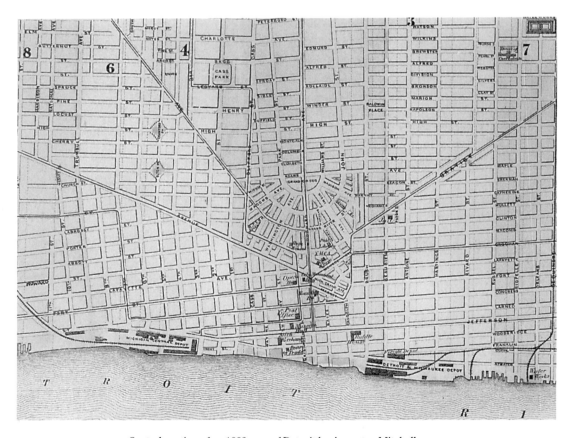

Central portion of an 1882 map of Detroit by Augustus Mitchell.
FROM THE STROH BREWERY COMPANY ARCHIVE.

tainly the Davis & Moore brewery listed as being on Woodbridge in the 1837 directory, probably at the corner of Atwater and Woodbridge.

By 1861, three decades later, there were "upwards of 40" breweries active in Detroit. The seven largest were mentioned by name in the *Advertiser.* Among these were John Carew's Detroit Brewery on First, W. C. Duncan's Central Brewery on Woodbridge opposite the Michigan Central Railroad, George Carne's on Atwater near the waterworks, and the Western Brewery of Rufus Brown on Abbott and Seventh. Probably not more than ten brewers were large enough to own a regular brewery building. Most of the others were either home brewers whose market encompassed a few blocks, or home saloon-brewery combinations. In those cases, the saloon keeper lived above the tavern and brewed his beer in the back rooms or in a shed in the yard. Many saloon keepers were tempted to brew their own at least for a few years. In 1861, Bernhard Stroh still lived and brewed on Catherine Street; his decade-old brewery was still too small to mention in the *Advertiser.*

The Detroit city directories of the 1840s and 1850s provided some of the names of other early local brewers: Elisha Avery, who was brewing when the second directory appeared in 1845; John Dash (1850); Richard Hawley (1845), John Mason (1852), and Patrick Tregent (1853). Hawley, Duncan, Mason, and Tregent all bought space in the 1853–54 directory to promote their ales. Duncan had his Steam Ale, while Mason advertised "Amber and Brown Ale." Brewing already had become a competitive industry. Most brewers operated on a very small scale and did not bother to advertise in the directory. The market was measured in blocks, and for everybody it was a draft business.

THE GERMAN COMPETITION

The second phase of brewery development began with the arrival of a wave of German immigrants after the political upheaval and repression of 1848 following the third French revolution. It was during this period that Bernhard Stroh arrived. Some German immigrants had settled in Michigan prior to 1848, but none had become a brewer in Detroit.

The beer brewed by the earliest German immigrants was not ale. As early as 1842, the Schaefer brothers in New York brewed a new German type called *lager,* from the German word for "storage" or "aging." Lager is pale beer with a pronounced hop flavor using bottom-fermenting yeast, made famous by the municipal brewery in Pilsen, Bohemia, hence the name *pilsenser* or *pilsner.* The original German top-fermented beer type has been revived to a modest degree in modern Germany. There it is called *Alt,* meaning "old," in the sense of historic.

Lager beer spread from Bohemia throughout the German states into northern France, Belgium, Holland, and up into Scandinavia. In the 1870s, it was sold under the name *Bohemian.* Several breweries, none in Detroit, named their Bohemian type after the town of Budweis, a competitor of Pilsen for good Bohemian beer. Some of the German brewers

Typical ale advertisements in the 1846 Detroit city directory.

also produced the darker Bavarian type and named brands after the Bavarian cities of Munich (München), Würzburg, or Ulm.

During the 1850s and 1860s, the English and German brewers coexisted. Breweries were still being founded by men with Anglo-Saxon names like Beal & Richardson (1864), Bowker & Blackmur (1862), or McRoy (1863), and there were also brewers such as Bonning-hausen (1864), Ruoff (1864), Stegmeyer (1864), Strehlinger (1865), or Voelkel (1860). However, there were more new German than English brewers arriving. By 1860, about half of the local breweries were operated by Germans. And by this time the German brewers were offering the pale bitter beer associated with the German brewing tradition.

Thus, by the 1870s, breweries were classified as either ale or lager brewers. A few specialized in the German wheat beer, called *Weiss* or "white," as wheat beer was much paler in color. The beer drinker was offered a whole range of regional types—pale Bohemian, dark Bavarian, amber Tivoli, and seasonal black-brown bock made with roasted malt—in addition to ale, brown stout, and strong porter.

THE RISE OF THE BEER BARONS

By 1880, ale brewers were in a small minority. The market had changed so completely with immigration that none of the relatively large ale brewers of the 1860s survived. Of twenty-eight brewers listed in the 1862 directory, only four were still there twenty years later, and many new names had appeared. Duncan's Central Brewery on Woodbridge, once the largest brewer in town and a dealer in malt and hops, was reduced to operating a malthouse only.

Several large German breweries and brewing dynasties had emerged by the mid-1880s. For the first time, the effect of economies of scale appeared, as batch size increased to several hundred barrels. The period from 1890 to about 1910 is considered the golden age for the industry. This was particularly true for the larger brewers. In an era free of income taxes, brewers could not only live the good life but also afford to beautify both the exterior and interior of their buildings.

In addition to the Stroh family, the Klings, Martzes, and Darmstaetters were the most prominent brewing clans, founding businesses that lasted three generations. Philip Kling started a brewery with Michael Martz and another partner. Michael Darmstaetter opened his small brewery about the time that Bernhard Stroh did, and his sons went on to operate independent breweries. His son Jacob's line also lasted three generations. August Ekhardt and Herman Becker took over a small brewery in 1883 and, through mergers, developed the operation into a sizable plant.

Not all brewers were Germans. Detroit had a significant Slavic community, and four breweries were owned by families of Polish ancestry, two of them of medium size. John Zynda did not start until 1885, but by 1890 his White Eagle brewery flew the flag of Polish kings. A large man who loved food, beer, and companionship—a picnic on a secluded beach was evidently his idea of combining life's essential pleasures—he fit in well with his German competitor-colleagues. His extended family permitted him to staff the brewery with brothers, sons, and nephews. The other large Polish brewery was Auto City, founded in 1910 by the Chronowski brothers.

The breweries operated by these families were quite different from the plants of the 1860s. Not only were they much larger four- or five-story brick buildings with fancy detailing, but they incorporated significant technical improvements as well. Mechanical refrigeration had replaced river ice as the cooling medium in all but the smallest plants. It also was a time of scientific improvement of the entire operation. Pasteur had published his studies on beer in 1876, and brewmasters had learned techniques to keep their yeast healthy. The brewery laboratory appeared in the late 1880s. While the methods were primitive by today's standards, brewmasters paid great attention to process temperatures and product quality. There were consulting laboratories, technical journals, and conferences.

The economic muscle of the large breweries presented a two-fold threat to the small ones. Large size meant that one could afford to go after the home trade. Even in the 1890s, many ads prompted buyers to call the brewery's telephone number to have cases delivered to their homes. Smaller brewers often found bottling too expensive and only supplied taverns with kegs.

Large size also meant that a brewery could acquire saloons, like the "tied houses" in England. With more saloons getting financing from their brewery owners, the small brewers had fewer outlets, and independent saloons were left with poorer backing and often poorer beer. This resulted in a movement to cooperatively owned breweries. Names including the words "Mutual" or "Consumers" indicate this type of joint ownership. Twenty or thirty independent saloons would pool their resources. The funds would be used either to finance the building of a new and larger plant such as the Union Brewing Company in 1888 or, more often, to

Pabst Bohemian Beer label for the Detroit Branch.
FROM THE STROH BREWERY COMPANY ARCHIVE.

acquire an existing plant whose beer was liked. The former owner-brewer at times assumed the salaried role of president of the cooperative.

The 1890s also saw the rise of the first major shipping brewers. Branches were established in other cities by renting depots and hiring staff. Kegs or bottles packed in straw were shipped to these branches for local distribution. Often the local agency put keg beer in bottles embossed with the branch name. Pabst in Milwaukee established a depot in Detroit in 1883, and Stroh had a substantial branch in Cleveland as well as branches throughout Michigan.

THE GREAT BRITISH BEER TRUST

In the late 1880s and early 1890s, there was a tremendous amount of interest generated by efforts of British investors to acquire control of U.S. breweries. British capital was readily available for investment abroad. American breweries were seen as a good investment because of the rapidly growing population and the opportunity to curtail competition and increase profits.

Adolphus Busch of St. Louis understood this very well. After being approached by an emissary from Baron Rothschild for the second time, he was asked by a reporter about the purpose of the proposed consolidation. "Why, to make money, of course," he replied. "Syndicates are usually formed for that purpose, are they not? The idea is by consolidation to decrease the expense of manufacture, enlarge the field to be supplied, and thereby to increase profits." Like most major brewers, however, Adolphus Busch chose to remain independent.

The British syndicate hit Detroit in the spring of 1889. Local newspapers covered efforts to corner the brewing market between March and May with a barrage of articles based on rumors, reports, speculation, interviews, and, finally, some facts. On March 6, an unidentified major Detroit brewer confirmed the existence of the syndicate, the London Investment Company. The source may well have been Col. August Goebel, who had been quoted as being strongly in favor of British capital.

Agents for James Grant, a New York broker, canvassed all breweries whose value reportedly had to exceed 100,000 pounds. A *Detroit Free Press* reporter called on the trade to learn who would be included. William Ratigan of the Bavarian Brewing Company and Fred Dittmer were evasive. A staff member of August Goebel & Company claimed "densest ignorance." On the other hand, Charles Endriss had submitted what he considered a fair value for his plant, Edward Ruoff had also provided figures, and E. W. Voigt declared that he was "ready to sell at any time." Jacob Mann, the Detroit Brewing Company, Philip Kling, and William Moloney made themselves unavailable. Thomas McGrath had not been approached. Only Julius Stroh, having achieved top rank in the city, was highly negative about an approach by a pool. He considered it "utterly impossible by reason of the relative value, good and indifferent, of beers now on the market."

On April 8, the *Free Press* reported a rumor heard in New York that four breweries had been sold. Knowing that Grant had obtained options on the Goebel, Michenfelder, Mann, and Endriss breweries, a reporter was able to interview one of the four. The source stated that Grant had options on the four properties for a total of $450,000, and that he hoped to sell these breweries in the East at a substantial profit. The interviewed brewer said he was willing to sell because "we are in constant dread of a Republican legislature giving us Prohibition."

With the options terminating April 30, speculation about the fate of the four breweries was building. Finally, on Monday, May 13, 1889, it was learned that sale of the four breweries had indeed been concluded on the previous Saturday. The purchasers were evenly divided between Detroit and British interests. The local investors were William B. Moran, Ralph Phelps, Jr., and Joseph B. Moore. The net purchase price was $475,000 for the four breweries. The investors were able to bypass Grant's scheme by negotiating directly with the brewery owners until the options had expired. A condition of the sale was that the retiring brewers not enter the brewing business within a radius of fifty miles of Detroit for ten years. August Goebel was to be charged with the overall management.

Rumors about options for other breweries circulated during the next week, but the only other transaction concerned E. W. Voigt. He later sold his brewery to the syndicate but kept the mortgage, and was able to repurchase the brewery later at a bankruptcy sale.

Goebel was a clear winner. He closed the Endriss and Michenfelder operations within a couple of years and focused on the Goebel brand. In 1897, he was able to erect a very large plant at the corner of Rivard and Maple, across the street from where the Mann home and brewery stood. At that time, the new Goebel brewery rivaled the Stroh brewhouse on the other side of Gratiot Avenue. The Goebel plant would last until 1964.

PROHIBITION

Prohibition, the fourth phase of brewing history, hit Detroit's brewers on May 1, 1917, almost three years before national Prohibition took effect on January 16, 1920. A combination of the Anti-Saloon League, industry leaders like Henry Ford who wanted sober and hard-working employees, and church officials, particularly the charismatic Reverend Billy Sunday, convinced Michigan voters that alcohol was evil and abstinence the solution to social problems.

Detroit brewers were particularly hard hit because Canada ended its partial prohibition in 1927. With decent beer only a motorboat ride away, the few breweries still open had a tough time. American, Schmidt, Stroh, and Tivoli replaced "Brewing" in their corporate names with "Products" and remained open with skeleton staffs.

After Canada outlawed beer and enforcement became stricter, the brewers who were still active turned to promoting the sale of canned hopped malt syrup for home brewing. Domestic brewing technology being on the primitive side, the quality of these beers was often unpredictable. The need for reliable products was met by organized gangs, as in other cities. In Detroit, the Purple Gang, headed by the Bernstein family, controlled beer distribution for several years.

Several cases of illegal brewing operation are known, but there were certainly others. One was the Auto City Brewing Company in Hamtramck, which the Chronowski family owned but leased to a relative when brewing became illegal. Prohibition could not have been a popular law in the Polish community. When the brewery was eventually raided, the Chronowskis were in the clear, but their front man had to serve time in Leavenworth. And when the owners of the Union Malt Products Company applied for a brewer's license in 1933, they were refused initially because its operators had been well-known Prohibition law violators.

Prohibition proved to be no threat to John Zynda, who, as former water commissioner, had political connections and was needed to provide libation for social events such as weddings and funerals in his part of town. Zynda also had the right logistical setup. An underground tunnel led from the bottling shop to the garage across the street. The tunnel was narrow and too low for someone to walk upright through it, but it was equipped with rollers, and cases or half-barrels could be sent across. According to

The "For Sale" sign and broken window add to the forlorn look of a brewery closed during Prohibition.

oral history from Zynda family descendants, an empty car was used as a decoy. Federal agents would follow the empty car; meanwhile, the loaded vehicle, which was parked half a block away at Grocholski's hardware store, would get a signal and could get away for a beer run.

The economic effects of Prohibition were devastating for local brewers. At a time when money was being made in almost any industry, brewers could not turn their fixed assets into income. Smaller brewers who were still in business in 1918 closed their plants forever. Several of the larger brewers rented out space to light manufacturing for some income. The period was to last fifteen years in Michigan, long enough for some families to lose key members or sell out for what little they could get.

RETURN OF BEER AND COMPETITION

The next phase started in a party mood. The euphoria over the repeal of the 18th Amendment and the pent-up demand was such that even cool heads overestimated prospects for starting up new brewing ventures. Within a year, a dozen breweries were competing for Detroit's thirst, others were upgrading old plants, and several more were on the drafting board.

The established names had no difficulty raising capital and thus had the resources to upgrade their plants, hire competent staff, and promote their brands. Of the major brewing families, only Kling and Voigt failed to restart operations in Detroit. The Kling and Breitmeyer families purchased and expanded the former Daley brewery in Flint, hoping to supply Detroit from there. The effort failed largely because Kling was now seen as an out-of-town beer, and distribution was difficult. The son of E. W. Voigt took a minority stake in a venture bearing the Voigt name, which turned into a race between construction and selling stock to pay for it. Unfortunately, investments dried up when the plant was only half finished, and the venture had to be abandoned.

Two well-known brewing scions, Ben Koppitz of Koppitz-Melchers and Armin Darmstaetter of the Mundus Brewing Company, started energetically but lost control when dissident stockholders ousted them. The Koppitz brewery on Atwater had been built from scratch after repeal, the only completely new major brewery in the area. Financial irregularities in acquiring the property were alleged. The reason for Darmstaetter's ouster was never told, other than to say that ownership disagreement existed. In both cases, the loss of family spirit contributed to business failure.

A couple of smaller breweries were also built from scratch. The Regal Brewing Company opened in 1935 with Canadian backing not far from the Pfeiffer plant. It was designed to last by noted architects Harley-Ellington, but brewing ceased after four years. The smaller Von Brewing Company on East Forest Avenue was closed after three years; the building is long gone.

The Ray Drug Company at 13247 Harper stocked seven Detroit beers in 1935: Goebel, Stroh's, Pfeiffer's, Schmidt's, Mundus, Regal, and Auto City.

FROM THE MANNING BROTHERS HISTORIC PHOTOGRAPHIC COLLECTION.

Some brewery ventures never got beyond incorporating a name and trying to sell stock. The Ziegler-Hutter Breweries filed articles of incorporation in 1934, but that was as far as it went. The following year, there was some publicity about turning the Stinson Airplane factory in Northville into an ale brewery. In 1935, J. K. Hofer, who had brewed in the Windsor area during Prohibition, wanted to build a brewery designed by Fred Martin.

The Fort Dearborn Brewing Company had probably the strongest backers of any uncompleted venture in Hiram Walker and Edwin R. Stroh, a grandson of the Stroh founder. Albert Kahn was retained to prepare architectural plans. Later the Walker family withdrew, and the remaining investors were either astute enough to see that demand was being met by the major existing brewers, or too slow in erecting a brewery to be seriously hurt.

The smaller brewers that reopened after Prohibition were soon outspent in the marketplace, even in a period of relatively benign competition compared with what was to come after World War II. The recession in 1937 curtailed income and beer consumption. Of twenty breweries that were active in 1934, only twelve were still in business four years later. Stroh, Pfeiffer, Goebel, and Tivoli dominated the local market just before the war, with Schmidt, E&B, and Detroit rounding out the roster of larger brewers.

The war years provided a hiatus from competition but brought other worries. With raw materials rationed to prewar levels, manpower and equipment difficult to obtain, and a strong demand, brewers had headaches they never expected. The temptation was to provide the product by whatever means available. The easiest route was to brew thinner beer. Customers were lining up at the store with cases of empties and were glad to have any brand, but memories of good beer were not erased.

POSTWAR SHAKEOUT

Before the 1970s, economically desirable plant size doubled about every ten to fifteen years in this century, from a quarter of a million barrels (of 31 gallons each) to 8 million. While half a million barrels was a very satisfactory plant size before Prohibition, business success required 2 million by 1950 and 4 million by 1965. The size of a brewery has leveled off at between 6 million and 12 million barrels, because transportation costs favor multiplant firms.

The postwar era was marked by a fight for survival when television advertising changed a largely regional business into a single national market. It took a period of adjustment and experimentation, but twenty years after the end of the war, even brewers that had been ranked in the top ten nationally had become casualties or were on the way out. Ballantine in New Jersey, Falstaff in St. Louis, and Lucky Lager in San Francisco all were large breweries that either closed or declined and were absorbed. This was not clear at first, because the early failures were smaller and weaker local and regional brewers, which had been at risk in any period.

Detroit was no exception to this trend. When settlement of a long brewery worker strike in 1958 permitted out-of-state shippers to enter the local market in force, all remaining Detroit brewers suffered, and existing weaknesses were aggravated. The failures of Koppitz in 1947 and Zynda the following year would have occurred within a few years in any case. The Detroit Brewing Company locked its doors in 1948. E&B, formerly Ekhardt & Becker, stayed in competition until 1952.

In the meantime, the Big Three—Stroh, Goebel, and Pfeiffer—fought for dominance. Stroh at first had a rough time. A conservative attitude, which had carried it through a century of brewing and preserved its good name during the war years, now put its management at odds with rapid changes in marketing. Such newfangled ideas as beer in cans and a lighter flavor were considered suspect at first. Both Goebel and Pfeiffer surged ahead in the early 1950s.

Customers lined up at Ray's Retail Beer Store, 10448 West Chicago Avenue, in 1944 when beer needed no advertising. FROM THE STROH BREWERY COMPANY ARCHIVE.

Goebel's business was so good that breweries were acquired in Muskegon and on the West Coast. The new Koppitz brewery also became a Goebel branch plant. In retrospect, it appears the technical staff for such an extensive production scheme may have been limited. Changes in the brewmaster's office were said to have caused changes in the beer also. For whatever reasons, sales declined in the late 1950s, which in turn inspired a variety of advertising campaigns. This loss in continuity further damaged the franchise. Goebel ceased operations in 1964 and all assets were purchased by Stroh.

Pfeiffer also grew tremendously during the late 1940s and early 1950s under the leadership of Alfred Epstein. The Kling brewery in Flint was purchased to supply draft beer, thus freeing production capacity at the Mack Avenue plant. It is difficult to pinpoint the reasons for the decline of the Pfeiffer brand within a decade. The long strike in 1958 came at the worst possible time for Pfeiffer, which had to service a debt incurred when it purchased the Schmidt brewery in St. Paul in 1954.

With the Pfeiffer brand under pressure in Michigan, management decided to become a regional brewer under the name Associated Brewing Company. It acquired the E&B brands; Drewerys in South Bend, Indiana, and Chicago; Sterling in Evansville, Indiana; and Piel with plants in New York and Massachusetts. While Associated's headquarters were in Detroit and the operation was profitable, the large home brewery was closed in 1966. The brands were sold to other brewers six years later, after it became evident that the plants and the brands were no longer competitive.

Tivoli, which had made so much headway after Prohibition, failed to grow after the war, when it became the Altes Brewing Company. Altes still was a good name with a loyal if local following. The firm was purchased by the National Brewing Company of Baltimore in 1960 in order to expand the market for its National Bohemian brand. While Altes drinkers in Detroit were in a minority, the entire city seemed to be united in wanting Altes much more than "National Boh." The campaign was a failure; in 1965, National was itself acquired by the G. Heileman Brewing Company of LaCrosse, Wisconsin. Altes continued to be brewed on Hurlbut Street until 1971. Then Heileman closed the plant and shifted production to its brewery in Frankenmuth.

During the last stages of this phase, Anheuser-Busch and Miller increasingly dominated the national market. Stroh beer sales doubled in the 1970s to 6 million barrels, and the sales territory was expanded to more than twenty states. By the decade's end, however, sales had leveled off. With its major competitors six and eight times larger and expanding, a "grow or go" scenario was inevitable. Stroh decided to grow and bought Schaefer of New York City in 1981 with its modern brewery near Allentown, Pennsylvania. A daring leveraged merger with the much larger Schlitz catapulted Stroh to third place nationally the following year. The Parke-Davis site at the Detroit River became available when the manufacture of pharmaceuticals was relocated, and the thirty-acre site was purchased for a corporate headquarters and development.

With Schlitz came many assets, including three very large and modern plants. Flat beer sales, the need to repay borrowing that had financed the Schlitz buyout, and the extra capacity in the acquired plants doomed the less efficient Detroit brewery. It became obvious that the historic Detroit brewery was a luxury the company could no longer afford. The proud history of brewing Stroh beer in Detroit ended in 1985.

History is often cyclical. During the 1980s, there was a rediscovery of more flavorful beer types. After a century or more of increasingly larger plant sizes, it again became possible to enter the industry with a very small microbrewery or brewpub. This movement started in Western and West Coast states, reaching Michigan in 1983 and Detroit in 1992. If the past is indeed prelude, there will be more specialty brewers, followed by competition and growth of the survivors. The new brewers will learn again that the heavier the body and the stronger the flavor, the less beer will be consumed, and that the larger market segments will have to be served. Most important is the fact that history repeating itself means that the Detroit area again has its local breweries.

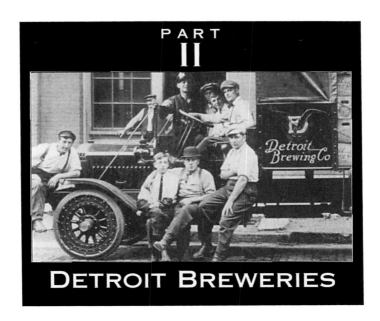

DETROIT BREWERIES

3

THE STROH STORY

Bernhard Stroh was no different from other German brewers who emigrated in the middle of the last century and started small breweries in American cities. Like several other Detroit brewing families, the second-generation Strohs operated a large plant and prospered, and the third generation had to survive the sixteen lean years of Michigan and national Prohibition. Unlike its local competitors, however, Stroh survived the postwar competition and grew to become the eighth-largest U.S. brewery. In the early 1980s, Stroh "bet the farm" and became a major national brewer by acquiring large competitors with plants in several states. The Stroh story thus follows the growth of sales and competition from a small local area in the 1860s, to a multistate region in the 1960s, and finally to the fiercely competitive national and international beer market of the 1990s.

BERNHARD STROH, 1850–1875
57 CATHERINE, 1850–1864
331 GRATIOT, 1864–1875
LION BREWING COMPANY, 1875–1885
B. STROH BREWERY COMPANY, 1885–1902
275 EAST ELIZABETH (OFFICE)
THE STROH BREWERY COMPANY, 1902–1920
253–257 EAST ELIZABETH
THE STROH PRODUCTS COMPANY, 1920–1933
909 EAST ELIZABETH (RENUMBERED)
THE STROH BREWERY COMPANY, 1933–1978
1 STROH DRIVE (RENAMED), 1978–1985
100 RIVER PLACE (NEW CORPORATE OFFICES), SINCE 1985

Founder Bernhard Stroh, 1821–1882.
FROM THE STROH BREWERY COMPANY ARCHIVE.

ANCESTORS IN GERMANY

In the triangle formed by the confluence of the Mosel and the Rhine rivers, north of the coalfields of the Saar, is a region of wooded hills, fields, and small towns, part of the Palatinate, or Pfalz in German. There is no autobahn or metropolis; Idar-Oberstein and Bad Kreuznach are the largest cities. It is here in the town of Kirn on the small Nahe River, in the shadow of the Kyrburg castle, that Strohs have lived since at least the middle of the sixteenth century. The family's original name was Strohschneider, meaning "straw cutter."

The four earliest documented generations of Strohs were shoemakers. In 1600, Culmann Stroh of the second generation (about 1550–1614) was given the status of burgher, a free resident who could own real estate. In the next generation, Johann Stroh (about 1590–1670), became mayor during the harshest period recorded in Central Europe: the Thirty Year War (1618–1648). Less than half of the town's prewar population of 1,050 could be recorded at the end of the conflict.

The town of Kirn and Johann Stroh recovered after payments of war debts to Sweden. Stroh was joined at his craft by his two sons, both also master shoemakers. They started selling shoes in surrounding villages. This brought Johann into legal conflict with the Shoemaker Guild. In order not to let any one master become more prosperous than his guild brothers, the guild restricted a master to one journeyman and one apprentice. Johann eventually won his case against the guild in the Lord's Court. None of his four grandsons took up the shoemaker's trade. They became bakers instead.

A grandson of one of the four bakers, Johann Peter (1746–1810), branched out to keep an inn, where home-baked bread, home-cooked meals, and home-brewed beer were served. Town records showed him to be living in Kirn with his family in a house with adjoining brewhouse beginning in 1775. The brewing tradition of the Strohs had begun.

Johann Peter Stroh had three sons and a daughter; two sons became bakers who also sold beer, and the second son, Georg Friedrich (1784–1853), inherited the brewhouse. Georg Friedrich's oldest son, Carl Peter, became innkeeper and brewer; Georg's daughter Anna Catharina would see her daughter marry into the locally prominent Andres brewing family.

Georg's youngest son was Johann Bernhard (1821–1882). He learned the brewing trade, but his father's brewhouse could support only one family. As the younger son, he was entitled to a financial stake but not the property. Bernhard, along with a group of local families, emigrated to Brazil, but that country did not appeal to him. He returned home, where he was required to serve in the army. The turmoil after the political unrest in 1848 caused a widespread emigration of Germans, mostly to the United States. Bernhard's prospects after military service at age twenty-seven were not good. Again, he said his farewell and left to seek his future and fortune in "Amerika."

BEGINNINGS IN AMERICA

Bernhard Stroh was one of the major brewers of Michigan in 1880 when he was interviewed by a trade journal published in Chicago. It was a short article, but it was the only time Stroh mentioned his beginnings in America for publication: "He came to the United States in 1848, and worked in Harrisburg, Pa., for two years at $12 a month. His capital on arriving in America was about $150 all told." Tax records in Harrisburg confirmed that he worked at the Barnitz Brewery there for a modest sum. That job permitted him to learn English and familiarize himself with U.S. brewing customs.

He settled in Detroit in 1850, probably in late summer or early fall. According to oral history, he had been on his way to Chicago via ship, but he liked Detroit and stayed ashore. The area just east of downtown between Jefferson and Gratiot avenues was settled largely by recent German immigrants. Stroh found a place to live on Catherine Street, near Hastings, just east of what is now Greektown, and he set up a small brewing operation. As early as the 1890s, 1850 was claimed as the brewery's founding year in ads. It must be assumed that Stroh's sons knew this from their father. In those years, there were few, if any, formalities required to start a brewery, so there is no date of founding as there would be later when federal licenses were required. Stroh arrived too late to be included in the 1850 city directory; he is listed in the next one, which appeared in 1852.

Bernhard Stroh left no journal or diary, so we do not know when or how he met Eleanora Hauser. They were married on March 28, 1853, which indicates that he felt confident about the prospects of his little brewery. The first child, Bernhard Jr., was born the following year; Julius arrived two years later, followed by Nellie, George, Emil, and Rose.

The small brewery prospered from the beginning in the growing German community. According to comments passed down in the family, Bernhard Stroh first delivered kegs in a wheelbarrow until his trade grew large enough to warrant a wagon and a team of horses. This small operation grew into a large frame brewery with a daily capacity of 80 barrels. After a decade of brewing on Catherine Street, he knew that even larger quarters would be required. He and Eleanora purchased property

The older children of Bernhard and Eleanora Stroh posed for a formal sitting with young Frederick, born in 1871 to Bernhard's second wife, Clothilde, probably shortly after their father's death in 1882. From left: Julius, George, Nellie, Emil, Bernhard Jr., and Rose.

FROM THE STROH BREWERY COMPANY ARCHIVE.

along Gratiot Avenue between Hastings and Rivard, within sight of the Catherine Street address. There he had the foundation and the basement storage cellars built for a large future brewery. The cellars were used to store the beer from the Catherine Street brewery.

In 1867, after fourteen years of marriage, Eleanora died. She lies buried beside her husband in Elmwood Cemetery, next to her parents and a child who died in infancy.

THE LION BREWING COMPANY

The year of Eleanora's death was also the year that the new brewery was finished after several years of construction. A reporter described it prior to installation of equipment. Designed by Joseph Gottle of Cincinnati in the Italianate style with Roman arched windows favored by brewery architects at that time, it was among the largest breweries in Detroit and the largest single brewery building for decades, with a daily capacity of 200 barrels. It had a frontage along Gratiot of 125 feet and a depth of 140 feet, and the cooling tower on the fifth floor rose 125 feet above the street. Two cellars were below street level, the top one 8 feet high for fresh beer and the lower stock cellar where beer was aged in 20- and 40-barrel casks. The newspaper reporter was glad to leave the freezing cold and dim lighting of the lower cellar.

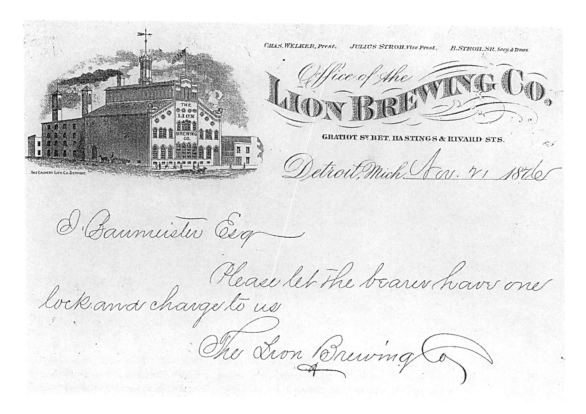

A note written in 1876 shows the earliest known view of the Lion brewery.
FROM THE STROH BREWERY COMPANY ARCHIVE.

The engine room was on the first floor, as was the "working room," presumably for brewhouse vessels. The second and third stories were designated for malting, and the fourth and fifth floors were for barley and malt storage, respectively. The sixth floor consisted of a 70-by-40-foot dome, where a 60-by-30-foot coolship, a giant shallow pan, would hold the freshly boiled and hopped wort. The sides of the dome consisted of hinged slats to permit cooling by air circulation. Many brewmasters preferred the shallow, open coolship even after the development of more efficient and sanitary cooling systems. The coolship provided good aeration of the wort for yeast growth and time for trub, the small particles formed during boiling, to settle in a low-tech, inexpensive manner.

On top of the cooling dome, a 40-foot high tower had no other purpose than to permit a visitor to be impressed by the view 165 feet from the ground, and to let the flag fly as high as possible. Of far more important use was an ice cellar at the rear of the main building, 53 by 14 feet and 40 feet high, with direct access to the upper beer cellar. A malt kiln was planned as part of the complex.

Two 12-foot-long crouched wooden lions guarded the roof, facing Gratiot Avenue in both directions. The lions were carved by the well-known Detroit sculptor Julius Melchers, whose wooden Indians are now

Management and workers of the Lion brewery, about 1885. Julius Stroh (sitting behind barrel) is flanked by his brother Bernard and Charles Welker, brother of the founder's second wife and a partner. To the right is brewmaster Konrad Koppitz. The crew included five teamsters, holding whips or a saddle, and four maltsters with wooden grain shovels. The round object on a long handle at right is a yeast skimmer used in ale fermentation.

FROM THE STATE ARCHIVES OF MICHIGAN.

held in high regard. Stroh had seen lions as part of the municipal crest of Kirn since childhood. "The Lion Brewing Company" became the name in December 1875, replacing "Brewery of B. Stroh" on the building. The Lion Brewery was incorporated for ten years. The two oldest sons joined their father in working at the brewery when Bernhard Jr. was twenty-one and Julius was nineteen.

THE SONS TAKE OVER

Stroh remained a widower for three years, then married Clothilde Welcker, a woman from an affluent German family. The Strohs lived in a large home next to the brewery with their son Frederick and seemed a happy couple for the twelve years of their marriage.

The brewery in the meantime experienced a quality problem which resulted in a sales decline, financial losses, and the need to borrow. A new brewmaster, Konrad Koppitz, was hired in 1878. The new product was well received, and sales exceeded 30,000 barrels in 1880. Two years later, on June 23, at the age of sixty-one, Bernhard Stroh died, leaving the majority of the brewery's stock to his widow. Bernhard Jr. became president, and Julius was secretary and treasurer. The plant was owned by the Connecticut Mutual Life Insurance Company under foreclosure at the time of Bernhard's death.

The B. Stroh brewery with the Stroh family residence, mid-1880s. The reason for the bunting and flag is not known.   FROM THE STROH BREWERY COMPANY ARCHIVE.

Julius Stroh married Hettie Melchers, daughter of sculptor Julius Melchers, in June 1883. The couple later resided in a large Italianate mansion fronting East Jefferson and the Detroit River across from Van Dyke, where their two daughters and three sons were raised.

The happy mood of a summer wedding was broken at an October meeting of stockholders, which also included Charles Welcker, Clothilde's brother. The problem was the distribution of surplus income. While Bernhard Jr. and Julius wanted to use these funds to repurchase the brewery from the insurance company, Clothilde, voting for the majority, chose distribution of dividends. It was the beginning of a serious rift between the widow and the two sons. Within a month, the sons personally repurchased the plant from Connecticut Mutual.

In December 1885, ten years after incorporation, the Lion Brewing Company expired by limitation of its charter. In the meantime, Bernhard Jr. and Julius had bought out other family stockholders, and they incorporated the B. Stroh Brewing Company, with Julius Melchers as vice president. Clothilde felt cheated by the transfer from Lion to B. Stroh. She was no longer a partner, and her son Frederick would have no stake. This resulted in a lawsuit in 1891. The judgment went against the widow, who received a settlement to assuage feelings, but no equity.

The B. Stroh Brewing Company continued to grow. Beer was shipped east as far as New England. Stroh became available throughout

The brewing crew poses with brewmaster Otto Rosenbusch (behind sign at right) and foremen (with bowlers) about 1895. Several men are holding swiveled oil lamps, useful in the dark cellars where beer was aged. FROM THE STROH BREWERY COMPANY ARCHIVE.

Michigan and around Lake Erie. In 1897, the brewery opened a branch in Cleveland on Bond Street, in what is now the downtown area. Beer was shipped from Detroit in barrels and either distributed to taverns or transferred to bottles and delivered locally. The Cleveland branch moved to larger quarters on 40th Street in 1899.

Such branches were forerunners of distributorships, but they were owned by the parent brewery, and the local manager was an employee. A large brewery such as Schlitz had perhaps a dozen branches, but regional Stroh had only the one in Cleveland. Stroh bottles embossed with "Cleveland Branch" are an interesting reminder of this operation. The brewery was also represented by agents in many towns and cities. These were store owners who handled liquor and tobacco and were local suppliers for Stroh beer.

The Cleveland Branch also designed an oval label for local use with a crackled glass pattern in the background. Called *craclé* by continental designers, it was a fairly common pattern on lampshades and other decorated items at the time. The Cleveland oval label impressed the management in Detroit, and it was not long before it replaced the large rectangular label there.

Brewmaster Otto Rosenbusch, the first of three generations of Rosenbusch brewmasters, in an 1897 convention brochure.

From The Stroh Brewery Company Archive.

The B. Stroh firm was the largest Detroit brewery at the turn of the century, when an annual capacity of 300,000 barrels was claimed. While all brewers inflated their capacities—it was probably the maximum daily production multiplied by 360 and hardly realistic, given the seasonal nature of beer consumption— none of the other brewers was in the same league. The brewery of Bernhard Jr. and Julius was prospering. The main Bohemian brand was well accepted. A low-alcohol Brown Stout, an amber Tivoli, and XXX Pale rounded out the product line. For a mascot, the brewery settled on a boy in a monk's habit with a brewer's leather apron. This was a popular figure at the turn of the century, when children were widely used in advertising. A boy monk was the symbol of Munich, and was often reproduced in a brewing context.

In 1890, Stroh's head brewer, Konrad Koppitz, teamed up with Hettie Melchers's younger brother Arthur, who was Stroh's cashier, and some partners to form the Koppitz-Melchers Brewing Company. A brewery was built about ten blocks east on Gratiot. Stroh found a reliable replacement in Otto Rosenbusch. Otto had come to the United States in 1883 at age seventeen. He attended the Schwarz Brewers Academy in New York, graduating in 1887, and was a Stroh brewmaster for thirty-five years. The Rosenbusch name would be associated with Stroh's for three generations and nearly a century.

JULIUS STROH
AND THE STROH BREWERY COMPANY

The first decade of the new century was one of continued growth. This called for an increase in the brewery's capacity from 300,000 to 500,000 barrels. In January 1902, the company was reincorporated as the Stroh Brewery Company by Bernhard Jr., Julius, and three employees, including brewmaster Otto Rosenbusch. The new entity then acquired all the assets of the old company. Julius assumed the presidency in 1908, when Bernhard Jr. was forced to retire because of ill health.

Patrons, bartender, and bystanders strike a relaxed and cheerful pose in front of Tonie & Cur-tis's Pleasure Club tavern, location unknown.   FROM THE STROH BREWERY COMPANY ARCHIVE.

With beer sales increasing, Julius foresaw that the brewery's capac-ity was limited. In 1911, he sent Rosenbusch, now superintendent, to Europe to get a feel for the newest trends and the best brewing equip-ment. Some of Otto's letters to Julius have survived. They tell in great detail whom and what he saw, how he was received, and how the Euro-pean beers seemed to him. He met other U.S. brewers on his tour and learned what sort of equipment was considered reliable. In the Munici-pal Brewery of Pilsen in Bohemia (brewers of Urquell), he observed the use of small copper kettles which were heated by direct fire as in the olden days. This method had been discarded by all but tiny breweries in favor of steam, but Urquell was brewed on a large scale and produced one of the finest beers on the continent.

With Julius Stroh and Otto Rosenbusch convinced that direct fire produced a superior beer, Stroh ordered a new brewhouse to be built in 1912 housing copper kettles designed to be heated by direct fire. The Ger-man firm of Topf & Sons in Erfurt was retained to manufacture six kettles and to provide the foundation design of refractory brick. The choice of fuel was between gas and oil. Gas was tried, but an explosion caused such a mess that no gas was permitted for the life of the brewery.

The new brewhouse was an imposing structure of eight stories, with a central atrium to permit heat to rise and escape through louvered win-

Two Rapid trucks are being loaded at the brewery in 1910, when drivers still sat on the right side. The building with sliding doors behind the trucks held the stables; the door above provided access to the hayloft.

FROM THE NATIONAL AUTOMOTIVE HISTORY COLLECTION, DETROIT PUBLIC LIBRARY.

dows in the roof. Such "heatstacks" were a feature common to large brewhouses built around the turn of the century. The brewhall on the ground floor was decorated with tile from the local Pewabic Pottery, and the ceiling sections had painted borders of hop vines. With the soft gleam of kettle domes, shiny brass fittings, and tiles in earth tones of moss green and ochre, the Stroh brewhall was a showplace, both technically and aesthetically. The building had space for two complete production lines of six kettles each, but only one line was installed since that was all that was needed.

The tall brewhouse evolved from the limited space available to an inner-city brewery. A central location was required for beer distribution by horse and wagon. Gravity flow was used as much as possible. Malt mills, malt hopper scale, and hot water tanks were typically placed at the top floors, with mash tubs and corn or rice grits cookers next, then lauter tubs and grants and finally kettles. In the new brewhouse, the boiled wort was pumped to the top floor, where the hop strainer was located, then to hot wort tanks for settling. Below these tanks was a large hall with closed and open heat exchangers to cool the hot wort to fermenting temperature. The brewhouse was large enough for malt and rice storage silos and refrigerated rooms for hop storage.

The gravity brewhouse fell out of favor after World War II, along with urban factories in other industries. Breweries built after the 1960s were so large that a suburban or exurban location with access to highways and

The first row of firebrewing kettles in the new eight-story brewhouse was photographed in 1918, shortly before Prohibition curtailed operations severely. Pewabic tile in earth tones, copper kettles, and brass fittings gave the brewing hall a beauty rarely seen in industrial settings. Additional rows of kettles were installed in 1936, and again as part of a major expansion in 1956 (see photo page 79). FROM THE STROH BREWERY COMPANY ARCHIVE.

rail was required. Modern brewhouses are still the tallest buildings in a brewery complex, but usually no more than four stories in height.

PROHIBITION

The new brewhouse opened in 1914, with time running out for the alcohol industry. The Prohibition movement had been active for decades and had been gaining strength for years, but it took the war to turn it into law. In spite of a determined effort by the major brewers to promote home consumption—"Call Main 316 for a case delivered to your home" was the Stroh text—and special bottled brands for home and hotel, breweries were tarred as businesses that permitted unsavory social conditions. Prohibition started as strictly a wartime measure supposedly to

The new brewhouse on Elizabeth Street is flanked by a new office building at left and an engine building at right. This photo was taken in 1927 when the word "beer" was prohibited, and Stroh's dealcoholized beer was called "lager." ➤
FROM THE MANNING BROTHERS HISTORIC PHOTOGRAPHIC COLLECTION.

conserve grain. Some leeway was given between the passing of the 18th Amendment and its effective date in 1920, but in Detroit the law took effect in 1917.

This left Stroh with a big brewhouse investment and a doomed market. Julius bought out the interests of his brother's heirs, as it must have seemed difficult enough to support one family. He really had little option but to remain open and try to maintain a foothold. Already in the fall of 1917, Otto Rosenbusch started brewing near beer at 0.5 percent alcohol, which was sold under the name "Temperance Beer." The technology for evaporating alcohol in those years was less sophisticated than now, and it was hard to avoid a slightly dull flavor. "Serve cold" was a common instruction on near beer labels to help mask the treatment; the Stroh text on a red band of Prohibition cereal beverages was "Serve Ice Cold."

The corporate name became the Stroh Products Company with the onset of Prohibition. The brewery launched many products to generate income: near beer under the Bohemian Lager label, Birch beer, Caledonia Dry ginger ale ("like champagne"), Old Gold Ginger Ale, Mattay

Stroh's display at a 1927 food show featured malt syrup cans and paper and metal signs.
FROM THE MANNING BROTHERS HISTORIC PHOTOGRAPHIC COLLECTION.

Orange soda was one of the beverages marketed during Prohibition, along with ginger ales, birch beer, club soda, and the almost alcohol-free lager.

Cola, and orange soda. The best seller was probably hopped syrup for home brewers. This was sold "for baking, confectionary or beverage use," but everyone knew it was for brewing. Stroh's malt syrup was sold in large tin cans, about the size of a 2-pound coffee can. Labels contained coupons that could be saved for prizes; the syrup market was quite competitive. There was local competition from the Kaiser-Schmidt Brewery nearby, and Pabst became a large shipper of its Premier brand syrup. Given the proximity of Canadian lager or ale and the pride taken in brewing an alcoholic beer at home, near beer found few takers.

Otto Rosenbusch retired in 1929, and his son Herman A. Rosenbusch took over; his tenure as brewmaster and superintendent lasted fifty years. Otto Rosenbusch still had brewing in his blood and became associated with the Riverside Brewing Company east of Walkerville, Ontario. In 1933, he returned to Detroit, sold his Stroh stock to Julius Stroh, and received a probably welcome offer for his expertise from Goebel to resume operations, which he accepted. He died in 1935 at age sixty-nine.

Another product which Stroh tried during Prohibition was ice cream. It may seem an unlikely item for a brewery to market, but it was tried in a few cities. Stroh purchased equipment, found space in the oldest brewery building standing (it dated from the 1870s) and started selling Alaska brand ice cream.

The first decade of Prohibition was a period of postwar boom and prosperity. Julius Stroh was determined not to lose out completely. He had the eighteen-story Stroh Building at 28 West Adams erected, a well-proportioned office building that still stands and until recently was occupied by Michigan Mutual Insurance Company.

BEER AND COMPETITION RETURN

Julius Stroh was seventy-seven, still dapper and energetic, when Prohibition was repealed in April 1933. His sons Gari and John were forty-two and forty and served as vice president and secretary, respectively. There was much work to be done to resume full production, but at least the syrup business had kept the brewhouse operating. Competitors who had shut down, such as Goebel across the street, lost at least six months getting started.

Only the ice cream, which had become something of a local favorite, was kept on from the Prohibition line. Having dropped the Alaska name, the Stroh ice cream department churned along in its own wing, concentrating on good quality.

Stroh's reentry into the beer market was rapid and very successful. Because Stroh had been the only Detroit brewery licensed to produce near beer, there was a cellar full of beer waiting for dealcoholization. This beer was ready for packaging as regular-strength beer on the date of repeal. Almost 440,000 barrels were sold in 1934; two years later, the volume was more than 700,000 barrels. Total sales of Michigan's fifty-four breweries that year was 3,093,000 barrels.

Julius Stroh pours the first legal glass of beer for Colonel Frederick M. Alger, one of the leaders of the repeal movement in Michigan, at an American Legion party, May 10, 1933.
ASSOCIATED PRESS PHOTO IN THE STROH BREWERY COMPANY ARCHIVE.

The Stroh Brewery in 1937, looking eastward along Elizabeth Street. A new beer stock house, where beer is fermented and then aged near freezing, was built on the site of the 1864 brewery in the right background.

A major building program was started in 1936 to accommodate the increased business. Only one floor of the old 1864 brewery on Gratiot was left. The others, considered a possible fire hazard, had beem demolished. The remaining structure was now razed for a large stock house. The new building contained four rows of glass-lined beer storage tanks on eight levels. It was the first stage of an immense block of fermenting and storage capacity to be built along Gratiot Avenue. The Stroh product line at this time consisted of the Bohemian Style beer, a seasonal Bock in spring, and a special premium Imperial Pilsener, available only on draft at selected bars.

GARI STROH

Julius Stroh died in June 1939 at the age of eighty-three. He had seen the very beginning of the family brewery as a youngster and guided Detroit's largest brewery through its most difficult period in his seventh and eighth decades. In his last years, he reacted vigorously to the opportunities created by the repeal of Prohibition.

Julius' older son, Gari, became president, with Gari's brother John as secretary. It fell to Gari to be in charge during the years of World War II, when one could sell all the beer one had several times over. The resources, however, were either rationed severely or very difficult to find, and this included workers. Rather than weakening the product to gain volume in a seller's market, he rationed his distributors. Quality would not be sacrificed for quantity at Stroh. This preserved Stroh's reputation immediately after the war, but this conservative approach to brewing became a liability later. Drinkers had gotten used to lighter and less flavorful beers. Stroh, however, maintained the prewar formula, which had changed little since it was awarded a gold medal in 1893 at the World's Columbia Exposition in Chicago.

At first, Stroh sales climbed sharply, and a second copper kettle line with supporting mashing vessels was ordered and installed in 1947. Beer sales that year were 877,000 barrels and stretched the existing bottling capacity to the limit. Gari's major contribution during his tenure was to have a new packaging center built. Construction of an impressive facility began the following year. The Stroh office building on West Adams Street was sold to raise the capital.

When completed in 1950, the new bottling hall was the largest unobstructed packaging plant under one roof in the country. In the basement were rows of tanks where finished beer was checked one last time for correct specifications before being pumped upstairs for packaging. This was the "government cellar," so named because beer passed through special meters for tax purposes. The main hall was an immense open space filled with rows of huge "soakers," to wash returnable bottles, fillers and crowners, long pasteurizers, labelers, and case fillers. It was a humid and often hot environment, but the work provided mostly unskilled employees with a good wage. Around the perimeter was a balcony where visitors could watch the continuous march of bottles; the balcony also led to offices and shops.

It was a sign of Stroh's conservative attitude and conviction about beer quality that the packaging center was equipped only for bottling. While cans had been first used for beer in 1935 and were well on their way by 1940, at the time, glass was considered best for flavor. Can linings improved greatly after the war, and the public found cans convenient. A can line had to be squeezed in when it became apparent that cans could be ignored no longer. Later, a large addition was built to handle the increasing demand for cans.

Gari Stroh barely saw the impressive structure completed; he died in June 1950 after a brief illness. The presidency went to his brother John, and Gari's son Peter was brought into the brewery. It was not, however, an easy time to join the family firm. Hardly had ground been broken for the new packaging center when sales began to slide, at first grad-

Newly appointed brewmaster Herman K. Rosenbusch shares a beer with his father, plant superintendent Herman A. Rosenbusch, in 1950.   FROM THE STROH BREWERY COMPANY ARCHIVE.

ually but then steeply. Only slightly more than 500,000 barrels were sold in 1950. This decline coincided with booming sales for Stroh's two major postwar competitors, Goebel and Pfeiffer. Both posted sales in excess of one million barrels. From being the leading Detroit brewer as the war ended, Stroh found itself a struggling number three.

JOHN STROH AND THE BEER WARS

After a delay caused by its shutdown during Prohibition, the Goebel plant across the street from Stroh's was upgraded and enlarged. Still conservative before the war, it became a very aggressively expanding firm in the late 1940s and early 1950s under its president, Edwin Anderson. The reason for Goebel's success was primarily its marketing. Anderson was also president of the Detroit Lions. This was the time when pro football and television came together as an excellent vehicle for beer advertising. The new rooster emblem was used to advantage, and the small

Billboard sign, October 1950.

Bantam bottle and cans were popular. The beer was considered lighter than Stroh's and seemed to meet current taste preferences.

Pfeiffer was brewed less than two miles away, on Mack Avenue. Like Goebel's, the brewery was closed during Prohibition, and extensive renovation was needed. Sales reached 400,000 barrels going into the war under the leadership of Alfred Epstein. Business grew rapidly after the war with clever advertising, based on the impish figure of "Johnny Pfeiffer."

Clearly, Stroh had to face a new set of circumstances. Lightening the beer proved easier than finding really good advertising. The slogan "You'll like Stroh's—it's lighter" may be short on creativity, but it was repeated often enough and in so many ways that the message got through. Sales picked up in the core market, and expansion into adjoining states restored Stroh to number one among Detroit's brewers. The stock cellars—a historic term, as the building was eight floors tall—were expanded by an addition along Gratiot in 1955, and a third kettle line was installed in 1956. Sales that year exceeded 2.7 million barrels.

Stroh's growth was shattered in the spring of 1958. A strike by unions against the Detroit brewers began April 1 and lasted 45 days. The immediate results were devastating for the five remaining brewers (Stroh, Goebel, Pfeiffer, Altes, and Schmidt). Stroh lost a quarter of its sales volume that year, but it was the long-term consequences that affected local brewers. Beer from other states gained such a strong foothold that the two-million-barrel level could not be significantly exceeded for a decade.

The strike dragged on because both sides refused to yield on a minor issue of the retroactive pay date, in spite of progress on substantive issues. The requirement had been for the unions to notify the brewers of requested changes by March 1, a month before expiration of the

Team bowling was a popular event from the 1930s through the 1960s, and the Stroh's Beer team included some of Detroit's best bowlers. This group photo of the 1953–54 team is from the Stroh Archive.

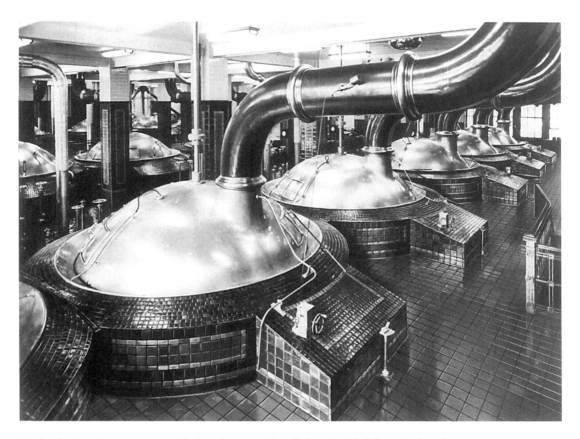

The kettle floor after expansion of the brewhouse and installation of a third direct-fired kettle line in 1956, eventually permitting a total of twenty-four brews of 1,000 barrels each per day.

FROM THE STROH BREWERY COMPANY ARCHIVE.

old contract. Normally, sufficient progress was achieved after a month to warrant retroactive dating to April 1. In 1958, the unions delivered a long list of changes only on April 12, and the brewers offered retroactive pay to April 15. This the unions flatly rejected, and 4,500 workers walked, the contract having expired and the expected retrodating having been denied. It took the presence of both state and federal mediators and a fourteen-hour bargaining session to agree on a three-year contract. Retroactivity was not even mentioned.

One indirect result of the strike was that it brought popular sportscaster Ernie Harwell to Detroit in 1960. Goebel had been sponsoring the Tigers as well as the Lions and, with declining cash flow, gave up Tigers sponsorship in September 1959. This was snapped up by Stroh. However, Stroh decided that long-time announcer Van Patrick would not be retained ("Benched by Brewery" was the caption under his photo in a *Detroit News* story). It was not because of his play-by-play but because of his long association with Goebel, explained Stroh advertising director Charles Derrick. In fact, Patrick continued to call the Lions games for

Goebel. That left the baseball play-by-play job to assistant announcer George Kell, a former Baltimore Orioles third baseman. He had started a new career in the booth that year and was well received. Kell had gotten his chance at the mike when he befriended the Baltimore announcer Harwell while Kell was recovering from an ankle injury. When the number one position opened in Detroit at a good salary, Kell called his friend in Baltimore. Harwell sent a tape, was one of three finalists to be interviewed, and became the voice of the Tigers for a generation.

Stroh took a hard look at acquisition when Pabst had to divest itself of Blatz in Milwaukee in 1968. Although Stroh entered a strong bid, Blatz was awarded to G. Heileman, in LaCrosse, Wisconsin. Stroh's opportunity came in 1964. Goebel was facing bankruptcy, and when it ceased operation, the brewery was acquired for $1,950,000. It was a very suitable purchase, because it was a local brand with sales of 200,000 barrels and an almost contiguous property. The Goebel plant was razed and production moved into the Stroh brewery. Goebel beer was not firebrewed, in order to preserve the Stroh brand as "America's Only Firebrewed Beer." It was slightly lighter in body than Stroh's and sold at a lower price. Slowly, the brand gained volume with minimal advertising, just by being a good beer at a good price.

"UNCLE JOHN" AND PETER STROH

John Stroh became chairman in 1967 and remained chief executive officer; his nephew Peter Stroh became president the following year. A team of highly qualified and capable executives had been assembled: Lester Freidinger, originally from Frankenmuth and later a Carling executive; Daniel Fraser, who rose from brewmaster to senior vice president of operations; Douglas Babcook, with an extensive brewing background from Canadian Breweries Ltd., who followed Fraser as brewmaster and vice president; and the third-generation Herman K. Rosenbusch. On the marketing side was the enthusiastic Harry Wagoner.

The Stroh Brewery Company was positioned to grow. When Doyle Dane Bernbach was chosen as the new ad agency, the combination of market expansion, innovative and memorable advertising, and sound technical support brought about tremendous sales growth. Three million barrels were shipped in 1970, and four million in 1972.

The year 1975 was a special milestone. The brewery celebrated its 125th anniversary, and Peter Stroh chose that time to visit his ancestral town of Kirn in Germany. The return of a highly successful descendant of one of Kirn's old families made local headlines. And in an industry where tradition still counts, the "German connection" provided a good marketing approach.

Back home, the team headed by "Uncle John" and his nephew Peter Stroh was enjoying increasing sales as Stroh beer was introduced into new states. John Stroh knew what he wanted—a first-rate staff and loyalty—and in return, he gave salary, wages, and benefits comparable to the Big

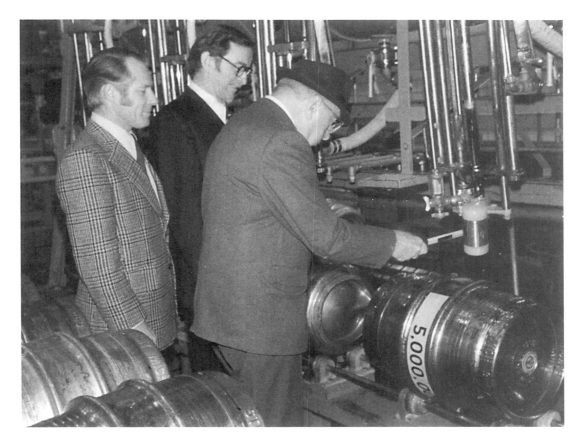

After filling a ceremonial 5-millionth barrel for a new annual record in 1975, the worker stepped aside to let chairman John W. Stroh finish tapping the bung. Looking on approvingly are master brewer (later senior vice president of production) Douglas R. Babcook and vice president of operations Daniel M. Fraser. Both Babcook and Fraser had extensive brewing experience with Canadian Breweries, Ltd.   FROM THE STROH BREWERY COMPANY ARCHIVE.

Three car companies. It took a long time for John Stroh to trust his staff to airplanes; in the 1960s, when other brewers would fly to attend a convention of master brewers, Stroh men still took the Pullman. John Stroh became stronger with age, and he developed a feel for what would work and what was too complex. He could deflate elaborate presentations with pithy comments, generating another "Uncle John" story. When discussion at one staff meeting continued aimlessly after decisions had been reached, John Stroh declared that he did not know what others had to do that day, but he had to get back to work. The room emptied in seconds.

As annual sales increased from three to five million barrels during the early 1970s, new brewhouse vessels, storage tanks, filters, packaging, and cooling machinery were being installed on a continuing basis. Stroh was now getting respect from the major brewers.

With respect came attention, and with attention came increased competition. Additional volume was getting harder to find. When sales

Chairman John W. Stroh (1893–1984), in 1975.
PHOTO BY BILL WILLIAMS, FOR
THE STROH BREWERY COMPANY.

reached six million barrels in 1977, the growth curve for the Stroh brand tailed off.

The old core territory of Michigan, Ohio, Indiana, and Illinois was being invaded by stronger competitors and could no longer be defended effectively. One problem was the pricing of Stroh's beer. The segment occupied by regional and local brewers was declining. It was deemed essential that Stroh be associated with premium beers, but raising the price also hurt sales. By the end of the decade, the prognosis for even a strong regional brewer was no longer what it had been ten or even five years earlier.

Efforts to develop new brands were only partially effective. Stroh Light never became a bright star in competition with Miller Lite or Bud Light. A better opportunity was the super-premium Signature. It was packaged in special bottles, wrapped in gold foil at the top, and both the taste and the package announced "top quality." But after a very good reception, the entire super-premium category began to decline in competition with imports.

BETTING THE FARM

Faced with a "grow or go" scenario, Stroh decided to grow. Helping to make up the corporate mind was new marketing executive Roger Fridholm, who came aboard in 1978. The first opportunity for growth came in 1980. The Schaefer Brewery in New York, started by brothers Frederick and Maximilian Schaefer in 1842, had stumbled badly.

Rudy Schaefer, who in 1933 had been the youngest brewery president and the driving spirit for decades, had retired. The business was no longer run by the family. A new plant had been erected on large acreage near Allentown, Pennsylvania, to replace the old brewery in Brooklyn, New York, which had been built in the 1910s and extensively enlarged and modernized as sales grew. By 1970, operating costs in the New York area had become too high, and Schaefer moved all brewing to Allentown. When sales declined from six to three million barrels in the 1970s, the large debt for the Allentown plant could no longer be serviced. Stroh acquired a significant interest and completed the acquisition in 1981.

With the modern plant at the Lehigh Valley location came the opportunity to brew Stroh's beer on the East Coast.

Nineteen eighty-two proved to be a memorable year for Stroh. By June, it had acquired the much larger Jos. Schlitz Brewing Company of Milwaukee in a leveraged buyout. Within two years, Stroh had catapulted itself from a 6- to 7-million-barrel single plant firm to a 22-million-barrel giant with seven brewing plants, five can plants, a significant interest in a Spanish brewery, and a debt of more than $500 million. Stroh was the number three brewer in the country, after Anheuser-Busch and Miller. The very air in the newly purchased corporate headquarters at the Detroit River was charged.

The purchase of Schlitz was the result of shrewd and gutsy moves, after Schlitz had made serious mistakes in an increasingly unforgiving business climate. It had been the number one brewer in the early 1950s but lost top rank to Anheuser-Busch. Try as it might, every sales increase was matched, and usually more than matched, by its arch-rival in St. Louis. With sales forces of both companies being pressured to get results, the Federal Trade Commission ruled that illegal competitive practices had been committed and indicted both firms. Anheuser-Busch pleaded guilty and accepted a fine. Schlitz's management considered the ruling unjustified and fought the charges. The case dragged on, consuming corporate energy and generating bad publicity, and was ultimately lost at great cost.

It was a poor decision to fight the federal government but minor compared to the visibility of a bad advertising campaign. Even though Schlitz could not catch up with its rival, it was the number two brewer in the country and had fielded great and memorable advertising slogans. There was "When you're out of Schlitz, you're out of beer," the notion that because you only go around once in life, you may as well make it Schlitz, and the idea that Schlitz had "gusto." In the background was always "The Beer That Made Milwaukee Famous," the old mantra that had the longest "legs" of any slogan in the industry. And suddenly there came a belligerent "So you want to take my gusto away!" which was not seen as amusing and had to be killed. It could not have happened at a worse time, because there was a public perception that there had been trouble with the beer quality for several years.

Most likely, a couple of other decisions were made at the same time: to mechanize the process of fermentation and to lighten the beer flavor. Schlitz announced an ABF (accelerated batch fermentation) process, which was later defined as "advanced balanced fermentation." The key element was the use of large low-speed stirrers during fermentation. This ensured that yeast in the fermenting batch would be uniformly distributed. While this agitation may reduce the last stage of fermentation, there is nothing wrong with a uniform yeast population.

What may have been very inadvisable was to talk about modernizing a process when consumers seemed to prefer hearing about tradition

"There's an impressionist exhibit at the Art Museum, an early Michigan pottery show at the Historical Museum, a musket drill at Greenfield Village and an azalea show on Belle Isle. But that gleam in your eye tells me you still opt for the Stroh brewery tour."

Cliff Wirth drew many cartoons for the Detroit News featuring Stroh's beer and the brewery during the 1980s. FROM THE DETROIT NEWS, APRIL 6, 1981. COURTESY CLIFF WIRTH.

and the chief competitor was stressing beechwood chips and parading draft horses. But there had been a decline in beer flavor, probably caused by a change in brewing ingredients. A haze problem in some Southern markets only added to the negative impression. Then came the unpopular ad theme, and suddenly the sales curve nosedived.

Among all these difficulties came the unexpected death of Robert Uihlein, a descendant of Schlitz's founder. A large, robust man with a florid complexion and a strong sense of leadership, he had been groomed for years by his uncle Edwin Uihlein, after Edwin's own son and a future logical successor had been tragically killed in a car accident. There was a loss of family leadership at a critical time. It was only after several years that a widely respected and qualified candidate was found to lead Schlitz. This was senior executive Frank Sellinger from Anheuser-Busch. Sellinger assembled a team that improved quality, and he personally became involved in advertising and generated enthusiasm. But sales and stock prices did not respond. The momentum that had kept Schlitz going for some time now delayed a turnaround. Members of the Uihlein family, who were major stockholders, were ready to sell. Stroh saw an opportunity and acted.

Wall Street described the acquisition with the usual images of "a minnow swallowing a whale" or "the canary eating the cat." Actually, Schlitz in 1982 was only a potential giant. True, three of its five breweries were state-of-the-art, and the plants in Van Nuys, California, and Tampa, Florida, were neither small nor old. But the sales of Schlitz, which for years had held at four and a half times the volume of Stroh, were only twice the combined volume of the Detroit and Allentown breweries.

The Justice Department had objected to a merger of Schlitz and G. Heileman of LaCrosse, Wisconsin, the previous year. It approved the merger with Stroh but required that Stroh divest itself of one of the southern Schlitz plants, either Winston-Salem or Tampa. In 1983, the Tampa plant was therefore traded to Pabst for the former Hamm brewery in St. Paul. This plant had been purchased by Olympia, which wanted to expand from its base in Tumwater, Washington, and ended up being owned by Pabst. To simplify the trade, employees stayed with their respective plants. Thus, it came about that workers in St. Paul had been employed by Hamm, Olympia, Pabst, and Stroh in a single decade without changing their jobs.

At Tampa, the trade for the St. Paul brewery suddenly turned everybody from a Schlitz/Stroh employee into a Pabst employee. After a few years, it became evident that Pabst no longer needed an entire brewery there. The Tampa plant was then reacquired by Stroh.

YEARS OF GLORY AND GLOOM

For a few years, Stroh could enjoy the prestige of being the third-largest brewer in the nation and among the world's top twenty. Fire-kettles were installed in Allentown and Van Nuys for the brewing of Stroh's and Signature. The company boasted brands in every segment, from regional Piel's, Schaefer, and Goebel to national brands, from light extensions to malt liquor.

When chairman emeritus John W. Stroh died on September 28, 1984, the *New York Times* carried his obituary. His sense for keeping things simple and sticking to basics was difficult to follow in a merged organization with a very large top management. Now president after the successful merger, Roger Fridholm had the difficult job of combining two groups with different cultures into one large organization, while facing a highly competitive and consolidating industry.

By 1985, the volume of the Stroh's brand had peaked. With sales of 24 million barrels and a 31-million-barrel capacity in the seven breweries, and the debt from the Schlitz purchase to service, the least efficient plant was at risk. Total industry sales were flat, there were no sales increases in sight, and, with very tough competition at every segment, the old brewery on Gratiot was a luxury at a lean time. The Detroit plant could be closed and its production distributed among the other breweries to realize significant savings. Schlitz had been forced to close its own home brewery in Milwaukee five years before for similar reasons. It was a bitter pill for old Stroh hands to swallow. The last working day was May 31, 1985.

Detroit beer drinkers did not take kindly to the disappearance of local brewing. The demolition of the historic complex in the fall was a reminder. It seemed that as long as an out-of-town beer had to be bought, it was not going to be Stroh's. The presence of 600 employees working at River Place, the corporate headquarters and former Parke-Davis plant, somehow had no impact. The Stroh's label, once distinct to the point of being odd with its antique script, had been gradually redesigned with a more contemporary look. It also became less unique. The creative work of Doyle Dane Bernbach was deemed too slow in coming, and a new agency was selected.

After a few years, the Stroh's brand was in trouble. The Schlitz brand maintained sales only in certain geographic pockets; it would take another five years before it started growing again. Old Milwaukee and Schlitz Malt Liquor held up well, but total sales volume kept declining. The large staff at headquarters was trimmed in line with lower expectations.

It was at this point, in the fall of 1989, that Stroh agreed to sell its breweries to Colorado brewer Adolph Coors. This firm had experienced meteoric growth in the 1960s and continued expanding at a slower rate. After several static years, Coors developed a popular light beer and again was growing. Coors, however, had no brand in the popular price category of Old Milwaukee. As the deadline for purchase approached in December, Coors terminated the negotiations, and the sale was called off. Stroh would have to sink or swim on its own.

THE HEILEMAN GAMBLE

The canceled sale served as a wake-up call. With vastly fewer executives, the Stroh family was again making its influence felt. Christmas a year after the aborted sale was much more cheerful. The label was redesigned in blue, and the package was again distinctive. Serious problems remained, but the staff was working well together and optimistic that solutions could be found. Of the five breweries that had come with Schlitz, Van Nuys, California, was closed and Memphis was sold to Coors. Meanwhile, the Schlitz interest in the Spanish brewery Cruzcampo had grown tremendously. At a crucial time, it was sold for more than $300 million, permitting the retirement of Stroh debt and renewed advertising. Stroh was determined to be a survivor of the beer wars.

The way to survive turned out to be entering into contract brewing and the export market, both of which Stroh managed very successfully, while searching for that magic message or brand. The microbrewery movement generated a need for breweries with known skill and extra capacity. Some of the larger craft brewers either outgrew their capacity or focused on marketing instead of investing in expensive plants.

A major competitor for Stroh among second-tier brewers was G. Heileman Brewing Company of LaCrosse, Wisconsin. The former re-

Peter Stroh, chairman and chief executive officer, sitting in the atrium of Stroh River Place headquarters in 1996. He retired in December 1997 after 45 years of service with the family brewery and related businesses.

THE STROH BREWERY COMPANY.

gional brewery at the Minnesota border grew significantly by acquisition in the 1960s and 1970s. Australian industrialist Alan Bond of America's Cup fame wished to enter the U.S. beer market and acquired Heileman in 1987 for an astounding 1.26 billion dollars in a highly leveraged buy-out.

The acquisition saddled Heileman with some $800 million in debt. Declining business forced the closing or sale of plants in St. Paul, Evansville, Indiana, and Frankenmuth, Michigan, and caused Heileman to file for bankruptcy in 1990. Stroh made a very serious attempt to acquire its rival in 1994, but was outbid by the Dallas investment firm of Hicks, Muse, Tate and Furst. An infusion of cash and new management could not reverse sales in a flat beer market, and the debt level on Heileman's business proved increasingly burdensome. After two years of losses, Hicks, Muse decided to sell. A second Heileman bankruptcy cleared the way for Stroh to finally purchase its competitor in July 1996.

The acquisition was a very good fit. In addition to obvious marketing and production advantages, Stroh inherited the traditions of many breweries and brands that came under the Heileman umbrella. The former Rainier and Blitz-Weinhard breweries in Seattle and Portland also benefited Stroh's growing Pacific export market. Unfortunately, 1997 saw the beginning of a lengthy price war, which eroded the benefits of the Heileman purchase.

Chairman Peter Stroh stepped down late in 1997 at age seventy, and the grandson of his uncle and former chairman, John W. Stroh III, assumed the presidency of the parent firm, Stroh Companies, Inc. He had been trained in brewing and business, but 1998 proved to be one of the most difficult years in Stroh's history. Sales suffered under increasing price competition, and lower earnings forced reductions in marketing spending, while the debt incurred in the Heileman acquisition became burdensome. On February 8, 1999, the Stroh Brewery Company

Mike Peters's cartoon about student protests against curtailment of beer drinking during football season was reprinted by the *New York Times*. Copyright 1998 Dayton Daily News & Tribune Media Services, Inc. Reprinted with permission. All rights reserved.

entered into a definitive agreement to sell its beer business to the Pabst Brewing Company and the Miller Brewing Company. The consummation of that transaction on April 30, 1999, concluded the Stroh family's long association with the brewing industry.

The modest brewery which Bernhard Stroh founded in 1850 overcame many difficult periods and went on to prosper as a family firm. In the 1970s, it grew to become the eighth-largest brewery in the nation, and Stroh's beer was widely admired by consumers and competitors. The strategy since the 1980s was to grow by acquisition. As Stroh approached its 150th anniversary in the year 2000, even award-winning beers, multiple modern plants, and a dedicated family were no longer enough to be a successful competitor.

MEMORABILIA

The Stroh brewery provided trays, glasses, mugs, and cork pullers to saloons before Prohibition. A vertical oval tray showing a small boy in a brewer monk's habit carrying a case of Stroh's up to a porch is considered the top collectible. The only small, round tip tray known advertises malt tonic. A stemmed and etched beaker and an early ale glass (a small Pilsener shape) embossed with the lion are very desirable glass items. German pocket knives are rare, and large signs, either lithographed or on glass, are usually unique. No lithograph showing the brewery has been located. Signs produced during the 1930s and 1940s are sought by collectors and are not inexpensive.

MANAGEMENT

1890s: Bernhard Stroh, president; Julius Stroh, secretary and treasurer; Otto Rosenbusch, brewmaster.

1900s: Bernhard Stroh, president; Julius Stroh, vice president and treasurer, president after 1908; Charles F. Raiss, secretary; Otto Rosenbusch, brewmaster and superintendent.

1940s: Gari M. Stroh, president; C. F. Raiss, vice president and treasurer; John W. Stroh, secretary; Herman A. Rosenbusch, master brewer and superintendent; Fred Flemming, chief engineer; Earl A. Bradley, bottling superintendent; William Kay, sales manager.

1950s: John W. Stroh, president; John W. Shenefield, secretary, later vice president and treasurer (1953); Harold S. Wagoner, vice president, sales (1951); Albert J. Klick, secretary; W. Edwin Mosher, Jr., assistant secretary; Herman A. Rosenbusch, superintendent; Herman K. Rosenbusch, brewmaster (1952).

1960s: John W. Stroh, president (1951–1967), chairman of the board (after 1967); John W. Shenefield, president (1967–1968), vice chairman (1970–1971); Lester M. Freidinger, executive vice president (1967– 1978); J. P. Leahan, vice president, administration (1967–1978); E. R.Zeisler, vice president (1961–1964); Robert P. Hyde, director of marketing (1964–1969) Herman K. Rosenbusch, director of brewing (1963– 1978); Daniel M. Fraser, brewmaster and director of packaging (1963– 69).

1970s: John W. Stroh, chairman (1967–1982); Peter W. Stroh, president (1969–1982); Lester M. Freidinger, executive vice president; Daniel M. Fraser, vice president and senior vice president, operations (1969–1982); Douglas R. Babcook, master brewer (1972–1976), vice president and senior vice president, production (1977–1983); Carl Holmer, master brewer (1977–1982); William E. Tily, director of brewing development; Edward F. Rohlin, vice president, marketing (1969–1973), Robert B. Hetrick (1974–1979); Wilfred C. Hugli, Jr., vice president, corporate development (1969–1974).

1980s: Peter W. Stroh, chairman; H. A. Ruemenapp, vice chairman (1983–1985); Roger Fridholm, president (1983–1990); A. J. Tonna, executive vice president, operations; J. Wayne Jones, executive vice president, sales and marketing; R. A. Caponigro, senior vice president, finance, and treasurer; R. J. Lodato, senior vice president, administration; J. H. Bissell, group vice president, marketing; K. A. Tippary, group vice president, sales operations. *Vice presidents:* James R. Avery, operations planning and control; Stephen F. Fehling, human resources; J. J. Franzem, corporate services; P. J. Fox, sales; H. Hastings, brand management; J. H. Hawley, brewing; M. John Hellweg, sales promotion; W. L. Henry, financial planning; R. B. Hetrick, market expansion; W. R. Hintz, controller; G. E. Kuehn, general counsel; N. J. Lewandowski, purchasing; C. W. Lole, planning; M. C. Meilgaard, research and development; R. Alan Murdoch, international treasurer; D. V. Van Howe, secretary; W. V. Weatherston, corporate affairs. *Detroit brewery staff:* O. Wiesneth, plant manager; A. L. Mclean, master brewer; W. Riethmeier, packaging manager; E. Turnbull, engineering manager; J. McDougall, quality assurance manager; R. Holloway, industrial relations manager; M. Shapiro, plant administration manager.

1990s: Peter W. Stroh, chairman (retired 1998); John W. Stroh III, chairman, Stroh Companies (since 1998); William L. Henry, president. *Executive vice presidents:* James R. Avery, operations; Joseph J. Franzem, customer marketing and administration; George E. Kuehn, general counsel and secretary; Christopher Sortwell, chief financial officer. *Vice presidents:* Stephen D. Anderson, quality assurance; John R. Curtin, packaging and logistics; Joseph D. Hertrick, brewing; Robert L. Pitcole, information systems and services. Vincent M.Abetemarco, treasurer.

Stroh Family

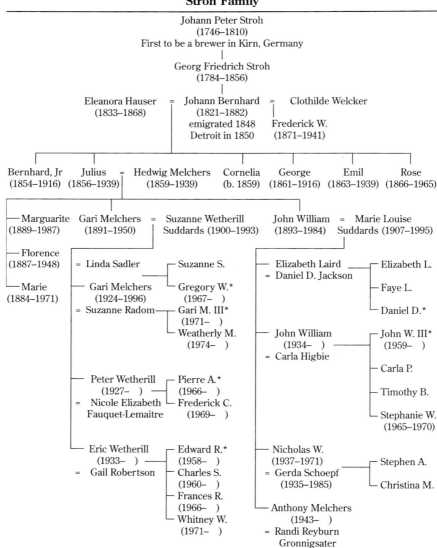

*Fifth-generation members active in brewery

4

SIX EARLY ANGLO-SAXON ALE BREWERS

Names and a few ads in old directories are all we know about most of the early ale brewers of Detroit. But there is enough information on six early English brewers to present at least the outlines of their lives and something about their brews.

Richard Hawley was the first Detroit ale brewer to be mentioned in a biography; he was already brewing in 1843. A dozen years later, he turned to making malt instead. It may have been a matter of pride—a real ale brewer would rather not switch to lager—but more likely it was the demand for malt by newly arriving brewers that brought about the change.

William Duncan started in 1850 and soon became the most prominent of the ale brewers. He also was very active in local and state politics, including a term as mayor of Detroit. Like Hawley, he later turned to malting.

Of the brewers included in this chapter, the Hawley and Moloney families showed excellent adaptation for survival and prosperity, moving respectively from ale to malt or lager to law.

None of these ale brewers survived into the new century, although ale continued to be brewed as part of the product mix by several Detroit brewers. Bernhard Stroh brewed some very heavy specialty beers in the 1860s, probably a stock ale and a porter, and his sons advertised a brown stout for many years. There was a time when ale, porter, and stout were king, and these brewers were an important part of that period.

Duncan listed the location of his Central Brewery on Woodbridge "opposite Mich. Central R. R. Depot." In this photo of the Michigan Central Railroad Yard from about 1868, the brewery's buildings can be seen just left of the smokestack, advertising ALE & PORTER on the west facade.   FROM THE BURTON HISTORICAL COLLECTION, DETROIT PUBLIC LIBRARY.

DUNCAN

W. C. DUNCAN, DUNCAN'S CENTRAL BREWERY, 1850–1864
LANGDON & COMPANY, 1864–1872
W. C. DUNCAN & CO. (N. WILLIAMS), 1872–1882
186–190 WOODBRIDGE
WM. S. DUNCAN & CO. MALTSTERS, 1882–1895
134–146 BEAUBIEN

William Chamberlain Duncan was one of the first major brewers in the 1850s and one of the few brewers to become prominent in local politics. He was born May 18, 1820, in Lyons, New York. When he was fifteen, the family moved to Rochester, New York, and in 1841, he served as steward on a lake steamer. He settled in Detroit in 1849. Duncan had no known brewing background, and details of his entry into the industry are lacking. However, in the early 1850s, he was brewing his own ales on Woodbridge and Second streets, opposite the Michigan Central Railroad depot. He advertised annually in the city directories, listing steam ales, porter, and brown stout in 1853; he mentioned stock ale for shipping and "the most delicate Pale Ale for family use" in the 1856 edition. The ales from Duncan's Central Brewery were popular enough for him to enlarge the brewery in 1860.

Duncan malted his own barley, which either was grown locally or came from Essex County, Ontario. His older brother, Elison Eli Duncan

(1818–1897), operated a malthouse at the corner of River and Fourth streets in which the brothers were partners. Later, Elison owned his own malting operation at the corner of Champlain and Beaubien. Duncan was probably also the first dealer in malt and hops, and he advertised these brewing ingredients to other brewers as early as 1853.

BREWER-MAYORS

As William Duncan's business prospered, he became active in city politics, serving as alderman for five years and as the first president of the Common Council. He was elected mayor of Detroit for a two-year term in 1862, and later for a term to the state senate. When asked again to run for mayor in 1873, he declined because of poor health. He died on December 18, 1877, at age fifty-seven.

Ale brewer and mayor of Detroit William Chamberlain Duncan.
FROM THE BURTON HISTORICAL COLLECTION, DETROIT PUBLIC LIBRARY.

In 1864, George C. Langdon bought the Duncan plant with Nathan G. Williams, and for the next eight years, he operated the brewery as Langdon & Company. Langdon was born in Geneva, New York, in 1833. He settled in Detroit in 1856 and began a varied business career. He was a bookkeeper, then a partner with a dealer in flour and grain, which must have led to contacts with local maltsters and brewers. In 1878, Langdon also became mayor of Detroit; the purchase of Belle Isle as a public park occurred during his administration.

When Langdon bought Duncan's Central Brewery in 1864, Sam Richardson, the brewmaster for nine years, left to join William Beal in a partnership. Their firm, Beal & Richardson, was located farther east on Woodbridge and also specialized in ale; with increasing competition from lager, it did not survive the decade.

ALE MAN WILLIAMS

The next owner of Duncan's brewery was Langdon's partner, Nathan Williams. He revived the Duncan name and was one of the few brewers who maintained the ale tradition. This business lasted ten years,

Advertisement for Duncan's Steam Ale in the 1861 Detroit directory.
FROM THE BURTON HISTORICAL COLLECTION, DETROIT PUBLIC LIBRARY.

and in 1882, he operated the malthouse only as Williams & Company. He refused to give up on ale, however, and in 1883, he reentered the brewing business as president of the Union Brewing Company, in addition to operating Duncan's old malthouse.

Williams was now in competition with Duncan's son William S. Duncan, who operated a new stone and brick malthouse at Lafayette and Beaubien in downtown Detroit. The local malt business was very active during this period. There were twenty-nine breweries listed in 1885, fourteen of which also included malthouses; the others had the choice of malt from one of six local maltsters or shippers from Buffalo or Chatham, Ontario.

In 1895, the Duncan malthouse on Beaubien was purchased by the Walkerville Brewing Company as its U.S. Agency. Canadian-brewed ale and stout were imported in bulk, at lower duty than bottled beer. The ale was then aged in wood, bottled, and distributed under the Robin Hood label.

MEMORABILIA
A few bottles embossed with "Duncan's Central Brewery" have been found and are considered very rare; these are the only artifacts known.

HAWLEY

RICHARD HAWLEY, 1843–1855
68 FIRST, 1843–1844

HAWLEY & Co.,
BREWERS OF PALE AND AMBER ALE,
PORTER AND BROWN STOUT,
AND DEALERS IN BARLEY, MALT AND HOPS,
Bates Street; south of Jefferson Avenue.
Orders by mail, accompanied by the cash, promptly attended to.   Casks should be corked as soon as empty, and returned promptly.

The only advertisement showing the brewery of Richard Hawley is in the 1853–54 Detroit directory. "Casks should be corked as soon as empty, and returned promptly" indicates that the cost incurred by slow cooperage return has a long history.

FROM THE BURTON HISTORICAL COLLECTION, DETROIT PUBLIC LIBRARY.

WOODBRIDGE NEAR WOODWARD, 1844–1846
RICHARD HAWLEY & COMPANY, 1846–1855
RICHARD HAWLEY & COMPANY (MALTSTERS), 1855–1873
THOMAS HAWLEY & COMPANY (MALTSTERS), 1873–1878
36 BATES, 1846–1855

This brief outline of Richard Hawley's life illustrates the very early days of brewing in Detroit. It could be assembled because he was included in a collection of biographies and because his first brewing experience in Cleveland was noted by Stanley Baron in his book on the history of American breweries and was researched by Carl Miller for his book on the breweries of Cleveland.

Richard Hawley was born December 10, 1815, in Shrewsbury, England. His family immigrated in 1818 and settled in Cleveland. At seventeen, he was associated with Joseph Hawley, probably his father, in the Cleveland Brewery, but they lost everything in the panic of 1837. Herrick Childs, who had recently relocated from Massachusetts, acquired the brewery, but late in 1840 Thomas Hawley and his son-in-law John Cooke leased the brewery until 1843.

Richard Hawley probably left Cleveland in 1840; by 1843, he was established in a Detroit brewery on First Street. He placed an ad for ale, porter, and beer in the 1845 city directory, listing an address on Wood-bridge near Woodward. The following year, he advertised ale, porter, and strong beer, at his final address on Bates just south of Jefferson Avenue. Hawley's name would be associated with ales for the next decade. The city directory for 1850–51 lists a familiar name, "Thos. Hawley," but no Richard. Later directories again list Richard.

In 1855, Richard Hawley turned to malting, most likely because the ale segment did not increase and Duncan had become the dominant ale brewer. There also was a strong demand for malt by the newly arrived German brewers. He brought his sons Thomas, John, and Richard Jr. into the business five years later. The family also traded in hops, not unusual in those early years.

Hawley retired in 1873 at age fifty-eight. The firm became Thomas Hawley & Company. In 1878, Henry Rickel leased the Hawley malthouse as part of his expansion program. By 1880, John had left the firm, having read for the law. Thomas also became interested in law. The last entry for the Hawley Malt Company is in 1884; afterward, both Thomas and John Hawley are listed as lawyers.

It is interesting that neither the Hawleys nor Duncan tried to shift to lager. They knew how to brew ale and their customers were ale drinkers, and they might have felt at a disadvantage competing with lager against German lager brewers. In later years, the ale brewer John Moloney did make the switch, but in the end, he, too, turned to law.

MEMORABILIA
Hawley's ales were almost certainly sold on draft only, and no artifacts are known or expected.

JOHNSON

JOHN MASON, 1851–1858
BOWKER & BLACKMUR, 1862–1866
EDWARD JOHNSON & SON, 1872–1888
MICHIGAN & SIXTH

The small ale brewery John Mason started in 1851 or 1852 in the Irish "Corktown" neighborhood never amounted to much in terms of size; six hundred barrels was as much as was brewed there in any year. But over a period of thirty years, several owners brewed the ale and porter pre-ferred by men in that neighborhood.

John Mason also advertised that beer was always available. This would be not German lager but the English "small beer," a much weaker and less expensive product than the ales.

Mason was listed in directories until 1858. The small brewery prob-ably stood empty until 1862, when Peter J. Bowker and John W. Black-

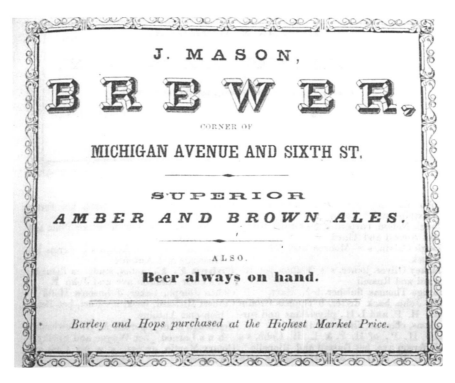

J. MASON,

BREWER,

CORNER OF

MICHIGAN AVENUE AND SIXTH ST.

SUPERIOR
AMBER AND BROWN ALES.

ALSO.

Beer always on hand.

Barley and Hops purchased at the Highest Market Price.

John Mason's ad in the 1853–54 Detroit directory lists amber and brown ales. The brewing of ales was revived in the 1980s by microbrewers, and more recently by many large brewers.
FROM THE BURTON HISTORICAL COLLECTION, DETROIT PUBLIC LIBRARY.

mur took it over. The firm Bowker & Blackmur brewed ale and traded in malt and hops. Another plant closing occurred between 1866 and 1872. Then Edward Johnson, Sr., and his son operated the plant for sixteen years. The Johnsons were natives of England who had immigrated in 1860. For the last twelve years, Edward Jr. was in charge.

The brewery property in 1880 consisted of a 50-foot frontage on Michigan Avenue, going back 175 feet on both Sixth and Baker streets. The Johnson ale business was for draft only and provided a living for the family, but the ale market did not grow. The business was last listed in 1888.

MEMORABILIA
There were probably signs printed when Johnson reopened the brewery in 1872, but nothing is known.

MOLONEY

WILLIAM E. MOLONEY, 1877–1891
VIENNA BREWING COMPANY, 1891–1896
MOLONEY BREWING COMPANY, 1896–1898
12TH & HOWARD

A bottle for Moloney's Dublin Stout, about 1885, has the typical shape and greenish-black color of imported English bottles used for that type. This is a rare example with perfect labels.

FROM THE STROH BREWERY COMPANY ARCHIVE.

William E. Moloney was a hardworking and personable Irishman. He was born in 1847 in County Tipperary, came to the United States with his parents about 1855, and arrived in Detroit in 1862. Four years later, when he was nineteen, he got married. The young couple operated a grocery store from their home at 321 Seventh Street in the early 1870s, and then at 12th and Sycamore. Moloney was first listed as a brewer in 1877, the brewery also being a part of his residence. Moloney liked the English brews—ale, stout, and porter—and he continued to brew them for twenty-two years in the face of competition from bottom-fermented types. He had German partners during the first couple of years—Matthew Hauck, Thomas Faichtenbeiner, and August Schneider—and probably they were responsible for his later acceptance of lagers.

Two years after Moloney started brewing at home, he acquired sole ownership of a small brewery on 12th Street and made his peace with Continental-style lager. Production almost doubled in his second year to 924 barrels. He started brewing the golden Vienna type and in 1880, with the goal of ethnic accommodation, named his plant the Vienna Brewing Company. Moloney did not abandon top-fermented beers; he also brewed ales and a porter under the Dublin Stout label.

Moloney's trademark was a hand holding up three fingers, and this appeared prominently on all labels. The Vienna brewery was now a 40-by-100-foot structure, two stories and a basement, set on a 78-by-196-foot lot. As his business prospered, he became active in local Democratic politics and was elected to two terms as alderman. His political career culminated in 1885, when he served a term as president of the city council.

In 1890, William's son John Edmund Moloney joined him as partner. John was not a brewer like his father. He had graduated from Canisius College in Buffalo, read law, and was admitted to the bar in 1892. He became a partner with Charles Flowers and James May in the law firm of Flowers, May & Moloney.

The Vienna name was formally adopted by incorporation in January 1892. At that time, it was reported that the brewery had a capacity of 30,000 barrels and twenty employees. In 1896, the Moloney name was reinstated. However, the plant was now antiquated and too small by 1890s standards. William closed the brewery in 1898. He was only fifty-one, but many of those years must have been filled with long days of hard labor as a hands-on brewer.

John was only twenty and had a job in the law firm, but perhaps he missed the smell of the old brewery. In the fall of 1899, John and several partners formed the American

The oldest bottle in the Stroh collection contained Scotch Pale Ale by the Western Brewery; new owners changed the name in 1883 to the East India Brewing Company.
FROM THE STROH BREWERY COMPANY ARCHIVE.

Brewing Company and tried to raise capital for rebuilding and enlarging the old plant. Plans were prepared for a 190-by-70-foot brewery, with the new part being four stories high. New machinery was to include a malt mill, a 150-barrel copper kettle, mechanical refrigeration, and more storage capacity. These improvements were estimated to cost $40,000. Completion was expected by summer 1900, but financing of this venture failed. The Moloney brewery never reopened.

William Moloney died in 1912 at the age of sixty-five, two years after his son's wedding. If he was disappointed by the failure of the brewery, he knew that his son was off to a good legal career as a partner with Flowers, May & Moloney, later with Moloney & Mendelsohn, and, after Morrey Mendelsohn's death, Moloney & La Joie. And like many second-generation Irish immigrants who did well, John expressed a preference for the Republican Party. When he was asked for biographical details for a book a decade later, he provided information about his father's political offices but never mentioned William's modest beginnings in Corktown or his brewery.

MEMORABILIA
Memorabilia of the Moloney Brewery are restricted to bottles and labels.

MANAGEMENT
1892 (Vienna Brewing Company): William E. Moloney, president and manager; John E. Moloney, vice president; John C. Donnelly, secretary-treasurer.
1899 (failed venture): Ferdinand Marshner, president; John E. Moloney, secretary; F. Marshner, James D. Burns, Norman B. Sharp, Charles Fry, directors.

ST. LOUIS

THOMAS MCGRATH, 1867–1894
ST. LOUIS BREWING CO., 1894–1899
500 GRAND RIVER AVENUE

Nicholas Klein, partner in the St. Louis Brewing Company, as shown in an 1897 brochure.
FROM THE STROH BREWERY COMPANY ARCHIVE.

The known facts about Thomas McGrath do not describe his appearance or personality, which must have played an important part in his development. Tom McGrath was born in Dublin but raised in Liverpool, and he arrived in the United States in 1849. He settled in Michigan, where he tried farming, but found carpentry more to his liking. He became a ship's carpenter in Marine City. How he moved from this trade to that of an ale brewer in 1867 is a mystery. His first year's production was recalled as being 150 barrels. In spite of his Anglo-Irish background, he switched to lager after a couple of years.

The brewery did not exceed 2,000 barrels until his twelfth year in business. By 1891, however, he was producing 10,000 barrels in a 110-by-

100-foot plant with refrigeration and its own steam power. His son Thomas F. McGrath was a graduate of Detroit University and assisted him in management. In 1890, McGrath became president of the Detroit Brewers Association and he assumed positions on the Board of Public Works and Education.

In 1894, he incorporated his business as the St. Louis Brewing Company and sold the brewery to Nicolas Klein and Neumann for $30,000. McGrath continued to operate the plant as president and manager. In retrospect, it turned out to have been a good time to be getting his investment out of the brewery. Trouble surfaced in 1899, when Klein brought suit against his partner Neumann. Klein asked for an accounting and the appointment of a receiver. William B. Hatch was named trustee, and the brewery, whose sales must have been sagging, was closed.

MEMORABILIA

Nothing related to this enterprise could be located in area collections.

UNION

WESTERN BREWERY, 1860–1877
ABBOTT & SEVENTH
EAST INDIA BREWING COMPANY, 1877–1883
630 WOODBRIDGE
UNION BREWING COMPANY, 1883–1890
621 WEST FORT STREET

The history of the Union name is complicated because it was used by two different companies. The first Union brewery had its origin with Rufus Brown, an ale brewer since 1860 at the corner of Abbott and Seventh streets on the west side. He named it Western Brewery for obvious reasons. In 1869, Alonzo C. Davis and Henry W. Newberry acquired the brewery and continued with ale and porter until 1876. Scotch Pale Ale was one of the advertised brands.

The brewery appeared in larger quarters at 630 Woodbridge and under new ownership in 1877. Newberry had died, and Davis sold out and became a partner in a wholesale grocery business, Garrison & Davis. Being no longer west of Woodward, the new partners chose the name East India Brewing Company. The managing partner was Charles I. Farrell; by 1879, there was an annual city directory ad for "Farrell's Famous East India Pale Ale" and for "Farrell's Old Country Porter." The ownership of the brewery showed a modern complexity: in addition to the East India Brewing Company, there was Farrell & Company, "Maltsters and manufacturers of East India Pale Ale." Production for the year in 1878–79 was 2,500 barrels.

Another change in location, name, and management occurred in 1883. The new location was 621 West Fort Street, the new name was

Union Brewing Company, and the new investor joining Farrell was president Nathan G. Williams. This was the Williams who had purchased the Duncan Central Brewery with George Langdon back in 1864 and, when Langdon shifted to malting, ran the brewery as Williams & Company.

After 1882, only the malt business was active, but Williams evidently was determined to return to ale brewing. The product line was expanded to include a Half & Half, indicating some lager, and a low-alcohol, high-malt health drink under the name Hoptonic. The Union brewery also acted as agent for Voigt's and Mann's Lager. The details of this arrangement are unknown; perhaps Union contracted for city delivery. This firm lasted seven years, until 1890.

MEMORABILIA
Two bottles with labels in the Stroh collection seem to be among the few surviving objects from this period.

MANAGEMENT
1880: James McGregor, president; C. J. Lloyd, secretary-treasurer; Charles I. Farrell, manager.
1885: Nathan G. William, president; Charles I. Farrell, vice president; Charles K. Jackson, treasurer; Charles R. Richardson, secretary.

5

Ten Small German Lager Brewers

Neighborhood brewers gave Detroit's early German community its character. The ten described here were small only by later standards, and they were great successes in their own time, having stayed in business an average of thirty years. Most started brewing between the late 1860s and the early 1870s, and they enjoyed good acceptance of their beers for a generation. The center of breweries founded by Germans was the corner of Rivard and Maple, across the street from Stroh's. Most brewed within a half-mile radius.

When the industry was mechanized in the 1880s and the scale of operation became much larger, these breweries fell behind. Only one of this group lasted until 1917; the others closed between 1889 and 1905. Yet for all the similarity in dates and tenure, each story is different. Some brewers were realists who sold out when the opportunity arose; others may have enjoyed life as it was and were comforted by the past into false hopes, and two families did their best to remain open in the face of tragedy.

BAVARIAN

ANTON MICHENFELDER & COMPANY, 1874–1884
BAVARIAN BREWING COMPANY, 1884–1890
71 SHERMAN

The brewery Anton Michenfelder started at Sherman and Rivard streets in 1874 was not a tiny operation. Production after four years was a respectable 5,000 barrels, at a time when many brewers produced half that amount.

Michenfelder incorporated the business in 1882 when he brought in W. P. Ratigan as an associate. He arranged for John Hock to bottle his beers, but he malted his own barley. Two years later, he changed the name to Bavarian Brewing Company. It was during this decade that John Zynda worked for Michenfelder and became skilled in malting and brewing.

A drawing of the brewery appeared in an 1885 feature article on Detroit breweries in the trade publication *Western Brewer.* It shows two adjacent four-story buildings; the left one, with few windows, is probably the malthouse. Michenfelder listed only himself as proprietor. Bernard Michenfelder, perhaps a cousin or a much younger brother, immigrated in 1881 at age seventeen, and learned the brewing trade at Bavarian.

Michenfelder sold out to the British syndicate in May 1889 (see chapter 2, above). He was ready to retire to his farm near Norris. His relative Bernard became brewmaster at the Walkerville Brewing Company across the Detroit River between 1895 and 1898, and then purchased the Upper Sandusky Brewery in Ohio. August Goebel, who was backed by the syndicate, closed the brewery along with those of Endriss and Mann.

MEMORABILIA
Old bottles with an "A. Michenfelder" slug plate are rare, and nothing else of a collectible nature seems to have survived.

COLUMBIA

MICHAEL, JACOB & WILLIAM, WILLIAM DARMSTAETTER, 1852–1885
COLUMBIA BREWING COMPANY, 1890–1917
92 (LATER 227) CATHERINE

Michael Darmstaetter immigrated from Darmstadt, Germany, and established a house brewery in 1852, almost across the street from Bernhard Stroh's place on 89 Catherine. The two men started brewing within a year or two and must have known each other well. They were no doubt competitors for the same market, but there has long been a tradition of brotherhood among men engaged in the brewing trade. Darmstaetter's first output was 10 barrels daily, the size of many microbreweries of the 1980s and 1990s. Stroh's first brewery may have been even smaller.

Darmstaetter retired in 1856 and left the business to his sons Jacob and William. Either the brewery was too small to support two families or each brother preferred to run his own shop, because William bought out his brother's share two years later. Jacob moved to the other side of Woodward Avenue and founded a brewery at 12th and Howard streets, and a dynasty of his own. Reflecting the local beer market, he named his new venture the West Side Brewery Company. Its story is told in chapter 9.

William Darmstaetter also built a new brewery at the Catherine Street location, which he operated for the next twenty years. The only production figures available are for 1878 and 1879. The brewing business could have been going much better; sales were given as 1,944 and 887 barrels, respectively. In 1885, he decided to stop brewing entirely and converted the plant into a malthouse to supply the growing demand for malt. Having been a brewer himself, he no doubt could speak the right language when selling malt to his former competitors.

After thirty-three years in the malting and brewing business, William Darmstaetter retired in 1885. The business was left to his sons Rudolph, Arthur, and William Jr. The brothers wished to return to brewing, and the name Columbia Brewing Company was chosen. Arthur and William Jr. continued to malt, brew, and bottle after Rudolph's death in 1901. Arthur is listed as a partner until 1911, then William Jr. carried on alone. The brewmaster was George Walker, formerly with Koppitz-Melchers. The brewery was rated at a capacity of only 20,000 barrels in 1914. It was last listed in the 1917 Detroit directory.

Columbia was typical of many small breweries that could provide a decent living for their owners and workers. The Darmstaetter brothers invested in mechanical refrigeration, as did almost everybody else, but the business never took off to a degree that a larger plant made sense. The "grow or go" scenario already operated a century ago; a 20,000-barrel brewery in the 1910s was no longer competitive.

MEMORABILIA

Collectibles from the Columbia brewery are limited. Old bottles embossed "W. DARMSTAETTER / DETROIT, MICH." are highly regarded by collectors of antique bottles. Newer bottles embossed "COLUMBIA" with a C in a double circle are more common. A Columbia shell glass showing a trademark of intertwined initials on a U.S. shield promotes the "Select Export" brand. A small tray with "Columbia" on a brown wood pattern is occasionally seen, but large trays are very rare.

ENDRISS

CHARLES, GOTTLIEB & JULIUS ENDRISS, 1866–1889
350–352 RIVARD

The Endriss family was another case in which several members ended up brewing independently, at times even competing against each other, after having worked together, thus generating a very confusing story. The key member, Charles Endriss, was born in Goeppingen, Württemberg, in 1831. He arrived in the United States in 1852 but did not reach Detroit until 1865. Two years later, he founded a brewery at 350 Rivard. The brewery prospered and had sales of 6,600 barrels in 1879, but claimed capacities of 15,000 barrels in 1880 and 16,000 to 18,000 barrels in 1887 are highly inflated compared with actual production. Endriss also owned a malthouse on Bates Street between Woodbridge and Atwater. His daughter Elizabeth was listed as bookkeeper.

Another Endriss, Gottlieb F., started as a partner with Jacob Mann at 20 Maple Street in 1866. In 1872, Gottlieb established his own business at 320 Rivard, and his address was 42 Maple between 1874 and 1878. These locations were all at the corner of Rivard and Maple, where Mann had his brewery. In the 1875–76 directory, he had himself listed in heavy type, in competition with Charles, and he also paid for a special ad. Anyone living near Rivard and Maple streets surely had his choice of beers!

For several years, Gottlieb Endriss worked with his brother Julius; in 1877, the brewery was actually listed as Julius Endriss & Company. Soon thereafter, Julius took over a small operation at 25 Macomb. It had been started originally by Joseph Voelker in 1862 and was later acquired by Joseph Kurtz. Julius Endriss operated it until 1885. It was then purchased by John Zynda, five years before he built his own brewery on Canfield. The plant was probably just large enough to make a living for one family and a few workers. Gottlieb Endriss later became a bottler, with the same address on Maple for both his home and his business. It is likely that he bottled the beers brewed by Charles Endriss. Also boarding at 42 Maple were bottlers Frederick and William Endriss.

In the late 1880s, Charles Endriss became discouraged by the prospects for the brewing industry. When approached by Eastern and British investors in the spring of 1889, he sold out, along with his neighbor Jacob Mann. Goebel, the surviving entity, closed both breweries after a year. According to a newspaper report, Charles Endriss planned to go into the wholesale liquor business with his son Herman. They realized their plans with offices in the Chamber of Commerce building.

Endriss sold at a time when staying with beer meant facing much larger competitors as well as growing prohibitionist sentiment. There is, however, a postscript indicating that beer gets into the genes. In the fall of 1898, a little more than one year after Charles Endriss's death at age sixty-six on May 2, 1897, a new Endriss brewery was incorporated with a capital stock of $25,000. The principals were Julius Schnoering and two very familiar names: Herman Endriss and Charles Mann, Jr. The Phoenix brewery at the corner of Russell and Sherman had become available, and the new Endriss Brewing Company was listed in both the 1898 and 1899 city directories. No evidence exists that the brewery actually reopened, although the 1899 listing implies production. Herman Endriss hedged his investment by staying in the wholesale liquor business.

MEMORABILIA

Embossed bottles are in only a few collections, and nothing else has surfaced so far.

GERMANIA

FRED AND ELIZA GRIESER, 1871–1888
GERMANIA BREWING COMPANY, 1888–1900
294 SHERMAN

The story of the Grieser brewery illustrates the determination to continue in the face of tragedy. Fred Grieser started a home-brewing operation at the northeast corner of Sherman and St. Aubin in 1871. His untimely death two years later left his forty-one-year-old wife Elizabeth with a ten-year-old boy, John. Eliza, as she was known, buckled down and became one of the few women to run a brewery. If she could make a go of it, perhaps John could take his father's place someday.

In 1874, Eliza Grieser's brewery turned out 1,237 barrels, 1,355 the following year. In 1876, she was also operating a saloon as part of the establishment. A relative, Louis Grieser, came to live in the house and helped to brew. Nicholas Grieser, another relative who was a bookkeeper for the Hawley Malt Company, boarded at the home.

Finally, in 1885, twenty-two-year-old John Grieser was ready to take his place in the brewery. The name was changed to Germania Brewing Company in 1888, with John in charge. Nicholas Grieser left Hawley to join the family firm. By 1890, John was married and living at 193 Chestnut with his wife, Ellen. The Germania brewery was small but provided a living for the Griesers. In December 1895 Eliza Grieser died at sixty-four. Tragedy struck again in March, when John died suddenly at thirty-three, leaving an even younger widow.

Nicholas Grieser took over as brewmaster. However, time was running out for Germania, and the family closed the brewery in August 1898. The following July, Karl Zahringer and John Honer either purchased or leased the small plant and resumed production. Brewing operation shut down permanently in 1900.

MEMORABILIA
Nothing with the Germania name seems to be known.

OCHSENHIRT/HOME

VOLLGER & OCHSENHIRT, 1871
ADAM OCHSENHIRT, 1872–1882
ADAM OCHSENHIRT & COMPANY, AMERICAN BREWERY, PROPRIETOR, 1882–1890
HOME BREWING COMPANY, 1890–1902
148 SHERMAN STREET

Charles Vollger and Adam Ochsenhirt started brewing lager in 1871 on a very modest scale. The following year, Ochsenhirt bought out his partner, and from then on it was an Ochsenhirt family business.

Adam Ochsenhirt, with a keg to his right and his son Albert to his left, posing with the workers of their Home Brewing Company in the 1890s.   FROM THE STROH BREWERY COMPANY ARCHIVE.

Information on Ochsenhirt's background is very sketchy. He was born in 1835 and immigrated in 1854. How he became a brewer is not known. It took him seven years to exceed 2,000 barrels, producing perhaps 80 barrels per week in the summer. This would be the output of a microbrewery in the 1990s. He had the space to expand, as his property occupied an area of 115 by 140 feet.

Ochsenhirt incorporated his brewery in 1882 under his own name, referring to himself as proprietor of the American Brewery. He changed the name to Home Brewing Company in 1890. There probably was a decent local trade, but the business did not develop sufficiently, and the brewery closed in 1902. An attempt to sell the plant brought a high bid of only $14,000, which Ochsenhirt rejected. It was expected that the brewery would become a warehouse or depot.

No photograph of Ochsenhirt's brewery is known, but an excellent photograph of the Ochsenhirt family and the workers has survived. Two aspects of the group photo are noteworthy: almost everyone has a nice ceramic stein for drinking beer, and outdoor tavern signs are displayed. The Home brewery was small, but it had style.

A single bottle embossed "A. Ochsenhirt/Detroit" in the locally famous Heckman collection is the only one known, and several bottles embossed "Home Brewing Co." have been located.

KOCH

JOHN KOCH, ULMER
LAGER BEER BREWERY,
1872–1883

EKHARDT & BECKER,
MICHIGAN BREWERY,
1883–1891

244 RUSSELL

Albert Ochsenhirt in an 1897 convention brochure.

FROM THE STROH BREWERY COMPANY ARCHIVE.

The story of John Koch is neither significant nor dramatic, but it illustrates the matrix of a small brewer's extended family. Koch was born in Germany in 1840 and claimed 1865 was the year he moved to Detroit and started brewing, although he did not appear as a Detroit resident until the 1871–72 directory. He was listed as "Koch, John brewer, 242 Russell h. same," meaning that he had a very small brewery in back of his house. By 1874, the address was corrected to 244 Russell. In 1875 he found a name for his enterprise: "John Koch's Ulmer Lager Beer Brewery"—Ulm being a town in Bavaria, perhaps the original home of the Koch family.

The address did not change over the years, but the property and the brewery grew. A description in 1880 lists the brewery property as 100 by 150 feet and the capacity as 12,000 barrels, although sales were less than half of this amount in the preceding year. Cellar stock capacity was given as 2,500 barrels with an ice capacity of 500 tons. A 15-horsepower engine provided power. He also did his own malting. These are all indications that Koch's plant was of modest size but fully equipped.

An undated early photograph shows the house at 244 Russell, which was obviously used as both office and home. Thirteen men in work clothes are standing with the proprietor. The brewery was probably in the back; the sign on the roof is further confirmation. The man holding a large block of ice shows that hard labor was expected. Two women can be seen standing in the doorway, too shy to pose with the men.

Over the years, several family members worked at the periphery of the local brewing industry. Jacob Koch was a cooper in 1872 who later became a bartender at Julian Strelinger's saloon. (Strelinger in those

John Koch, standing in the center in front of the steps, poses with his workers in front of his brewery on Russell Street in the 1880s.   FROM THE COLLECTION OF JAMES L. KAISER.

years combined the unlikely careers of saloon keeper, brewer, and florist.) A Fritz Koch worked for John Koch in 1883, and Julius Koch became a cigar maker at Fred Toelle's shop. (Toelle later bought Henry Arndt's brewery on Gratiot Avenue.)

But it was J. William Koch, John's younger brother by seven years, whose work was closely linked with the brewery. A bottler since the middle 1870s, he handled the Ulmer Lager at his shop and home on 129 Sherman. In 1880, the dimensions of the bottling property were given as 150 by 150 feet. When John Koch changed the name from Ulmer to Michigan Brewery and then sold his business to August Ekhardt and Herman Becker in 1883, J. William Koch became proprietor of the Michigan Bottling Works. Ekhardt & Becker kept the Michigan Brewery name and bottling arrangement. J. William Koch brought his son into the business and added a saloon to his home. Ekhardt & Becker operated Koch's brewery for eight years and then closed it in 1891. By 1895, they had built a new brewery on Winder in the Eastern Market area.

John Koch could not keep from being a brewer. A year after selling out in 1883, he purchased a ten-year-old brewery on Monroe Street in Manchester, twenty miles southwest of Ann Arbor. He named his plant Michigan Southern Brewery and Bottling Works. His ads in the *Manchester Enterprise* for lager beer showed a trademark of intertwined initials and brewer's tools in front of a barrel. After seven years, in 1891 when John Koch was fifty-one, he sold his brewery to Charles Adrian. The brewery survived until 1919 as the Manchester Brewing Company. John Koch gave brewing one more fling in his sixties. In the early years of the new century, he was vice president of the Michigan Union Brewing Company in Ann Arbor.

MEMORABILIA

Nothing from the Ulmer or Michigan Brewery period has surfaced so far. Bottles embossed "J. W. Koch/Michigan Bottling Works" are known, and the single known bottle of the Michigan Southern Brewery and Bottling Works/ Manchester is in the Don Limpert collection.

Newspaper ad in the *Manchester Enterprise,* May 26, 1887.   COURTESY DON LIMPERT.

MANN

MANN (JACOB) & ENDRISS (CHARLES), 1866–1872
20 MAPLE
JACOB MANN, 1872–1889
28–30 MAPLE, 1872–1878; 343–351 RIVARD (MAPLE AND RIVARD), 1878–1889
CHRISTIAN MANN, 1874–1876
278 RUSSELL
C. MANN & COMPANY, FT. GRATIOT BREWERY, 1876–1879
DANIEL WALTZ, 1879–1881
GEORGE BLOSS, 1881–1897
2000 GRATIOT

Members of the Mann family, Jacob, Christian, and Lewis, at times competed with one another but also formed partnerships. Jacob Mann was born in Germany in 1843 and arrived in the United States with his parents four years later, first settling in Buffalo. Jacob is on record as a coppersmith at least since 1862. This must have brought him into contact with brewers, and in 1866 he opened a small brewery with Charles Endriss.

The partnership of Mann & Endriss lasted a dozen years, and then both started independent breweries. Jacob Mann located his brewery

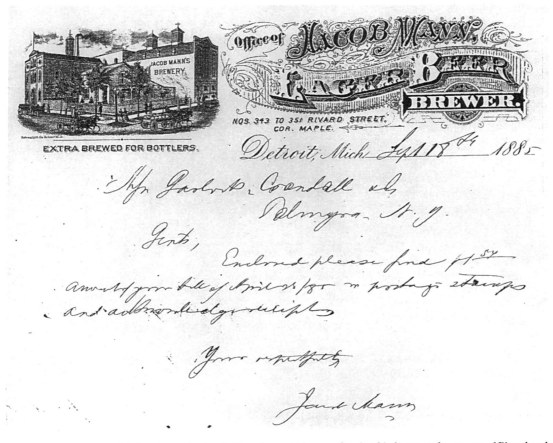

A letter signed by Jacob Mann is on stationary showing his home at the corner of Rivard and Maple streets, flanked by brewery buildings. Mann's house was replaced by Goebel's office building in 1893.   FROM THE COLLECTION OF TERRY WARRICK.

nearby, at the southwest corner of Rivard and Maple streets. It was not a tiny operation; his sales were 5,000 barrels the first year. He brewed lager, and although he added ale in 1885, he preferred to be known as a lager brewer. It is not known how the original brewery looked, but the 1878 plant was lithographed by Tuchfarber in Cincinnati in great detail and was also etched for stationery use during the 1880s. The corner lot was taken up by his residence, flanked on each side by brewery buildings. The brewhouse was on Rivard. According to the lithograph, there was an ice vault with adjoining storage shed on Maple, evidently part of the original brewery. The etching shows this was replaced by a three-story stock house with the false triangular roof frontage that was to become popular again a century later. A large malthouse formed the back corner of the property. The brewery was described in 1880 as occupying 100 by 110 feet with a capacity of 10,000 barrels and employing ten to twelve men.

Both Jacob Mann and Charles Endriss sold their businesses to the British syndicate in 1889, which placed August Goebel in charge, and he closed both breweries a few years later. Mann expressed a desire to move to California and cultivate fruit trees. When Goebel erected his new brewery across the street, he had the home demolished and replaced it with an office building. The structures on either side were still part of the Goebel complex in the late 1940s. The office building did not survive Prohibition.

An early competitor of Jacob Mann was Christian Mann. He started by brewing out of his home at 278 Russell in 1874, not far from Bernhard Stroh's brewery. Two years later, Christian Mann opened the Fort Gratiot Brewery at 2000 Gratiot under the business name of Christian Mann & Company. Production was about 1,400 barrels in 1879. The following year that plant was sold to Daniel Waltz. His widow took over when he died unexpectedly and continued as owner for another two years. It was then acquired by George Bloss. Nothing else seems to be known about this brewery; no description, photographs, bottles, or other artifacts have been located. The plant closed in 1897.

Another member of the Mann family, Lewis Mann, was listed in 1874 at 351 Rivard. This was the place where Jacob Mann had his beer bottled. Lewis Mann did not remain a brewer or bottler, but started a brewer's supply business in 1880. He later rejoined Jacob Mann at Maple and Rivard. He advertised extensively in the 1890 Detroit directory that he had "The Best Temperance Drink for Family Use," listing 105 Catherine near Rivard as the address.

MEMORABILIA
In addition to the lithograph, a very impressive black curved tavern sign with elaborate gold print is in the Warrick collection, which also includes stationery showing an etching of the home and brewery.

MANAGEMENT
1880: Jacob Mann, proprietor and brewer; Peter Babo, bookkeeper; Frank Tasche, foreman since 1874.

DITTMER/PHOENIX

FRANK BILZ, 1874–1876
FREDERICK DITTMER, WOLVERINE BREWERY, 1876–1884
FRED DITTMER BREWING COMPANY, 1884–1888
MILLENBACH BREWING COMPANY, 1888–1890
PHOENIX BREWING COMPANY, 1890–1896
230 RUSSELL STREET

The modest brewery at the northwest corner of Russell and Sherman streets had four owners during its twenty-two years of existence, but mostly it was Fred Dittmer's brewery.

Frank Bilz was the first on record, from 1874 to 1876. The following year found him brewing at 237 Mullet; no reason for the change is known.

For the next twelve years, the brewery was the property of Frederick Dittmer. His family immigrated in 1848 from Prussia when he was six years old, and they settled in Detroit in 1855. In 1867, at the age of twenty-five, Dittmer invested in a cigar manufacturing operation which became Sullivan & Dittmer. He may have been a partner in John Hock's saloon, because when he became a brewer as the proprietor of the Wolverine Brewery eight years later, Hock was the bottler of the "Celebrated Wolverine Lager Beer."

Dittmer's brewery prospered. Production in 1878 was 4,400 barrels, and a very respectable 7,400 barrels were produced the following year. Only Voigt, Kling, Stroh, and Goebel brewed more beer in 1879, and twenty-three breweries were smaller. In 1884, Dittmer incorporated the business as the Fred Dittmer Brewing Company, with Matthew Millenbach as vice president. The brewery building measured 50 by 100 feet and consisted of two floors and two cellars with a capacity of 10,000 barrels; it employed eight to ten men. There was mechanical cooling to a limited degree. Joseph Oberstadt was hired as foreman to supervise a crew of eight men and four wagons for the brewing and delivery of "Saazer Beer," Saaz being a region in Bohemia known for its fine aromatic hops.

Dittmer retired in 1888 at sixty-six. He sold his equity to his former associate Matthew Millenbach, who renamed the brewery after himself. Millenbach was the owner for two years only. In 1890, Peter Koenig acquired the property and changed the name again, to Phoenix Brewing Company.

Sales had not grown since the days of Dittmer, and the brewery was now marginal in size and sales. The new owner tried to promote his beer with etched tavern glasses advertising Velvet Beer. They show the rising Phoenix bird emblem and Koenig's name. His efforts, however, were too late or too modest. The establishment was sold at auction in February 1893 for $19,200 to Frank D. Andrews, who held a mortgage on the property and foreclosed on it. A fire in 1894 causing $5,000 damage was a further blow. The last directory listing for Phoenix was in 1896. Herman Endriss wanted to reopen the plant in 1898, but he could not obtain sufficient backing.

Fred Dittmer retired from all business in 1892, and lived in Detroit until his death at seventy-two in 1914. Head brewer Joseph Oberstadt became brewmaster in Mount Clemens.

MEMORABILIA

Only Wolverine bottles are known from the Dittmer years. A single beautiful brass tray from the Koenig period is in the Terry Warrick collection, the heraldic Phoenix bird matching the glasses advertising Velvet Beer.

MANAGEMENT

1880: Frederick Dittmer, brewer; John Jungert, bookkeeper.
1887: Frederick Dittmer, president; Matthew Millenbach, vice president;

August Ruoff, at left, sits surrounded by his workers. An unusual etched-glass sign is propped up behind a three-place barrel washer. As was customary in such group photos, booted cellar men are sitting in front while teamsters are standing in the rear.

Charles L. Beck, secretary and treasurer; Joseph Oberstadt, superintendent.
1888: Matthew Millenbach, president and treasurer; Joseph F. Dunnebach, secretary.
1890: Peter Koenig, proprietor

RUOFF

RUOFF BREWING COMPANY, 1861–1905
335 GRATIOT

August Ruoff was born in Württemberg in 1828 and, like Bernhard Stroh, was also an immigrant of 1848. Ruoff arrived in Detroit in 1849, and later he even became a close neighbor of Stroh's brewery on Gratiot Avenue. The histories of the two breweries, however, are vastly different.

While new arrival Stroh had a brewing background and lost no time in establishing himself as a brewer, Ruoff became a brewer by chance. For several years, he worked as a silverplater for John Rankin on Third Street and later opened his own silverplating shop. As a sideline, he bought a saloon on Monroe Street, and this led to contacts with brewers. The shift from saloon to what today is called a brewpub was quite common.

Ruoff's home brewery had an initial capacity of four half-barrels. This venture prospered and led to the building of a proper brewery and a saloon-residence on Gratiot Avenue. With time, Ruoff added a small malthouse and icehouses. However, he did not take the critical steps to enlarge his operation to become a shipping brewer and the owner of a larger, more modern plant. This meant investing in a new brewhouse, cellars, and an ammonia compressor. It meant expenditures for ads, signs, and trays, and going after the home delivery trade. But Ruoff never added a bottling operation, nor, for that matter, does he seem to have invested in merchandising items.

It seems that Ruoff was comfortable with who he was, a hands-on brewer who had started with very little and now had a decent living from his brewery and saloon. Production figures for 1878 and 1879 show that he sold 4,500 and 4,700 barrels. In 1880, he reported a staff of eleven men and operated three teams for delivery. Machinery was powered by an 8-horsepower engine. A great many breweries were smaller.

August's only son, Edward (there were six daughters), tried a jewelry business, which his father had started when he was a silverplater and had turned over to two half-brothers by the name of Traub. Later, Edward Ruoff went to work at his father's brewery. August Ruoff incorporated it in 1888, with himself as president, thirty-one-year-old Edward as vice president, and his wife, Bertha, as secretary and treasurer.

An interesting photograph of the Ruoff crew is in the Warrick collection. It shows the white-bearded Ruoff with a crew of sixteen. As was the custom when posing for such photographs, most of the men are holding their tools or glasses of beer. There are four teamsters in leather aprons with delivery record books in their breast pockets. The only equipment shown is a three-place keg washing station. The two round items on the barrel are swivel oil lamps for use in the beer storage caves.

A truly unusual promotional bar piece is shown—an etched glass plate for Salvador Lager Beer. Judging by the three full glasses being held, Salvador was an amber brew with a good head of foam. The photograph makes one important point. When it was taken, sixteen men and a working boss could brew 5,000 to 10,000 barrels a year and look at a camera with self-assurance. But even then, the economically viable size of a brewery was changing. The future would not accommodate August Ruoff's scale of operation.

August Ruoff retired in 1895 after 45 years in the business, and he let Edward run the shop. The Ruoff Brewery lasted ten more years, until Edward was forty-eight and August was seventy-seven. Ten years later, August Ruoff had lived to be Michigan's oldest living brewer. He died at age eighty-seven. Edward died in 1935 at age seventy-eight, and the Ruoff name died with him; he was survived by four married sisters.

There is a postscript. In 1956, Stroh started construction of the easternmost addition to its huge eight-floor beer storage (aging) building along Gratiot Avenue. Excavators uncovered the Ruoff caves, a reminder of another period when beer was aged underground in casks and cooled by river ice. The tunnels were lined with limestone to waist height, then with brick and brick arches. One tunnel went under Gratiot Avenue.

MEMORABILIA
No object from this brewery has been located so far, although trays, glasses, and saloon signs are known from breweries of similar size.

WESTPHALIA

ANTON KUHL, ANNA KUHL, 1871–1884
CITY BREWING COMPANY, 1884–1887
WESTPHALIA BREWING COMPANY, 1887–1895
425 CLINTON

This is the story of another small brewery taken over by a widow. Unfortunately, very little is known about this brewery in spite of a continuous operation for twenty-five years. In the end, it became one of several acquisitions by Ekhardt & Becker, who probably bought it for the saloons it supplied.

Anton Kuhl's operation in the early 1870s was very small, probably producing 1,000 barrels at most. It was just enough to make a living if all one did was fill barrels for local saloons and the family did much of the work. Kuhl was not to see success; he died in 1874. His widow, Anna, carried on bravely for ten more years, assisted at least for part of this period by brewmaster Robert Kiessel, who had had a falling out with E. W. Voigt.

For the next three years, the plant was called City Brewing Company, and in 1887, Anna Kuhl sold it to Joseph

Former Voigt brewmaster Robert Kiessel became Westphalia's brewmaster after a patent disagreement with E. W. Voigt. He later was brewmaster in West Bay City and at a large New York brewery.
COURTESY WILLIAM KIESSEL.

Nagel. He operated the brewery for eight years as the Westphalia Brewing Company. The treasurer of Westphalia was Joseph J. Noecker, who was succeeded by Anthony Kaiser in 1890. When Ekhardt & Becker acquired Westphalia in 1895 and closed it, Kaiser became vice president. After leaving Westphalia, Noecker invested in the Mount Clemens Brewing Company and served a term as its president. Brewmaster Kiessel moved to West Bay City, where a suitable position was available.

MEMORABILIA

It would be under Nagel's ownership that small merchandising items such as glasses, trays, or saloon signs could be expected, but nothing has turned up so far.

6

FOUR POLISH BREWERS

The early breweries were started by English-speaking men, and later came the Germans, but by the 1880s, a strong Polish community was established in Detroit as well. Its members also liked their beer.

The Auto City Brewing Company was not founded until 1910, but it became the largest of the four breweries operated by Polish immigrants. It had sound financial backing and had a strong if brief revival in the 1930s. Felix Talarowski and Teofil Marcinkowski produced liquid malt during Prohibition under the Wayne Products Company name and wanted to become real brewers after repeal. Their modest venture lasted only a few years. A Hamtramck competitor of Wayne for the home brewing trade was C&K, named after Casimir Kocat; his story is told under the successor firm Wagner Brewing Company in chapter 8.

Thomas Zoltowski operated a small brewery before Prohibition only. Almost nothing is known about this venture, although he considered his brewery to be a part of the mainstream local brewing industry. We know most about John Zynda and his White Eagle Brewery. John became the "Big Daddy" of an extended family. Several descendants have maintained an interest in family history, and have provided photographs and information for this book.

AUTO CITY

AUTO CITY BREWING COMPANY, 1910–1941
8214 McDOUGALL, HAMTRAMCK

Stanislaus Chronowski, about 1915.
COURTESY OF MARYLOU MARTIN.

The Chronowski brothers, Stanislav and Joseph, were born in Poland, Stanislav in 1875 and Joseph in 1880. Stanislav arrived in the United States in 1898, and he became a contractor. The brothers organized a brewery in the predominantly Polish enclave of Hamtramck in 1910, incorporating it as Auto City Brewing Company with a capitalization of $75,000. Stanislav took charge of the construction of a three-story brick building on an 80-by-100-foot area. The plant was designed for an initial capacity of 25,000 barrels and opened in December 1911 with Stanislav as president. Business was good from the start. Prospects continued to be favorable, and the capacity was doubled. Output was estimated at 40,000 barrels in 1914.

RIGHT PLACE, WRONG TIME

While 1910 seemed an odd time to enter the industry, with anti-saloon sentiment increasing, Hamtramck was a very good location for a brewery. A working-class neighborhood, Hamtramck became the location of the great "Old Main" Dodge plant. Slavs were known to like their pivo (beer). Workers could identify with the name "Auto City," the wheel emblem, and the Polish ownership.

When Prohibition became law in 1917, Joseph Chronowski left the brewery and organized the Liberty State Bank, also in Hamtramck. It was a smart move in the booming postwar economy. Stanislav and younger family members tried soft drinks for a couple of years, and then the plant was leased to a relative. During this period, brewing was resumed on the sly, and federal agents raided the brewery. The relative in charge had to serve time in Leavenworth. In 1928, the Chronowski brothers reopened the plant to produce liquid malt for home brewers. As the national mood swung toward repeal in 1932, Joseph took over as president and started to prepare the plant for brewing. Stanislav became vice president, and Joseph's son Alois was secretary. Funds for reopening the plant were raised by a stock issue in 1933.

An Auto City truck with a Bock Beer ad, 1935.

FROM THE MANNING BROTHERS HISTORIC PHOTOGRAPHIC COLLECTION.

THE BEER WITH VITAMIN B

The brewery reopened in 1934 with a refurbished brewhouse, consisting of an old combination mash-lauter tun, a new grant with fourteen taps (to collect the wort), and a new 330-barrel brewkettle in a clean and airy setting. New glass-lined storage tanks and bottling equipment with a capacity of 500 cases an hour were also installed.

Auto City had the exclusive local license for the Fischer process of restoring vitamin B to beer with surplus yeast. These were the years when vitamins were a popular issue and new vitamins were being discovered. The concept of adding back the vitamin B, which yeast is known to absorb during fermentation, is not without merit. This became a moot subject when the Food and Drug Administration banned vitamin advertising on the grounds that no health claims could be made for an alcoholic beverage.

Annual sales during the first three years were around 75,000 barrels. The best year was 1936, when Joseph reported net income of $119,000. The plant had a theoretical capacity of 250,000 barrels. Production would have to double to generate enough income to promote the Auto City and Altweiser brands adequately in the new competitive market. Unfortunately, the automobile industry weakened, and the strikes and layoffs in 1937 and 1938 had a serious impact on Auto City. Sales volume fell 36 percent in 1937. The brewery was never able to reverse this trend. One of the last brands tried was Bartosz, named after a patriot of the Old Country, but even his fiery and windblown visage, on a product launched in 1940, failed to arouse sales. A Canada Black Horse brand was either bought or leased from Cleveland's failing Kings Brew-

The Auto City brewery had been closed about a dozen years when this photo was taken from the rear in the mid-1950s. FROM THE COLLECTION OF ERNEST OEST.

ery in 1941, but Hamtramck was not horse country. Auto City closed late in 1941.

Auto City was the largest brewery operated by and for people of Polish ancestry. Like Zynda and a great many breweries of medium size, it catered to a specific ethnic and socio-economic segment. Its product was mostly a workingman's beer, and when the economy weakened and competition heated up, Auto City suffered.

MEMORABILIA

Auto City had a colorful "tin-over-cardboard" sign for its Altweiser brand, and one for the Bartosz brand is also known. Attractive labels from the 1930s are in many collections, but almost nothing seems to have survived from the pre-Prohibition years (1910–1917).

MANAGEMENT

1912: Stanislav Chronowski, president; Joseph Chronowski, vice president and treasurer; Charles Huhn, secretary and brewmaster.

1937: Joseph Chronowski, president, manager, brewmaster; Stanislav Chronowski, vice president; Alois Chronowski, secretary; Charles Huhn, treasurer; Thomas O'Hagan, sales manager; T. Pistrowski, chief engineer; Anthony Joss, bottling manager; Philip Ewald, draft manager.

1941: Joseph Chronowski, president, manager, purchasing agent; Joseph S. Chronowski, treasurer; Michael Schachtner, master brewer; John F. Kostuch, chief engineer.

Chronowski Family

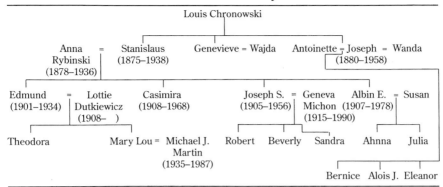

WAYNE

WAYNE PRODUCTS AND BREWING COMPANY, 1933–1936
WAYNE BREWING COMPANY, 1936–1937
3603 EAST HANCOCK

Felix Talarowski and Teofil Marcinkowski were partners in a liquid malt business to supply home brewers during Prohibition. The partners incorporated their venture in 1926 as the Wayne Products Company. With the return of beer in 1933, the liquid malt business ceased practically overnight, and the two Polish entrepeneurs obtained a license to manufacture beer. They changed the name of the business to Wayne Products and Brewing Company, later to the simpler Wayne Brewing Company, and set about to supply their former customers with the right stuff.

Much of 1933 was spent in erecting a three-story brewhouse. Designed under the direction of Detroit architect Louis Cantor, it was scaled to an initial capacity of 33,000 barrels. Wayne's brands Alt Pilsener and Bishop's Ale were among the lower-priced beers in the area. The first master brewer was Adam Wolfrum, formerly from Chicago; later came Eugene Kazmark. Initial sales of 40,000 barrels in 1934 were encouraging enough for plant capacity to be expanded. A premium Champagne Type Extra Pale brand was launched in 1935. Adam Blake, the former president of C&K, was taken on as draft beer manager. Total employment was about fifty to sixty. Sales in 1935 were 38,000 barrels, but the number decreased sharply to 20,000 barrels in 1936 after supply had caught up with demand. In January of the following year, the company petitioned for reorganization under Chapter 77B. The assets were sold at public auction in November, netting about $30,000.

Wayne beer is little more than a somber footnote in the brewing history of Detroit. But, for a group of partners in the liquid malt business during hard times, it was an opportunity to become brewers. Now little is left but the memories of elderly widows or grown children, whose husbands or fathers at one time were associated with a small Detroit brewery.

MEMORABILIA
Only a few labels and a single bottle opener are known.

MANAGEMENT
1934: Felix Talarowski, president and treasurer; Teofil Marcinkowski, vice president and secretary; Michel A. Roth, managing director; William A. Gant, sales manager; Adam Wolfrum, brewmaster.
1937: John F. Conroy, president; Teofil Marcinkowski, vice president and secretary; William M. Walker, treasurer; Felix Talarowski, assistant treasurer; Eugene Kazmark, brewmaster.

ZOLTOWSKI

THOMAS ZOLTOWSKI, 1891–1919
733 HASTINGS

Thomas Zoltowski was born in Poland in 1844 and was first listed as a Detroit resident in 1885, when he operated a grocery from his home at 743 Hastings. By 1891, he had changed the store into a saloon, and he soon started brewing a few buildings away from his residence.

Zoltowski was not the only brewer who came up by way of a grocery store and then a saloon. He was very serious about his trade as a brewer, and when the brewmasters had their annual convention in Detroit in 1897, he took a half-page ad in the program booklet. Unfortunately, it gives only his name, his address, and a highly inflated capacity of 30,000 barrels. The 1898 supplement to *Western Brewer* lists him as a lager brewer with an annual capacity of 12,000 to 14,000 barrels. Five years later, "about 20,000 barrels lager beer" was mentioned.

In spite of his brewery's modest size, Zoltowski considered himself part of the local mainstream brewing industry. He employed a series of German-American brewmasters over the years (Gustav Ladensack, Charles Ackerman, John Osser, Oscar Doerr, and Oscar Lang); otherwise, management was a family affair. He was never listed as a bottler, and no bottles or labels are known. The brewery remained active until Prohibition. Zoltowski died in March 1918 at age seventy-three, and the brewery ceased operation the following year.

MEMORABILIA
No tavern sign, glass, or tray has surfaced so far. No photograph of Zoltowski or his brewery could be located.

MANAGEMENT
1897: Thomas Zoltowski, brewer.
1918: Thomas Zoltowski, president; B. Zoltowski, secretary-treasurer; J. Zoltowski, manager; Oscar Lang, brewmaster.

ZYNDA

John Zynda,
White Eagle Brewery,
1886–1891

25 Macomb

John Zynda & Bros.,
White Eagle Brewery,
1891–1919

John Zynda & Sons,
1919–1932

Zynda Brewing
Company, 1933–1948

862 (later 4232)
Riopelle

John Zynda, in an 1897 convention brochure.
From The Stroh Brewery Company Archive.

When slender, twenty-one-year-old John Zynda arrived in Detroit in 1880, no one would have guessed that he was destined to become a "Big Daddy" in the Polish community and a corpulent presence in the brewing fraternity. Zynda was born into a Polish family in Berent, East Prussia, which after World War I was ceded to Poland. Having been educated in the art of brewing early in life, he found employment in the Anton Michenfelder brewery at Sherman and Rivard, where he became foreman. His brother Theophilus followed Zynda to Detroit in 1882.

THE WHITE EAGLE

In that year, John Zynda married Augustine Eichler in Detroit. In 1886, he purchased a small brewery from Joseph Kurtz at 25 Macomb Street at the corner of Brush. The business prospered, and in 1891, he opened a much larger plant at the corner of Riopelle and Canfield, a few blocks northwest of Eastern Market. Local architect Peter Dederichs, Jr., designed the brewery, which also contained bottling facilities. Zynda called it the White Eagle Brewery in honor of the national emblem of his homeland. Engravings show minuscule people and horses in relation to the extensive building. Photographs, however, indicate that not everything shown was built, such as the malting wing. Zynda was president, and his brother Theophilus, who joined him in 1891, was secretary.

GOOD LIFE IN THE NEW WORLD

The union of John and Augustina Zynda was blessed with nine children: Anna, Helena, John Jr., Paulina, Joseph, Leo, Charles, Rose, and Aloysius. As his family and his fortune grew, Zynda bought a large house

The Zynda brewery building at Riopelle and Canfield, which closed in 1948, was photographed in the mid-1950s, when the neighborhood was still residential.

on Bellevue with extensive grounds, which became like an Old World farm estate with fruit trees, ducks, geese, and chickens. John smoked his own meats for the winter holidays, and stories of sons sneaking sausages to be eaten in the barn are told by now-elderly grandchildren.

Family members also describe the house during the gaslight era. The living room and the master bedroom had large fireplaces. The grand piano, grandfather clock, and curio cabinet impressed the grandchildren. An open staircase led to a long hallway with bedrooms and John's card room, where he kept his stein collection. At the top of the stairs was a chapel with two or three pews; a priest would come over on occasion to hold mass for Zynda. Two bathrooms, with old-fashioned wooden tanks, were upstairs, and the kids would get into trouble for flushing the toilet too much.

Zynda is remembered as a strict paterfamilias of the old school. There was no talking at dinner until the meal was over. The girls had to polish the silver and feed the fowl; the boys had their chores as well. After Christmas dinner, all the children would form a circle in the living room. Zynda would dress as Santa and dump bags of apples, oranges, and nuts onto the floor, which had to be grabbed quickly, and then he would hand out presents.

STAN'S ALASKAN ADVENTURE

A younger brother, Stanislaus, had arrived in 1890. He, too, went to work at the brewery, where he was foreman. While John Zynda's other brother, Theo, stayed with the brewery, Stanislaus heeded the call to go west. Alaska had become the frontier, and Stan ended up in Seattle and then Juneau, which had several small breweries. He was the brewmaster of the Douglas Brewery in 1914; later, he bought the Juneau Brewery and changed its name to the Eagle Brewery. Alaska must have been a difficult place to brew, with its $1000 license fee, uncertain supplies of raw materials, and a boom-or-bust economy. Brewing ceased in 1919, and Stan returned to Seattle.

Back home in Detroit, the second generation had gone to work, and John Zynda, Jr., became manager of the brewery in 1903. The original Pilsener and Culmbacher brands were replaced by Crystal Pale and Zyndapride.

LADIES MAN

In 1912, John Zynda, a widower for five years, left on a trip to the Old Country. In his hometown of Berent, the fifty-three-year-old brewer, still an imposing and handsome man with a full beard, met and married Anna Sanger, a woman in her thirties. This caused a scandal on his return to Detroit. A thirty-seven-year-old widow, Valeria Gizynski, instigated a $20,000 breach of promise suit claiming that he had wooed her ardently—a newspaper account left little to the imagination regarding his alleged impulsive nature—and that she had expected to be the next Mrs. Zynda.

Zynda himself was described as calm; he was no doubt waiting for the furor to subside. He probably settled out of court, as his relationship with Valeria Gizynski must have been widely known and there is no further mention of legal action.

A GAME OF COPS AND BREWERS

John Zynda served on the Detroit Board of Water Commissioners for eight years and was an important member of Detroit's Polish community. Many local weddings and funerals of note were made more sociable by the delivery of a complementary keg of Zyndapride Lager.

When Prohibition became effective in 1919, Zynda converted his brewery to the manufacture of soft drinks, including Birch Beer and a chocolate drink. At that time, the business name was changed from John Zynda & Brother to John Zynda & Sons. We know from family oral history that Zynda and his sons did not feel that soft drinks and near beer would "cut the mustard" in Hamtramck. It was far more likely that Zynda would go on a diet than that he would stop providing beer to his customers.

It so happened that the garage across the street was connected to the brewery by an underground tunnel. Up the street was Grocholski's hardware store, a former saloon whose owner was only too happy to serve as lookout. When federal agents were watching, a truck filled with near beer would leave in a hurry, chased by the agents. The former saloon keeper then signaled when the coast was clear, and the real shipment would be sent on its way.

Usually the Zyndas would be tipped off before a raid, so everything would be cleaned up, and there would be nothing to show. One time, a new agent came to inspect. He went to watch empty half-barrels being washed, and he found a keg full of good beer. John Zynda and one of his brothers had to go to a downtown hotel and pay off the feds, who had tapped the confiscated keg and were busily drinking up the evidence.

The Zyndas also ran a small illegal brewery operation at their Bellevue Street property, which had large grounds and a barn. A tinsmith by the name of Jake Knapp made a tank of about 50 gallons' capacity to fit behind the rear seat of John Zynda's limousine. By one means or another, the Zyndas brewed and sold real beer.

Local policemen also looked out for Zynda shipments. One day, when a beer truck was unknowingly approaching a crime scene, a policeman stopped the truck with the warning that he knew what was inside the vehicle and told the driver to clear out fast.

THE EAGLE GETS OLD

Zynda died in December 1927 at the age of sixty-eight. His four oldest sons continued with the manufacture of soft drinks until shortly after the crash of 1929, when the plant was closed.

The Zynda Brewing Company was reopened in 1933 with John Zynda, Jr., as president and other family members as officers. The brands were the old Crystal Pale, a new Zynda's Lager, and a dark Muenchener. The peak year was 1934, when almost 48,000 barrels were sold. Two years later, the bubble burst, and sales were only half that amount.

In 1943, Joseph Zynda took over. He added an Old Eagle brand, which became the only brand in wartime 1944. Sales hovered around 12,000 barrels. Joseph Zynda remained president until the brewery closed in 1948, when larger breweries started to advertise heavily. In the

Zynda newspaper advertisement ca. 1936.   COURTESY FRANK ZYNDA.

words of John Zynda, Jr., "The plant was too small to brew enough beer to pay for the advertising to sell the beer."

That comment begs the question "Why did the family fail to enlarge the operation when business was good in the teens?" Actually, John Zynda was reported to have purchased land in Toledo in 1895 for a second brewery, and in 1902, building was supposed to have begun. The reason for abandoning this project is not known. John Zynda had started with next to nothing, and by age fifty, in 1909, he had achieved wealth and status in his community. He had fought the good fight and no doubt wished to enjoy the rewards. He and his sons carried on gamely during Prohibition, but two years after beer returned, they faced vastly larger and more aggressive brewers. Zynda outlasted its larger competitor Auto City seemingly by inertia. The Zynda brewery had been very much a part of the Polish community before Prohibition; after repeal, the old loyalties of Hamtramck were weaker, and the scale and cost of competition escalated after the war.

The brewery stood empty for many years and then was used by a plumbing supply firm before being demolished as part of a renewal project. A small bottling building was not torn down until the early 1970s.

MEMORABILIA

Older material is very scarce. The most desirable and unique item is a large, vertical, oval serving tray showing John Zynda's portrait, with a full flowing beard in profile, and a bottle of Crystal Pale in the foreground. Round metal trays with etchings of the White Eagle Brewery are known. Bottles and labels from the 1930s are relatively common.

MANAGEMENT

1897: John Zynda, president and treasurer; Theophilus Zynda, secretary. 1943–1948: Joseph J. Zynda, president and purchasing agent; John F. Zynda, vice president; Charles Zynda, secretary; Leo Zynda, treasurer; William. J. Schneider, brewmaster.

Artist's drawing of the White Eagle brewery, greatly exaggerated. The section at right was never built.

Zynda Family

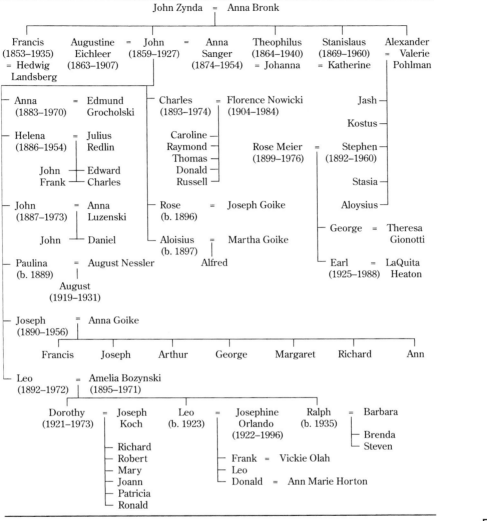

7

FOUR MUTUALLY OWNED BREWERIES

Federal law in the United States prohibits a brewery from owning saloons, with the recent exception of a small brewpub. This was not always so, nor is it the rule everywhere. Most pubs in the United Kingdom are "tied" to breweries. In Munich, you may order from five or six brands in any beer hall, but all will have been brewed by the specific brewery that leases out the premises. Before Prohibition, it was common practice for breweries in this country to own saloons in order to ensure a steady business.

Not all tavern keepers liked this arrangement. Breweries at times set prices according to their view of what constituted a decent return. Many small saloon owners had little or no say in matters affecting their income. Switching to another brewery would be no help; brewers set prices as a cartel.

The answer, tried in many cities, was for a group of saloon keepers to pool their resources, buy a small brewery, and hire a brewmaster to brew only for them. As part owners of a brewery, they controlled costs and knew what was a fair price. Names such as "Peoples Brewery," "Mutual Brewing Company," or "Consumers Brewing Company" indicate such arrangements.

Detroit had four breweries that were jointly owned during part of their life cycle. None of these was large, because both capitalization and needs were modest. Their stories illustrate the determination to be independent. However, they did not expect Prohibition any more than their larger competitors, and they had to close. The largest of the four reopened

The Union brewery in 1921.

after repeal, but by then it was just another small brewery in a market that soon became saturated.

UNION

UNION BREWING COMPANY, 1898–1919

UNION BEVERAGE COMPANY, UNION MALT PRODUCTS COMPANY, 1919–1933

CADILLAC BREWING COMPANY, 1934–1936

UNION BREWING COMPANY, 1936

24 (LATER RENUMBERED 3520) MITCHELL

Eight years after the original Union Brewing Company on West Fort Street closed, a group of saloon keepers revived the Union name. They organized a new corporation with a board of trustees and raised $75,000 to build a brewery for their own supply. Joseph Aiple, the former brewmaster at Goebel, headed the new venture. Aiple was then forty-two years old; he liked to hunt on two hundred acres of farmland he owned near Novi, and he was designated to cull the wild pigs on Belle Isle. His granddaughter, now in her mid-eighties, recalls a stuffed tusked boar's head in his home on McDougall from such a hunt.

The brewery was erected near the northeast corner of Gratiot and Mitchell, with a four-story, 150-barrel brewhouse. The building featured the crenellated roof line and highly decorated corbeled cornices of the Rhine castle architecture then popular. The first beer reached the taverns in June 1899. During the twenty years that the Union brewery was operating, the brand of the lager was Gilt Edge, and,

Goebel brewmaster Joseph Aiple, shown in an 1897 convention brochure, left soon thereafter to head the Union brewery.

FROM THE STROH BREWERY COMPANY ARCHIVE.

except for seasonal Bock, no other type was evidently brewed. The corporate name was changed to Union Beverage Company after the Michigan Prohibition Amendment in May 1917, and near beer and soft drinks were produced. When it became obvious later that the only viable Prohibition product was "liquid malt" for home brewers, the name was changed to Union Malt Products Company.

Investors bought the plant in 1933 and remodeled it for a capacity of 60,000 barrels. It was reopened in 1934 as the Cadillac Brewing Company. The labels show the automobile brand's crest, which was the crest of Detroit's founder, de la Mothe Cadillac, and was copied freely in those years to denote quality. The brewmaster was Homer Emory, formerly with the Riverside brewery near Windsor. Sales started off that year with 29,300 barrels, which generated $25,000 in operating income. Only a modest increase of 2,000 barrels could be achieved in 1935. Tivoli in the same part of town posted sales of 154,000 barrels in 1934 and 218,000 in 1935.

Clearly, Cadillac was not going to survive the post-repeal shakeout. A reorganization in 1936 brought the Union name back, but the small brewery could not compete in the same market, and production ceased later that year. The main buildings have long been razed. Only the two-story structure at the north end is still standing.

The brewery commissioned a very attractive serving tray with patriotic and brewing symbols to promote its Gilt Edge beer in gold letters. With a shield of stars and stripes superimposed on a large star, the Union tray is a colorful and highly desired collectible. A few delicate etched glasses depicting the brewery have survived. Little except labels are known from the Cadillac period after repeal. Small rectangular metal signs for store or tavern use ("tin-over-cardboard") were produced, but they are among the scarcest signs from the 1930s.

MANAGEMENT

1899–1918: Joseph Aiple, president, manager, and brewmaster; William Schook, vice president (to 1904); Lawrence Einhauser, vice president (after 1904); Oscar Kretchmar, secretary-treasurer; August Stieber, Peter Greiner, Albert Maas, initial board of trustees.
1933: F. C. Sebulke, president; William Schook, vice president; John De Schepper, secretary; Gustave J. Maertens, treasurer; Homer Emory, brewmaster.

EAST SIDE

CLEMENS BROTHERS, 1880–1882
JOHN CLEMENS, 1886–1891
115 CHESTNUT
CLEMENS BROTHERS, 1882–1885
EXCELSIOR BREWERY, 1886–1888
J. F. CLEMENS & COMPANY, 1888–1893
34 JAY
EAST SIDE BREWING COMPANY, 1893–1904
468 GRATIOT

The four Clemens brothers—John, Joseph, Peter, and Raymond—were descendants of one of the early settlers in Michigan, Joseph Clemens (1820–1865) of Eagle River in the Upper Peninsula. His son Peter owned one of the two breweries there. A grandson, also named Peter, was born in Eagle River in 1864, and came to Detroit at age five when his father relocated.

Brothers John and Joseph Clemens, like other brothers of early brewing families, were sometimes partners and also competitors. They were brewers at 115 Chestnut Street in 1880, producing a very modest 1,000 to 1,500 barrels per year.

The Chestnut Street brewery was originally started by Robert J. Marsh in 1874. Its ownership history is complex: in the 1880s, John Clemens was brewing there either with his brother, with a partner named August Naecker, or as sole proprietor for eleven years. The brewery ended up as the property of Frederick Frey.

From 1882, the Clemens brothers were also briefly associated with a brewery at 34 Jay Street. Between 1884 and 1891, John is listed as brewing at the original Chestnut Street address, while Joseph continued on

Jay Street. Between 1886 and 1888, Joseph called it the Excelsior Brewery, then J. F. Clemens & Company. In 1893, Joseph operated a saloon at his home on Gratiot Avenue.

THE EAST SIDE BREWERY

A number of saloon keepers east of Woodward formed a corporation with $25,000 under the name East Side Brewing Company to brew their own beer. Joseph Clemens was approached, and he joined the venture as president, with Peter Clemens as brewmaster. It was a small brewery with a listed capacity of 6,000 to 7,000 barrels. Peter's older brother Raymond also may

East Side brewmaster Peter Clemens, in an 1897 convention brochure.
FROM THE STROH BREWERY COMPANY ARCHIVE.

have worked there in the office. He later became manager and then secretary-treasurer of the brewery in Pontiac. Frank Clemens, the fourth brother, succeeded Peter as brewmaster in 1901.

The East Side brewery advertised its taproom where one could sample Pale Select and a darker Würzburger. It did not help enough, however. The saloon trade was very competitive, and East Side went out of business in 1904. Joseph was appointed receiver of the firm. In the same year, Frey also closed the Chestnut Street brewery.

In 1905, Peter Clemens joined his brother Raymond in Pontiac to become brewmaster of the Pontiac Brewery. He became vice president and was probably a part owner. When Prohibition loomed, Peter moved back to Detroit and opened a billiard hall at 2966 East Jefferson. He died in February 1929 at age sixty-four; a few more years, and there would have been real beer to go along with the click of rolling balls. Of the four Clemens brothers, only Raymond survived him.

MEMORABILIA

Only a few etched glasses and embossed bottles are known. No photographs of the brewery have surfaced. Peter Clemens's membership diploma in the Master Brewers, dated 1897 and printed in German, has been saved by the family.

MANAGEMENT

1893: Joseph F. Clemens, president; Frank Radke, vice president; Raymond Clemens, secretary.

INDEPENDENT

INDEPENDENT BREWING COMPANY
MICHIGAN CENTRAL R.R. & SPRINGWELLS, 1907–1919
CENTRAL NEAR W. WARREN, OFFICE AT 814 PENOBSCOT BLDG., 1934–1936

Thirty saloon keepers in southwest Detroit were so dissatisfied by the strong position of breweries in the summer of 1906 that they collected $75,000 and incorporated their own Independent Brewing Company. The stockholders then authorized $70,000 for the construction of a brewery in the Springwells district to serve the needs of member saloons at a time when many taverns had no choice of brands and prices. The beer was a lager named Ideal. Beer production was mostly draft, and capacity was estimated at 40,000 barrels in 1914.

FROM BEER TO BEEF

Prohibition closed the brewing operation, but the story does not end there. A group of cattle breeders bought the property cooperatively, also hoping to save money. It became a meat packing house, the Detroit Packing Company. This is not the only instance where a brewery became a meat processing and storage facility. Both products require large refrigerated spaces. With beer tanks removed, insulated and refrigerated buildings from several breweries located near the Eastern Market are still used for meat storage.

The Independent brewery was not reopened for lack of interest and effort. After repeal, two groups submitted bids for the former brewery building to William S. Sayres, the federal master in Chancery. One bid was from a group of meat processors headed by O. L. Smith, the other from Ben P. Jacobs and associates, who wanted to reopen the brewery. Independent had a good chance, because Sayres had recommended them even before repeal, if Congress were to relegalize beer. Although the Jacobs group bid $16,000 more than Smith, the ruling in federal court went against using the buildings for brewing because the Federal Farm Credit Administration had agreed to advance $320,000 to the Smith group.

Determined not to give up, former brewmaster George Schmitt headed a group of investors interested in raising funds for building an entirely new brewery. Operating from an office in the prestigious Penobscot Building, a new Independent Brewing Company was incorporated, with Schmitt as president.

FROM IDEAL TO IDEALISTIC

A contract to build a plant with a capacity of 180,000 barrels went to the J. G. Jarman Company for $150,000. Ground was broken in 1934 on Central Avenue in the west side industrial district for "the first really new brewery since Prohibition." In the spring of 1935, Schmitt reported that the new plant was "progressing toward completion." The brewery never made it to the finish line. A year later, in March 1936, Pros't acquired the assets by a stock exchange. As Pros't itself merged with Voigt in 1936 and failed in 1937, the original investors received stock of very questionable value.

MEMORABILIA

Independent items are all but impossible to find, and no photograph of the brewery could be located. A tray and a label are known, and an etched glass shows that the tavern owners had at least the thin-walled glasses promoting the Ideal brand. Member saloons probably had the customary corner signs flanking their doors. Rare embossed bottles show the hop cone trademark.

MANAGEMENT

1906: John P. Cole, president; William F. Zoeller, vice president; William Unruh, secretary-treasurer; Martin Schaefer, brewmaster (1906–1909).

1908: William F. Zoeller, president; William Daley, vice president; Thomas R. McCreery, secretary-treasurer.

1914–1918: William Daley, president and manager; August Grunan, vice president; Edward R. Weipert, secretary-treasurer; George H. Schmitt, brewmaster (1910–1919).

Bottle label, ca. 1910.

COURTESY ROBERT KAY.

MUTUAL

JULIAN STRELINGER, 1865–1894
MUTUAL BREWING COMPANY, 1894–1915
625 HASTINGS STREET

Julian Strelinger was a lager brewer on record since 1865. For many years, he brewed at his home at 113 Bates. He also operated a saloon on Monroe and a florist shop and greenhouse on Griswold. The home on Bates later became the office, with a brewing operation at the corner of St. Aubin and Jay streets.

In 1891, when he was probably in his fifties, he had a new brewery built at the corner of Mt. Elliott and Hastings, and he achieved what had eluded many house brewers: a proper brewery. The building was small, only two floors above a cellar. For unknown reasons, perhaps failing health, he retired two years later. The brewery was leased to Adam Klein and Frank Dierkes.

In 1894, the Mutual Brewing Company was organized, mostly by saloon keepers, to operate the former Strelinger plant. Klein and Dierkes were the managing partners. The brewery was a small and primitive

The Mutual Brewery in an 1897 convention brochure. The policeman on horseback no doubt knew where to go for refreshment.   FROM THE STROH BREWERY COMPANY ARCHIVE.

operation for the 1890s, without mechanical cooling, but it served the purpose of brewing for its tavern owners. A capacity of 20,000 barrels was claimed in 1897. The plant closed in 1915 after two decades.

MEMORABILIA

No point-of-sale merchandising items have survived. A photograph of the brewery was published in 1897. An adjoining tavern has curved outdoor metal signs; all member taverns must have been similarly equipped. Embossed bottles are known but rarely seen.

Mutual Brewing Company partner Adam Klein in an 1897 convention brochure.
FROM THE STROH BREWERY COMPANY ARCHIVE.

8

EIGHT THAT TRIED
AFTER REPEAL

The euphoria of finally seeing the end of Prohibition tempted large and small investors to cash in on the demand for beer. These ranged from William Bache's very small operation in Ecorse to well-financed ventures by big names on both sides of the Detroit River. Malt syrup facilities were bought by would-be brewers, or the owners tried to continue the brewing process to the finished product.

Unfortunately, failure was their common destiny. By 1936, the pent-up thirst had been slaked and the old established names were again dominant. It now required a good product and advertising to stay in business. A new name, no matter how sound the investors behind it, could not generate enough sales by 1938 to be competitive. Small brewers could have supplied a strictly neighborhood tavern business, but it was now illegal to brew and also sell the product directly to consumers.

One firm included here actually belongs to a separate category. The Michigan Brewing Company was started in 1912 by the Koerber family when their former brewery in Ionia had to close because of local Prohibition; it lasted about a decade. Family members continued brewing after repeal, but not in Detroit.

These stories, though sad, are also interesting and even inspiring. Small brewers did their very best to compete and be part of an industry they loved.

The former Bache brewery in Ecorse, photographed in 1955.

BACHE

W. S. BACHE COMPANY, 1935–1936
IMPERIAL BREWING COMPANY, 1936
240 SALLIOTTE, ECORSE

William Bache opened a small brewing operation after repeal of Prohibition in the industrial downriver community of Ecorse, with himself as president and brewmaster. Almost nothing is known about this brewery. A 1955 photograph of a rectangular two-floor brick building at 240 Salliotte suggests that it must have been built after World War I. At least one batch of Bache's Stratford Stout was produced, and 1935 sales of 66 barrels were reported. The name was changed to Imperial Brewing Company, probably in 1936. A label of Imperial Stout has survived in a condition suggesting actual usage, and a few unused labels of Stratford Stout are known.

This was probably a family venture with several partners in the manner of many current microbreweries, and stronger on hopes than financing. While Bache had no competition for stout, its market must have been small and dispersed. And Ecorse was the wrong community to promote what today would be called a very upscale or crafted malt beverage. With hindsight it is not surprising that William Bache failed early. The building is no longer standing.

MEMORABILIA

For a long time, it was assumed that nothing was known; the brewery was somewhat of a secret even to local collectors. Then the labels and photograph turned up.

MANAGEMENT

1936: William S. Bache, president and master brewer; William C. Liddle, vice president; Harry A. McKnight, secretary-treasurer; William S. Bache, Jr., assistant brewer.

FORT DEARBORN

FORT DEARBORN BREWING CORPORATION, 1933–1937
12001 EAST JEFFERSON, 1933–1936
530 PENOBSCOT BLDG., 1936–1937

It was not only the old breweries that were dusted off after Prohibition and readied for quenching the anticipated thirst for a foamy brew. Quite a few investors considered starting with a new plant, but often with inadequate capital. The venture with the strongest resources, the best-known names, and the widest business experience was the Fort Dearborn Brewery.

In the fall of 1933, Edwin Ralph Stroh, a grandson of founder Bernhard by son Bernhard Jr., applied for a brewing license. Edwin Stroh headed an insurance business out of an office in the National Bank Building. His father had sold his interest in the family business to his younger brother Julius when faced with ill health before Prohibition, and Edwin Stroh saw an opportunity for his branch to reenter the brewing industry.

A small and antiquated brewery would be no match for the major brewers with their six-digit barrel outputs before Prohibition. So Stroh went to the best industrial architect that Detroit could offer—Albert Kahn Engineering—for a design of a 200,000-barrel brewery with room to expand. The Kahn design called for a tall building with strong vertical lines for the brewhouse and stock house. A two-story building would serve for offices, and a large, low building was designed for packaging.

HENRY FORD'S NEW NEIGHBOR

The plant was to be erected in the western suburb of Dearborn on Schaefer Road, where an 11-acre site had been purchased. This was in the heart of Henry Ford's industrial park, and, in fact, the site chosen was across from the administration building of the Ford Motor Company. It was estimated that $1 million would be needed for land, buildings, and equipment. The City of Dearborn requested approval of the license from the Treasury Department, as the automotive sector was then weak and unemployment high.

Edwin Stroh set about getting financing, and he approached Hiram Walker Ltd. Harrington E. Walker was in charge, and he liked the idea so much that he took it over from Stroh. In January 1934, Harrington Walker announced the organization of H. E. Walker Distillers and Brewers, Inc., with offices on East Jefferson. The new firm planned to build a distillery capable of a daily capacity of 9,000 gallons on a site adjacent to the brewery, which kept the corporate name of Fort Dearborn Brewing Corporation. Both it and the Imperial Distillers Company were divisions of H. E. Walker Distillers and Brewers.

The officers, in addition to H. E. Walker, consisted of Edwin Stroh, Stephen L. Fitzpatrick, and Edwin's brother, Bernhard Stroh. These and Hiram H. Walker, Albert Kahn, Jerome H. Remick, Jr., Maynard D.

Smith, James Vernor, Jr., and Fritz Goebel constituted the board. Vernor was president of the ginger ale company and a transportation expert, and Fritz Goebel was slated to be brewmaster. It was a strong board, both in terms of talent and finances.

At that time, nothing came of the great plans for the Dearborn site. It is highly unlikely that Henry Ford, who neither drank nor smoked and was not shy about enforcing his views, wanted a distillery in what today would be called his face. One can only imagine what transpired. Hiram H. Walker decided to build the distillery in Detroit instead, and he then dropped out.

A SECOND EFFORT

Following a board of directors meeting in the summer of 1936, the Fort Dearborn Brewing Company became an entirely separate entity, which planned to build the brewery on the site purchased for that purpose in Dearborn. Stockholders in the former parent company were given shares in the brewery at no extra cost. The president of the new brewing company was again Edwin Stroh, now working out of an office in the Penobscot Building. But without Hiram Walker's backing, there was insufficient funding; the window of opportunity was closing, and the venture folded. Albert Kahn Engineering was probably one of the few winners in this venture, using the sketch of the proposed Fort Dearborn brewery to promote brewery design work in an industry publication.

MANAGEMENT

1934: Harrington E. Walker, president; Edwin R. Stroh, vice president; Stephen L. Fitzpatrick, vice president-secretary; Bernhard Stroh, treasurer.

1937: Edwin R. Stroh, president; Stephen L. Patrick, vice president.

B. Stroh Jr. Family

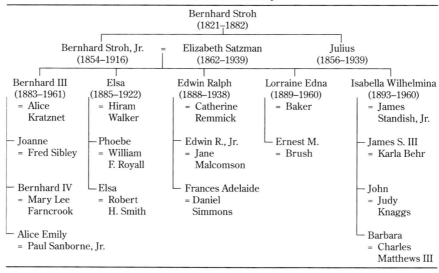

KRAFTIG

VON BREWING COMPANY, 1933–1935
KRAFT BREWING COMPANY, 1936–1937
KRAFTIG BREWING COMPANY, 1937
1800 EAST FOREST AVENUE

Von is a clear case of a brewing operation started from scratch with modest capitalization and an excess of optimism. The large building at the corner of Forest and Orleans on Detroit's east side was newly equipped for a capacity of 60,000 barrels. A reputable brewmaster with forty years' experience, Matthew Stegmeyer, was hired, and brewing began in 1934. The hoped-for market niche for superior beer either was very small, failed to be developed, or was being tapped by others. While the Von label was very attractive and provided a quality image, the name failed to generate sufficient sales. The preposition *von* means "of" in German and denotes nobility in family names. Probably it was meant to supply an aristocratic touch. Von sold 32,700 barrels in 1934 and 26,900 in 1935.

New investors took over the operation, who changed the name to Kraft Brewing Company, *Kraft* being German for "strength." Two adjoining buildings were acquired. Kraftig ("strong") Bohemian Type beer was placed on the market in July 1936. Sales were hurt by the changeover and amounted to only 6,500 barrels. The following year, the corporate name was also modified to Kraftig Brewing Company. By July, it was apparent that Kraftig was too weak to survive. A petition was filed asking for dissolution. Production was suspended in August, and sales ended in October after 15,000 barrels. The order for dissolution was approved in December.

Stegmeyer retired, but he had the satisfaction of seeing his son William work his way up in the craft to become a brewmaster of the Detroit Brewing Company in the early 1940s.

MEMORABILIA

A single tin-over-cardboard sign is the only item known locally from the Von period. Very little has survived of Kraft or Kraftig advertising. A small Kraftig plywood sign, a tin-over-cardboard sign, and a wall plaque are known. Even labels are hard to locate; only 5,000 barrels of Kraftig beer were bottled out of 21,500 barrels in total sales.

MANAGEMENT

1933: Ralph F. Foster, president; Sidney B. Berger, vice president; George W. Luke, secretary-treasurer; W. Burt Hollingworth, general manager; Anthony Maiullo, director (attorney); Matthew Stegmeyer, brewmaster.

1936: Jean C. Stuhr, president; P. Hugh Brevier, vice president; Edmund J. Boell, secretary-treasurer, Michael Rottenkolber, brewmaster.

1937: Karl F. Bergmann, president and permanent receiver.

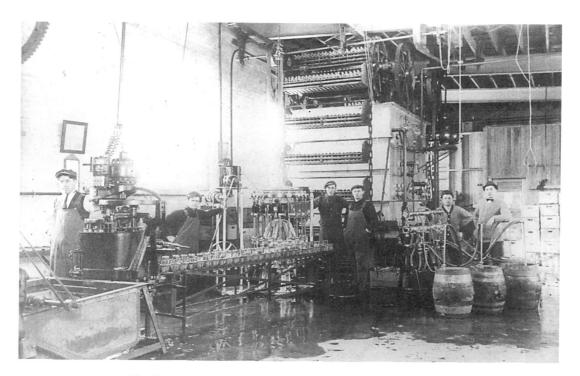

The Koerber brewery packaging area. The third man from the left, standing in front of the pasteurizer with his arm on the filler, is bottler Clarence "Click" Koerber. Brewmaster William Koerber is at right.

COURTESY JAMES KOERBER.

MICHIGAN

MICHIGAN BREWING COMPANY, 1912–1923
1262 MILITARY AVENUE

After building the Akron brewery, an attractive building that is still very much in use as a warehouse visible from Interstate 76, John Koerber was invited by authorities in Ionia, Michigan, in 1906 to consider rebuilding the defunct local brewery. John Koerber must have liked Ionia and the opportunity it offered. He sold his share in the Akron Brewing Company and resettled his family of seven children in Ionia. In 1906, he incorporated the firm as the Grand Valley Brewing Company with a capitalization of $100,000, which was later increased by $25,000. The brewery was in bad shape and had to be completely refitted. Beer production resumed in Ionia in 1907.

What Koerber had not known from talking with Ionia planners was that Ionia County contained a large rural population that favored Prohibition. All his plans for a family brewery collapsed when the county voted to go dry by local option in 1909. The Grand Valley brewery had to close, and the Koerber family was out of work. His dream broken, Koerber died in 1911 at age forty-eight.

A Standard truck loaded with new wooden cases of Michigan beer, about 1913.

DESTINATION DETROIT

There were seven Koerber children between the ages of thirteen and twenty-four who had expected to work in the family brewery. The five oldest decided to relocate the brewing operation to Detroit, and they approached Charles Ley, a family friend from Akron, for financial support. John Koerber and Charles Ley had both owned saloons there and had been very close.

A facility suitable for converting to a brewery was found on the west side near Livernois, next to the Kelsey Wheel Company. With Ley's backing and much family enthusiasm, the brewing equipment was moved to the new location. Installation of a 40,000- barrel plant was completed in 1912.

Today the Michigan Brewing Company would be considered a very large microbrewery, in the sense that family members were operating the plant and producing a special product on a modest scale. Charles Koerber, the oldest son, was treasurer, William was brewmaster, Clarence ("Click") was head bottler, Marie kept the books, and John at eighteen was a clerk. A teaser ad in December 1912 spoke of "A New Product with an Old and Delightful Flavor." This turned out to be Michigan Beer, which was ready for sale and advertised on July 4th, 1913.

The trade press reported annual elections of officers. These showed the same principals rotating positions among themselves. There was no other news about the plant after 1913, when the installation of eight additional chip tanks and the purchase of a new 3-ton Standard truck was mentioned.

NEAR BEER FROM TOLEDO

The brewery may have closed temporarily in 1917, when both William and John Koerber were in the army, but it continued to be listed in Detroit directories. An attempt to generate business in the early days of Prohibition with "In Lu," "Michigan Near Beer," and liquid malt failed. However, by this time, the brewery was completely surrounded by the Kelsey Wheel plant; entrance was through the Kelsey gate. In this protected site, according to family oral history, brewing of real beer continued unbeknownst to the federal authorities.

Family members still chuckle over stories of the early Prohibition years. The code name for a truck loaded with full-strength beer was "near beer from Toledo," a sort of password the police honored, no doubt for a share of the goods. One day, a new cop stopped a Koerber truck and asked what was being transported. "Near beer from Toledo" was the confident reply. The policeman, not yet having been told of the arrangement, decided to investigate, and the frightened driver ran away. Back at the station, the captain was told about the abandoned beer truck.

"What did the driver tell you was in it?" he asked the new officer.

"Near beer from Toledo, sir."

"Well, that's what it is!" said the exasperated captain. And Bill Koerber was called to get his truck picked up.

COMPETITION AND CLOSURE

After a few years, distribution of illegal beer was organized by the notorious Purple Gang, which did not care for competition. When a loaded Koerber truck was highjacked one day, it was obvious that sides had to be chosen. The Koerber family may have had few qualms about supplying beer in violation of an unpopular law in order to stay in business, but a turf war with an armed gang was much too risky. The Koerbers reluctantly closed the brewery in 1923. The buildings were sold to the Kelsey Wheel Company, which razed them for expansion of its operation.

Charles, William, and Arthur Koerber went to Toledo after repeal and purchased the Home Brewery. While this plant was being refitted as the Koerber Brewing Company, Clarence Koerber moved to Ionia and resumed operation at the Grand Valley brewery. Prohibition was a dead issue; he was now welcomed as a provider of jobs and suds. He became a local booster at a time when much needed to be done. Later he bought the larger Kern Brewery in Port Huron and combined production of his Friar's Ale and Clix Malt Liquor labels there in 1943. The Port Huron brewery continued to operate until 1960, when it was completely destroyed by fire. The Toledo operation had some good years but succumbed in 1950 during the period of postwar competition.

WARTIME MEMORIES

In June 1994, when ceremonies were being held for the fiftieth anniversary of D-Day at Anzio beachhead and in Normandy, John Koerber's grandson Charles reminisced about his special wartime service in Italy. Called from the front lines to restore two bombed Italian Peroni breweries and to supply front-line troops, including those at Anzio, with an occasional morale booster, Charles continued the Koerber tradition of brewing good beer under difficult conditions.

Unlike other Detroit breweries, the Michigan Brewing Company is only a short chapter in the history of the Koerber family; it neither originated nor ended in Detroit. But for a few years, until Prohibition closed the doors, five very gutsy young people rolled up their sleeves and worked hard for a small share of market.

MEMORABILIA

The Michigan Brewing Company is typical of smaller firms that purchased a limited number of merchandising items. One is the Chrysanthemum Girl, a very attractive stock tray with the Michigan Brewing Company name.

MANAGEMENT

1913: Michael Neckel, president; Charles A. Ley, vice president; Charles H. Koerber, secretary-treasurer and general manager; H. Sarbinowski and Frank Larkowski, directors; George Schmidt, brewmaster.

1917: Charles A. Ley, president; John C. Lensky, vice president; Charles H. Koerber, secretary-treasurer and general manager; Peter J. Neckel, secretary; William G. Koerber, superintendent and brewmaster.

1919: Charles A. Ley, president; Henry Malesky, vice president; P. J. Neckel, secretary; Charles H. Koerber, treasurer.

OLD HOLLAND

OLD HOLLAND BREWING COMPANY, 1934–1938
563 EAST LARNED

Almost nothing now remains of the old near east neighborhood on Larned where one of Detroit's most obscure breweries opened in 1934. Old Holland was mentioned in the trade press only when it went into receivership. In spite of being ignored as a very small brewery, Old Holland had four good years: sales ranged between 31,000 (1938) and 39,000 barrels (1937). The brands were a Bohemian Type Lager and an Empire Crown Ale. Brewmaster William Keinarth had learned the brewing craft at John Hauck's brewery in Cincinnati, where he started in 1887. He would have been at least sixty-five when he got the opportunity to brew again in 1935, and this assumes he started working at seventeen. He had a couple of decent years late in his life, and must have enjoyed the smell of a boiling kettle and hops once again. He was replaced by William J. Schneider in 1937.

The brewery was started by Abraham Kaufman, who had sold homebrew supplies in the early 1930s under the New England Malt & Hops Company name, but his Old Holland venture ran into debt very early. In the late fall of 1935, the firm sought protection from creditors, and a reorganization was ordered under Section 77B. The court jurisdiction was lifted the following summer, when creditors accepted $40,000 worth of stock in full payment.

MEMORABILIA

Rhomboid-shaped bottle labels are in several collections. A paper sign and a thermometer are the only other items known so far.

MANAGEMENT

1935: Abraham Kaufman, president; Frank Hoffman, vice president; William Keinarth, brewmaster; Otto Wolf, assistant brewer; William Miller, chief engineer.

REGAL

REGAL BREWING CO., 1934–1938
3220 BELLEVUE AVENUE

A few blocks from the corner of Mack Avenue and Mt. Elliott Street, not far from the old Pfeiffer brewery, is the remaining building of the former Regal Brewing Company. If there ever was a case of virulent post-repeal optimism, it was Regal. They wrote the book.

This was not a case of renovating an old plant closed since 1919. Regal was a new 100,000-barrel plant designed by Harley-Ellington of Detroit and built to last, with Albert Kahn bearing columns, the kind that flare out at the top. (Harley-Ellington designed much of the post-Prohibition construction for Stroh.) The Regal plant had thick cork

The former Regal brewery, photographed by the author in 1993.

insulation and concrete floors that probably could support armored tanks, never mind tanks full of sparge water, hot wort, or beer. Construction was completed in 1935.

The force behind the venture was Raymond Irion, second son of A. L. Irion, who headed the British-American Brewing Company in Windsor. William C. Stempel, an experienced brewmaster whose tenure at the new Voigt plant was cut short by insufficient funding, again took the challenge of a newly erected brewery. Less than 10,000 barrels could be sold that year. Regal had one good year, with sales of 60,000 barrels of Regal Old Style Lager and XXX Ale in 1936. By the following year, it was again a buyer's market, with the old strong names once more dominant. Irion sold the brewery in February 1937 to Ekhardt & Becker, who closed it in 1938.

Regal brewmaster William Stempel, who had tried to get the Voigt-Pros't plant on stream. *Michigan Volksblatt*, Sept. 26, 1910.
From The Stroh Brewery Company Archive.

The stock house still stands, and is likely to stand for a very long time. It has been used for light manufacturing for decades, mostly paper and cardboard products. There is no direct evidence that the building was a brewery, but on the third floor some of the wall finish has fallen off, exposing the cork insulation. In the back is a little yard, where in a sheltered corner there stood until recently two plugs of barrel pitch which had filled 5-gallon cans. Some local businesspeople remember that there was a brewery there at one time with a taproom.

MEMORABILIA

Collectibles from Regal are exceedingly rare except for labels, which are in several collections. A horizontal oval sign is the only merchandising item found. It had long been assumed that Regal did not fill cans, given the short span of operation and the fact that no Regal cans were known. However, a single can in fair condition was located in 1990 and is a highly prized item in a Michigan collection.

MANAGEMENT

1936: Raymond Irion, president; T. I. Sweetwine, vice president, secretary-treasurer, and sales manager; William Stempel, brewmaster; Charles Rhodes, chief engineer.

Bottle label, probably 1936.   From The Stroh Brewery Company Archive.

WAGNER

C&K Brewing Company, 1934–1936
Wagner Brewing Company, 1936–1937
11627 Klinger, Hamtramck

The story of C&K begins in Sault St. Marie, Ontario, where Andrew J. Short and Casimir Kocat established the Soo Falls Brewing Company in 1901. Lager and porter were the first products, with ale being added in 1902. The plant had a capacity of 15,000 barrels. This small brewery had no future, but fortune would smile on Kocat.

In 1923, Casimir Kocat appeared in Detroit, where he started a manufacturing plant for liquid malt in Hamtramck. This time, he was the sole owner. When beer became legal again ten years later, he was getting on in years and wished to move to a warmer climate. Kocat was able to find buyers for his plant. Investors sold stock and bought the business for $158,000. Kocat retired a winner in an otherwise ill-fated venture.

The property consisted of three modern buildings. The new owners named the firm C&K Brewing Company, as Casimir Kocat's name was known in the Polish community. Brewmaster William Becker was charged with reconditioning and enlarging facilities with the surplus from the stock sale, about $65,000.

C&K sold 37,000 barrels in 1934, not a bad beginning. The crucial year was 1935, when a planned expansion including a 200-barrel brew-kettle was completed. Philip G. Benjamin was brought in from Marx in Wyandotte to manage the plant. Sales were expected to climb but fell off after some initial gains, and the year ended up with a 10 percent decline instead. A Nottingham Ale was added to the product line, with the necks of bottles wrapped in tin foil to give the ale a premium look.

Then a new management team took over. The new owners had no roots in Hamtramck; their names were Alders, Larsen, Grant, and Brown. They renamed the brewery Wagner and the beer Hofburger Lager. Everything was set to go, but the customers did not respond. Sales plunged; only 19,000 barrels had been sold when production was halted in September 1936. In October, Wagner Brewing Company filed for bankruptcy. The property was liquidated at public auction in 1938.

Somewhere in Florida, Casimir Kocat was probably baking the memory of Soo winters and Hamtramck slush out of his body.

MEMORABILIA
Items are mostly restricted to embossed C&K bottles, and C&K and Wagner labels. Only a few C&K signs are known.

MANAGEMENT
1934: Adam Blake, president, later sales manager; E. Waltz, elected president after Blake.
1936: Arthur J. Alders, president; Clarence E. Larsen, vice president and secretary; Harry Grant, treasurer; John L. Brown, director; William Becker, brewmaster.

WALKER

WALKER BREWING COMPANY, 1934–1940
8561 TEN MILE, CENTER LINE

Center Line is now very much a part of greater Detroit, some ten miles north of downtown and easily reached—or bypassed—by interstate. In the 1930s, however, Center Line was considered a very separate community. Lower land values may have influenced John George Walker (known by his middle name) in his decision to locate his syrup and, later, his brewing operation there.

Walker was born in Germany in 1884 and arrived in Detroit in 1905. Nothing is known about his upbringing in Europe, but he must have had some experience in brewing. He was a brewer for Stroh, according to family oral history, and his obituary mentions a connection with the brewery in Mount Clemens. One of his daughters recalled that Ben Koppitz encouraged him to attend brewing school in New York. He took the advice and went there with his wife, Pauline. He was appointed brewmaster for the Koppitz-Melchers plant on Gratiot Avenue in 1917, but his tenure was cut short by Michigan's Prohibition law.

During Prohibition, George Walker produced malt syrup for home

George and Pauline Walker celebrate completion of the first brew with family and friends in 1934.

COURTESY GERTRUDE RICKABUS.

brewing. The Walker Products Company was located in a modest factory building at Ten Mile and Van Dyke in Center Line. He probably had a partner during those years, but in 1931 he incorporated the Walker Brewing Company by himself with a capitalization of $200,000. The brewery opened in 1934 with Walker as president and brewmaster, and his oldest daughter, Florence, as secretary-treasurer.

Initial sales were 21,700 barrels during 1934, and, according to family, Walker enjoyed being a brewery owner. He was even said to have rejected a good offer for the brewery on the grounds that he wanted to leave a going business for his son and four daughters. But sales volume declined every year, to barely 9,000 barrels in 1937. The last year of operation was 1940.

Walker opened a family bar in Mio. He tended bar and enjoyed chatting with friends, and his wife, Pauline, prepared meals. So the family had some decent years after all. Walker later retired to Berkeley, where he died in 1953 at age sixty-nine. The former brewery building still stands and is used as an appliance store.

Walker's surviving daughters have many fine memories of attending large Master Brewers picnics when there were still a couple dozen breweries operating in the area, of their parents leaving for the annual Master Brewers conventions, of their father's pride in having his own shop, and of growing up as a part of the brewing community in a great city.

MEMORABILIA

Except for labels, which are rare, almost nothing seems to have survived. The brewery is known to have given away bottle openers, and a rectangular tin-over-cardboard sign hung behind the bar in Mio.

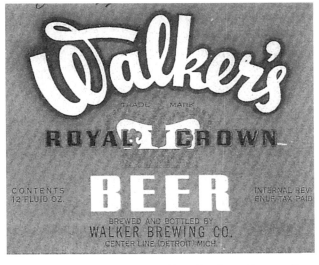

Bottle label, ca. 1938.

FROM THE STROH BREWERY COMPANY ARCHIVE.

9

FOUR THAT FAILED
BEFORE THE WAR

The time between repeal of Prohibition and the start of World War II was a difficult passage even for many brewers who were prosperous before Prohibition. Sufficient capital had to be obtained for plant renovation or new construction, qualified technical staff and workers had to be assembled, and a place had to be found in a market that was rapidly becoming crowded. Detroit, with its large labor force in the automotive industry, offered a good market for beer. However, labor unrest after a few years and a long recession in the late 1930s depressed discretionary income and dampened beer consumption. With many brewers competing for a flat market, effective advertising became an important requirement for survival.

Two brewers with very solid reputations, West Side (renamed Mundus and later Albert) and Philip Kling, opened plants but failed for different, partly self-inflicted, reasons after a few years. Voigt was the largest brewery in Michigan in the 1870s, but it lost rank steadily. A successor firm was caught in a losing race of selling stock to finish construction of a new plant. The smaller American Brewing Company in Delray had less difficulty in starting up, because it had produced "near beer." It suffered the fate of smaller suburban brewers that at one time had a local market but now found their territory invaded by larger Detroit brewers. Old brand loyalties were just not bankable anymore.

The West Side brewery in the 1890s. The posed wagons show the two types used: the large open wagons carried up to forty half-barrels; the enclosed wagons delivered cases to homes, with the slogan "Bottled Beer for Family Use." COURTESY THE DETROIT NEWS.

WEST SIDE

JACOB DARMSTAETTER, 1865–1886
HERMAN DARMSTAETTER & BROTHER'S CHICAGO BREWERY, 1886–1893
WEST SIDE BREWERY COMPANY, 1893–1919
MUNDUS BEVERAGE COMPANY, 1919–1933
MUNDUS BREWING COMPANY, 1933–1938
ALBERT BREWING COMPANY, 1933–1938
412 (LATER 1735) HOWARD

The Darmstaetter family, named for their Old Country home in Darmstadt, was active in the malting and brewing business in Detroit for about eighty years. Michael Darmstaetter was the first to enter the trade. He probably arrived in Detroit soon after 1848 and was already listed as a brewer on Catherine Street in 1852, a couple of blocks east of the small brewery of Bernhard Stroh. Between 1856 and 1865, after he retired, his sons Jacob and William brewed there. The two brothers soon split up. William took over the operation at 92 Catherine, and his story is that of the Columbia Brewery described in chapter 5.

EARLY BEGINNINGS

Jacob Darmstaetter set up shop on Howard and 12th streets on the west side. This was the beginning of the Darmstaetter line who owned what became the West Side Brewery Company. Jacob had married Luisa

Koch, and they had five children: Herman, Gustav, Otto, and two daughters whose names are not known. Herman, born in 1859, joined his father's business in 1877 at age eighteen. In the late 1870s, the plant was listed as a lager brewery with malthouse and bottling facilities. Sales were a modest 1,500 barrels.

Jacob Darmstaetter operated the Howard Street brewery under his own name for twenty years until 1886, when he retired and sold it to his two sons Herman and Gustav. The two partners named their business Herman Darmstaetter & Brother and their plant the Chicago Brewery, and set out to build up the business with brewmaster Oswald Kulewatz.

Herman Darmstaetter.

While the west side was not primarily German—much of the then predominantly Irish area is still referred to as Corktown—there was probably also less competition in an age when proximity to the brewery was a significant factor.

By the late 1880s, the Chicago Brewery employed ten workers and two teams in manufacturing and distribution, and it claimed a 20,000-barrel capacity. The main building was three stories high and measured 100 by 150 feet. In the basement were five vaults 16 feet high which contained the aging casks.

THE WEST SIDE PERIOD

The Darmstaetter brothers incorporated the business as the West Side Brewery Company in 1893 and dropped the Chicago Brewery name. At that time, a capacity of 30,000 barrels was claimed, with an estimated annual production of 15,000 to 20,000 barrels. When Jacob Darmstaetter died in June of 1898, the small business he had started in 1866 had become one of the major breweries of Detroit.

Sales of West Side beers increased in the 1890s. Noted brewery architect Louis Lehle of Chicago was retained to design a new wash and racking house for cleaning and filling returned kegs; this was completed in June 1900. Lehle also built a new stock house and other additions. Sales in 1914 were estimated at 140,000 barrels, well placed in the second tier after Stroh and Goebel. The main brand was Mundus (Latin for "world"),

Brewmaster Oswald Kulewatz, in an 1897 convention brochure.

registered in 1909. Another label was Waldbrau Style (German for "forest brew").

The family decided to keep the business open during Prohibition under the Mundus Beverage Company name and produced nonalcoholic beverages as well as Zaka coffee. Then there was a changing of the guard. Brewmaster Kulewatz retired in 1923 at age sixty-eight. He lived to see beer return, and before his death years later, he was the oldest brewmaster in Detroit. Herman Darmstaetter, four years younger than his long-time brewmaster, was not blessed with such a long life. He died in November 1921 at age sixty-two, leaving four children: Meta (Mrs. Tom J. Thorpe), Armin, Elsie (Mrs. Hay Langenheim), and Carl. Armin, who was born in 1888 and attended Amherst and the Wahl-Henius Institute, took over as chairman at thirty-three. Carl was also active, Meta was secretary, and her husband, Tom Thorpe, also participated in the firm.

THE MUNDUS PERIOD

A reorganization in October 1932 transferred the assets of the Mundus Beverage Company to the Mundus Brewing Company, and a stock issue was authorized to enlarge the plant. The Darmstaetter family was still very much involved, with Armin as president, and Carl as treasurer. It was decided that the existing old equipment would be discarded, and new brewhouse vessels would be installed. This trade-off between an earlier start versus greater capacity, efficiency, and better equipment delayed the opening until the late fall of 1933.

The revival of the Mundus name for the company and the label might be questioned now, but it made sense then to tap the loyalty of former customers and perhaps to avoid the geographic limitation of "West Side." A company newspaper, *The Month at Mundus,* was started in September 1933 to provide information to employees and stockholders about progress at the brewery. The October 1933 issue indicated that Mundus was brewing the genuine hoppy article as it was popular before World War I. Brewmaster Hans Havemann, combining "the most expensive brewing materials that the market affords, together with his years of

Home beer delivery in 1916.

FROM THE MANNING BROTHERS HISTORIC PHOTOGRAPHIC COLLECTION.

brewing experience and his intimate understanding of public taste," came up with the "only genuine old-fashioned hop-flavored lager beer being brewed in Detroit." It could have been simply that Havemann—or Armin Darmstaetter himself—was serving Detroit's beer drinkers a more bitter beer than many preferred.

Still, the brewery got off to a good start, and the mood was optimistic. In the January 1934 issue of *The Month at Mundus* is a story about the opening of a Rathskeller. A feature article is devoted to the new truck fleet, painted bright red with gold lettering on a black background. The truck bodies were built according to the original design of Mundus transportation expert Preston Tucker, who also designed a near self-loading and self-unloading system for kegs. After the war, Tucker generated much publicity when he designed a car and tried to compete with the established auto industry. Detroit architect Louis Kamper was busy revising plans for a new brewhouse and the addition of smaller buildings.

THE DEMISE OF THE DARMSTAETTERS

It all came apart in the fall of 1934, when the Darmstaetter interests lost control of Mundus after a bitter internal fight. The year ended with sales of 85,000 barrels. The critical year for Mundus was 1935. The new board under president Van Grant tried to improve sales with a spring newspaper advertising campaign that emphasized change: "A different beer—a better beer from Mundus" and "My—how Mundus has changed!" Flavor was said to be "checked and double-checked" by showing two check marks on the label. A new brand, Royal Amber, was launched. Sales for 1935 were 59,000 barrels; while still respectable, the momentum was lost and so was the Darmstaetter presence.

By that time, Havemann was long gone. His assistant, Frank

The West Side brewery was revived as Mundus in 1933. This photo shows extensive plant additions erected in the 1910s.

Schachtner, stayed on in 1934, when the change in management brought in Adolph Beschoner as brewmaster. The brewery tried to capitalize on his reputation with the caption "by the famous brewmaster Beschoner" on the label, but he died later that year. Another change came in 1935, when John Merkt was hired as brewmaster, with Schachtner again the assistant.

There still was dissension among the directors. Early in 1935, four stockholders sued Mundus, charging that management had engaged in a scheme to obtain title through mortgage default, that purchase of the plant was negotiated through a dummy, and that Darmstaetter had purchased the brewery from the Mundus Beverage Company in 1932 at an inflated price. On March 31, 1936, the assets and business of Mundus were taken over under Section 77-B of the Bankruptcy Act.

A CANADIAN LAST HURRAH

Control of Mundus passed to a group headed by Albert T. Montreuil, a Canadian who lived in Windsor and had retired in 1926 after being collector of customs for twenty-five years. This must have brought him into contact with the beer trade; he developed an interest in the brewing industry, and he obviously had the capital to invest. In 1933, he joined Mundus as second vice president, then was chairman at Pfeiffer briefly, and returned in 1936. Montreuil was not a bashful entrepreneur, and he liked "Albert" better than "Mundus." He also liked ale better than German-style lager. After the earlier management infighting, it must have been a relief to have somebody completely in charge. Unfortunately, Montreuil had been born almost a century too late for ale to carry the day on the Detroit side of the river.

With a bad sense of tim-
ing, the brewery was shut
down at least partially from
May to October, while $200,000
was spent on converting some
of the fermenting cellars to ale
brewing. In December 1936,
the new products Sir Albert Ale
and Albert Lager Beer joined
Mundus in the trade. And in the
brewhouse, assisting the Canadian brewmaster John McCormick, was again Frank Schachtner, who also had his son Frank
Jr. working for him and training
in the brewer's craft. McCormick had been with Molson,
where ale was king, for seventeen years. He was elected a
vice president and director in
July. Former brewmaster John
Merkt found employment at
the new Koppitz brewery and
ended his career as the Goebel

Armin Darmstaetter was photographed by
Bachrach in 1926.

FROM THE MANNING BROTHERS
HISTORIC PHOTOGRAPHIC COLLECTION.

brewmaster of the Muskegon plant. Sir Albert Ale and Albert Lager Beer
hit the market too late for Montreuil. He died unexpectedly after a week's
illness at age sixty-six on October 4, 1936, never having tasted the ale. The
year ended with sales of 25,400 barrels of Mundus beer and 15,200 barrels
of Albert products.

In the spring of 1937, the firm again petitioned for reorganization.
McCormick returned to Canada, and Schachtner stayed on as brewmaster while the brewery was operated by trustee William T. Skudyzycki
under Section 77-B. There was one final effort to turn sales around. Plans
called for resuming the original West Side name. Sales manager Ralph
Nadell proposed the slogan "Put West Side Inside," but it was too little
and much too late. Sales during 1937 were barely 10,000 barrels. West
Side closed in 1938.

Journeyman brewer Schachtner never got a chance as brewmaster
of a soundly managed plant. When Albert closed, he became assistant
brewmaster at Altes until he retired in 1955 at age seventy-five. His son
Frank Jr. grew up in a brewery atmosphere; his uncle Michael was
brewmaster at Frankenmuth, where young Frank helped out, and after
repeal Frank Jr. also worked briefly at Goebel and Koppitz, and then
found steady employment at Pfeiffer. He retired from the industry in
1953. His recollections of the time at Mundus working for his father

give a feel for the turmoil caused by the many management changes and shareholder squabbles.

West Side certainly should have been a survivor after Prohibition by virtue of its former market and family involvement. When one reads the Company newsletter, the impression is very strong that the Darmstaetter family was committed to the company and was its driving spirit. Most breweries failed because competitive forces favored increasingly larger plants. It is sad to read about a failure caused by ownership disagreements.

Carl Darmstaetter became sales manager of the Flint Hill Brewery Company in 1937. After he was ousted, Armin Darmstaetter looked after the family's finances as president of Herman Darmstaetter Heirs, Inc., and he was also president of the S.& D. Engineering Company. Armin had married Priscilla Schotten in 1914. Their two children, named after their parents, were Armin A. Jr., who became a physician, and Priscilla, later Mrs. William A. Blodgett.

Armin Darmstaetter, Sr., died at the relatively early age of fifty-five in May 1943. Former employee Charles Walker became assistant brewmaster at Zynda and later owner of a successful plating business, but he saved the interesting copies of *This Month at Mundus*.

MEMORABILIA

Attractive trays and shell glasses are known. A tray divided into quarters and showing seasonal scenes (the "Four Seasons" tray) is a very desirable Detroit brewery collectible from the West Side period.

MANAGEMENT

1886: Herman and Gustav Darmstaetter, proprietors; Oswald Kulewatz, brewmaster.

1914: Herman Darmstaetter, chairman and treasurer; Armin A. Darmstaetter, secretary; Chris. J. Berg, manager; Oswald Kulewatz, brewmaster.

1934: Armin A. Darmstaetter, president; Carl J. Darmstaetter, vice president and secretary; Albert F. Montreuil, second vice president and treasurer; John Faber, assistant secretary-treasurer; Hans Havemann, brewmaster.

1935: Van Grant, president; George T. Albright, James Ford, M. Stark, and Jerome S. Freund, directors; John Merkt, brewmaster.

1938: M. P. Hyndman, chair; John P. McCormick, vice president and brewmaster; William G. Lewis, secretary; W. C. Wood, treasurer.

Darmstaetter Family

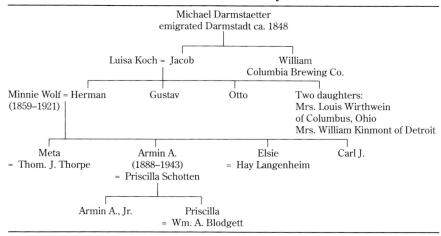

Michael Darmstaetter
emigrated Darmstadt ca. 1848

Luisa Koch = Jacob   William
                            Columbia Brewing Co.

Minnie Wolf = Herman   Gustav   Otto   Two daughters:
(1859–1921)   Mrs. Louis Wirthwein
                                             of Columbus, Ohio
                                             Mrs. William Kinmont of Detroit

Meta   Armin A.   Elsie   Carl J.
= Thom. J. Thorpe (1888–1943)   = Hay Langenheim
                  = Priscilla Schotten

Armin A., Jr.   Priscilla
                       = Wm. A. Blodgett

AMERICAN

EXPOSITION BREWING COMPANY, 1880–1900

AMERICAN BREWING COMPANY, 1900–1919

AMERICAN PRODUCTS COMPANY, 1919–1933

AMERICAN BEVERAGE COMPANY, 1933–1934

CHASE AND MECHANIC, DELRAY

AMERICAN BREWING COMPANY OF MICHIGAN, 1935–1938

1000 CARY (RENAMED)

The Exposition Brewing Company, Delray, in an 1897 convention brochure.

FROM THE STROH BREWERY COMPANY ARCHIVE.

Anton Schmitt, manager of the Exposition Brewing Company, in an 1897 Convention brochure.
FROM THE STROH BREWERY COMPANY ARCHIVE.

Fred Kraft, together with Charles and Anton Schmitt, opened a small brewery in the near downriver community of Delray. The attractive and compact building was located at the southwest corner of Chase and Mechanic streets, and it looked more like a school than a brewery. Anton Schmitt had the title of general manager and was also brewmaster. The partners incorporated the firm as the Exposition Brewing Company in 1890, a name suggested by the Detroit Industrial Fair and Exposition held in Delray. Capacity was listed at 20,000 barrels in 1897. Except for a photograph of the brewery and of Anton Schmitt, nothing seems to have survived from the Exposition period.

The name was changed in 1901 to the American Brewing Company. Disagreement among board members surfaced, with a minority threatening litigation. This was averted when the minority investors were able to purchase a majority of the stock in 1902. Edward Stange, one of the organizers of the Exposition Brewery and secretary-treasurer for two years, was elected president of the reorganized company. When the slogan "Operated by the Stange family for 48 years" was used by his son in 1938, the truth was stretched a bit.

Edward Stange's family originated in Nordhausen, in the kingdom of Saxony, where he was born in 1842. His father immigrated two years later and continued his trade as mason contractor in Detroit. Young Edward became a prosperous grocer and manufacturer of cider vinegar, and later saw an opportunity to invest in the Delray brewery. He took an active role in the incorporation of the American Brewing Company, became a director, and remained its president until his death in 1913 at seventy-one. His two sons, Fred and Hugo, were treasurer and superintendent, respectively.

The new owners added porter to the Cream Top Old Style Lager which had been the main brand in the Exposition period. In line with the new name, a new crest was adopted. It consisted of an eagle perched on an American shield, with a large A superimposed on the stars and stripes. This emblem appeared on all embossed bottles and labels.

The firm survived Prohibition as the American Products Company.

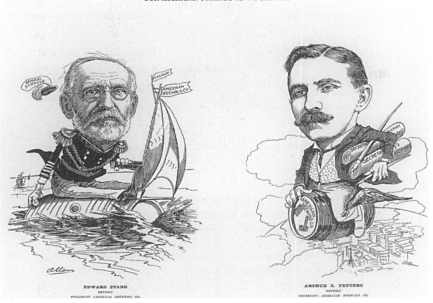

Edward Stange, president, and Arthur Fetters, secretary, of the American Brewing Company.
FROM OUR MICHIGAN FRIENDS AS WE SEE 'EM, C. O. YOUNGSTAND, ED., 1905.

Birch beer and Tang-Ee ginger ale were among the products marketed. Leo Taube and Fred C. Stange managed the firm after repeal and supervised an investment of about $100,000 in new brewing facilities. The Cream Top brand was revived, but the eagle and shield were replaced by two concentric circles containing the letters A, B, and C arranged in a triangle. The text "AMERICAN BEVERAGE COMPANY DETROIT" was inscribed between the two circles. The shield and eagle design, once used by many breweries, was now well established and heavily promoted as the trademark of Anheuser-Busch. The American Beverage Company in Detroit would have been in conflict with a major shipping brewer.

In 1936, the final name, American Brewing Company of Michigan, was adopted. In spite of efforts at market segmentation by producing ale, bock, and a Dutchman brand in addition to Cream Top, sales slipped a little each year from the 1934 peak of 54,600 barrels. A steeper decrease occurred from 49,800 in 1936 to 35,400 the following year. The brewery closed in late 1938, another early victim of the beer wars. Delray, once a very long trolley ride from downtown and home to the Hungarian community with its own identity, had become largely an industrial suburb of Detroit.

MEMORABILIA

Artifacts from pre-Prohibition times are mostly thin shell glasses. American Products Company commissioned an interesting and unusual tray to promote soft drinks during Prohibition, showing the dirigible ZR-1 and the text "Above Them All."

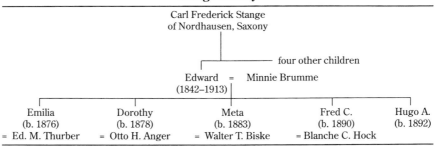

Stange Family

Carl Frederick Stange
of Nordhausen, Saxony

———— four other children

Edward = Minnie Brumme
(1842–1913)

Emilia	Dorothy	Meta	Fred C.	Hugo A.
(b. 1876)	(b. 1878)	(b. 1883)	(b. 1890)	(b. 1892)
= Ed. M. Thurber	= Otto H. Anger	= Walter T. Biske	= Blanche C. Hock	

MANAGEMENT

1884: Louis Drebes, president; Charles Schmitt, vice president; Anton Schmitt, brewer and manager; George H. Clippert, secretary; Fred Kraft, treasurer.

1899–1902: Fred Kraft, president; Charles Schmitt, vice president; Anton Schmitt, brewer and manager; George H. Clippert, secretary; August Quast, treasurer.

1903: Edward Stange, president; William Zimmerman, vice president; Arthur S. Fetters, secretary and treasurer.

1914: William Zimmerman, president; Leo Taube, vice president; Frederick C. Stange, treasurer; Arthur S. Fetters, secretary and manager; Oscar Lamsens, brewmaster (1909–1918).

1937: Fred C. Stange, president and manager; Leo Taube, vice president; Hugo A. Stange, treasurer; Walter T. Biske, secretary; Philip J. Halm, brewmaster.

KLING

PHILIP KLING, PARTNER IN PENINSULAR BREWERY, 1856–1868
PHILIP KLING & COMPANY, 1868–1879
PENINSULAR BREWING COMPANY, 1879–1890
PHILIP KLING BREWING COMPANY, 1890–1919
KLING PRODUCTS COMPANY, 1919–1921
1424–1438 JEFFERSON AVENUE

Philip Kling was one of the very early German settlers in Detroit, having arrived alone in 1836 at the age of eighteen. He was born in Kehl, on the Rhine across from Strassburg. His father had been a cooper, and Philip must have learned the barrel-making trade from him, because he supported himself by working in a New York cooper shop. Twenty years later, he had his own barrel shop on Gratiot Avenue. Bernhard Stroh, who brewed only a mile away, may well have been a customer, but according to reminiscences by Philip's son Kurt, most of Kling's business was with Hiram Walker.

The start of Philip Kling's brewery was claimed by him to be 1856. Eighty years later, when his son Kurt revived brewing operations after Prohibition, there was a series of print ads relating noteworthy events to 1856 when "Kling's Beer with the taste that satisfies" was born. Unfortunately, Philip Kling was surprisingly shy about his brewery connection during the 1850s and 1860s and preferred to be known as a cooper.

According to real estate records, in 1856 the shoemaker Michael Martz and the furniture store owner Henry Weber became Kling's partners in acquiring property between East Jefferson and the Detroit River near the future location of the Belle Isle bridge. That property later became the Philip Kling brewery, but what exactly happened in 1856 and the years immediately following is largely conjecture. The land had belonged to the ale brewer Patrick Tregent a few years earlier, and the beginning of a small brewery may have been there already, or the partners had one erected. What is certain is that in 1863

Philip Kling.   COURTESY PAULA SARVIS.

there was a brewery on that property, which the partners named Peninsular Brewery. Kling seems to have been more of an investor than actual brewer, because he still listed himself as a cooper until 1871, the year his new brewery was built.

PHILIP KLING TAKES OVER

Philip Kling, a handsome and able man, served a term as alderman from 1866 to 1868 and was the first president of the Detroit Brewers' Association. The late 1860s was a period of change for the Peninsular Brewery. Philip Kling brought in F. Louis Dohmstreich in 1868, perhaps in preparation for the departure a few years later of Michael Martz, who joined his brothers in a brewery established that year. The Peninsular Brewery continued to prosper. A large, attractive four-story brewery was completed on Jefferson Avenue, with the name P. Kling & Co. 1871 prominently chiseled in stone. When Henry Weber died the following year, his widow Caroline took his place for seven years. Kling then bought out the Weber interest and incorporated the brewery as the Peninsular Brewing Company. Sales of Kling beers reached 14,000 barrels in the late 1870s, making Kling one

Kling brewmaster Charles Daab, in an 1897 convention brochure.

of the most successful and prominent brewers in Michigan. The plant measured 200 by 60 feet with a capacity of 30,000 barrels. It stood on a 275-by-75-foot lot, which included an ice house, a 50,000-bushel malthouse, and a loading dock on the river. Thirty employees brewed Pilsener, Gold Seal Export, Extra Pale Ale, and Porter.

A major change occurred in 1887 following the death of Dohmstreich. Kling reincorporated the firm with a capital of $200,000, with himself as president. Kling was now sixty-nine; he had outlived his early associates with the exception of Michael Martz, and it was time to consider succession. The four children by his first wife, Margaret, were all considered unqualified for management by their gender. He did hire his oldest daughter, Julia, as bookkeeper, and she is listed as secretary-treasurer in 1890, the year that the name Philip Kling Brewing Company was formally adopted. Philip Kling's older son, August, by his second wife, Josephine, joined the firm as vice president the following year and remained with the brewery until Prohibition. Business had more than doubled in the last dozen years, but the 33,000 barrels sold in 1891 placed Kling only in the middle of his competitors.

August Kling's younger brother, Kurt, was only twelve in 1891. Kurt Kling later studied business for two years at the University of Michigan and in 1900 completed a brewmaster's course in brewing science in New York. Upon returning to Detroit, he worked in various departments at the brewery and was promoted in turn to brewmaster and superintendent.

The brewery was severely damaged by a fire in April 1893; only the malthouse behind the brewery could be saved. A new six-story brewhouse was erected toward the river, which gave the plant a capacity of 150,000 barrels. A reopening ceremony was held on April 19, 1894. The brand name was Pros't, "The Beer for Guest and Host." Kling also claimed to be "The original chill-proof beer," referring to beer remaining clear when cooled. Philip Kling died in 1910 at age ninety-two; his widow, Josephine, assumed the presidency, and Kurt became general manager.

The Philip Kling Brewery at its peak in the 1910s.

FROM THE BURTON HISTORICAL COLLECTION, DETROIT PUBLIC LIBRARY.

Kurt Kling tried to maintain a beverage operation during Prohibition as manager of the Kling Products Company, but he gave up after a couple of years. He sold the business to his brewmaster, Nick Frank, who then manufactured near beer under the Pros't Cereal Beverage name and sodas as Frank Products Company.

The part of Jefferson Avenue where Kling's brewery stood had been near the edge of town in the 1860s when the original Peninsular Brewery was erected, and later East Jefferson had turned into a street of large homes. The nearby Belle Isle Bridge drew a lot of traffic and created a very desirable site for recreational activity. Anheuser-Busch was not the first to combine a brewery with family entertainment: Kurt Kling's Luna Park even offered a roller coaster next to the brewery. With no early repeal of Prohibition in sight, the brewery on Jefferson was torn down in December 1921. The amusement park stayed in business until 1927.

KLING'S FLING IN FLINT

Anxious to get back into the beer business after repeal but without a plant in Detroit, the Kling family purchased the Dailey brewery in Flint, which had been built in the 1910s and reopened in 1934. Kling increased the capacity to 120,000 barrels, and brewing was resumed in 1936. That was probably a year past the desirable time to reenter the industry, but it was also a time when small and weakly financed breweries were on their way out.

Kurt Kling assumed the chairmanship, his son Philip became vice president, and his son-in-law John "Jack" Sutton was secretary-treasurer. There were only two outside stockholders. William Breitmeyer, former president of Pfeiffer, became president, and attorney Fred A. Behr served as counsel and director. Christian Jetter, a graduate of the Weihenstephan School of Brewing at the University of Munich, was hired as brewmaster.

Kurt Kling sounded optimistic when he stated that he had no intentions of seeking an extensive volume—there was insufficient capacity for this in any case—but wanted to brew for a discriminating clientele. The company, he said, hoped "to recapture those customers who were its steadfast friends prior to Prohibition and to enlist the younger generation of beer drinkers who have not found exactly the flavor they seek in any existing brew."

PAYOFF PROBLEMS

Business started off well with 55,000 barrels of sales in 1936 but had slipped to 23,600 by 1940. According to family oral history, the major difficulty was obtaining truck delivery in the home market of Detroit. Prohibition had created a network of people engaged in illegal alcoholic beverage distribution. With beer legal again, former bootleggers drifted into certain labor unions. Jack Sutton understood what had to be done to get drivers to deliver Kling beer to Detroit outlets, and he agreed to a small "loading fee" for every case delivered. But Kurt Kling was furious when he heard about this, and he nixed the agreement. Unfortunately for Sutton, the deal was considered binding by the other party, who let him know that trucks and possibly drivers who delivered Kling could expect a shortened life span, and that he was in for trouble. Sutton evidently convinced his accusers that he had acted in good faith, but his granddaughter still recalls how she and her brother were escorted to and from school by a bodyguard during this period.

Kling was history. The Kling management leased the plant in 1942 to David Rott. The last brewmaster was Joseph Hofer, who had operated a small brewery during Prohibition south of Windsor in La Salle. Hofer continued to brew in Flint for Rott, turning out the D. R. Premier and Kling's Premier brands. An entirely new chapter started in 1947. Pfeiffer bought the Flint plant when its sales were booming and converted it to packaging draft beer only. Operations ceased in 1958 after Pfeiffer had peaked.

The Flint brewery made economic sense regarding capital outlay for a short-term solution, but marketing beer in Detroit was no longer the business Kurt Kling remembered. In 1936, he was a fifty-seven-year-old gentleman, when what was needed was a "young Turk" with a determination to overcome any obstacle. His competitors were not young Turks, either, but at least they had breweries in the city. The loss of the Jefferson plant during Prohibition doomed the brewing efforts of the Kling

Beer delivery during the winter on early trucks could be a very cold job, as drivers worked with the same lack of protection teamsters had faced in prior years.

The closed Riverside roller coaster and brewery were deserted during Prohibition. The old Belle Isle Bridge is at left.

Kling trucks line up to begin delivery of Flint-brewed beer in Detroit.

family. There was a silver lining to this gloomy ending: Kurt Kling had a knack for investing, and he was able to provide handsomely for his family without the headaches of operating a brewery.

MEMORABILIA

Pre-1900 Kling memorabilia are attractive. A rare tray exists with a portrait of the founder as an older gentleman with a trimmed white beard, looking steadfastly ahead. Export and Pilsener beers are mentioned. Trays from the 1910s are more common. Their design is either an intricate Art Deco pattern surrounding the Pros't brand name or the face of a man and his hand holding a bottle, pouring beer into a glass, a dramatic composition against a deep blue background. A highly unusual tray depicts a couple, dressed in the most formal of evening wear, "After the Theatre."

MANAGEMENT

1873: Philip Kling, proprietor, Peninsular Brewery (Philip Kling & Company), with Henry Weber and F. Louis Dohmstreich.

1887: Philip Kling, president; Julia Kling, secretary-treasurer; Emil Horner, brewmaster.

1897: Philip Kling, president; August P. Kling, vice president; Jacob Baumann, secretary-treasurer; Louis Kamper, general manager; Charles Daab, brewmaster.

1914: Josephine (Mrs. Philip) Kling, president; August P. Kling, vice president and manager; Kurt Kling, treasurer and superintendent; Emile Kamper, secretary; Nicholas Frank, brewmaster.

1938: Kurt Kling, chairman; William G. Breitmeyer, president; Philip Kling, vice president; John Robert Sutton, secretary-treasurer; Christian Jetter, brewmaster.

Kling Family

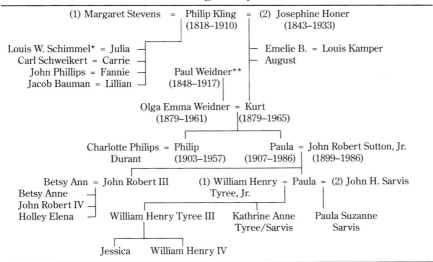

(1) Margaret Stevens = Philip Kling = (2) Josephine Honer
(1818–1910)   (1843–1933)

Louis W. Schimmel* = Julia
Carl Schweikert = Carrie
John Phillips = Fannie
Jacob Bauman = Lillian

Emelie B. = Louis Kamper
August

Paul Weidner**
(1848–1917)

Olga Emma Weidner = Kurt
(1879–1961)   (1879–1965)

Charlotte Philips = Philip   Paula = John Robert Sutton, Jr.
Durant   (1903–1957)   (1907–1986)   (1899–1986)

Betsy Ann = John Robert III   (1) William Henry = Paula = (2) John H. Sarvis
Betsy Anne   Tyree, Jr.
John Robert IV
Holley Elena   William Henry Tyree III   Kathrine Anne   Paula Suzanne
Tyree/Sarvis   Sarvis

Jessica   William Henry IV

*Louis W. Schimmel was associated with Ekhardt & Becker (Later E. & B.) and became a partner in the Tivoli Brewing Company.
**Paul Weidner was a prominent dealer in brewery supplies.

VOIGT

MILWAUKEE BREWERY, 1866–1883
VOIGT BREWERY COMPANY, 1883–1889, 1903–1918
VOIGT BREWERY COMPANY, LTD., 1889–1903
VOIGT PRODUCTS COMPANY, 1918–1919
213 GRAND RIVER
OAKMAN BREWING COMPANY, 1933–1936
VOIGT-PROS'T BREWING COMPANY, 1936–1937
9920 KNODELL AVENUE

Carl William Voigt immigrated from Doebeln, Saxony, in 1854 with his second wife and ten-year-old son Edward from his first marriage and settled that fall in Madison, Wisconsin. There he established a small ale brewery with a kettle capacity of four barrels. By 1856, business had grown to warrant a shift to lager. Edward learned the brewing trade at a very early age by working in his father's brewery after school; at age sixteen, he became a head brewer.

William, as the elder Voigt was known, sold the brewery in 1863 to Joseph Hausmann and moved to Milwaukee. After spending two years in the grain shipping trade on the Great Lakes as owner of the schooner Columbian with only modest success, he moved to Detroit in 1865. The following year, he started a 2,000-barrel lager brewery with his son. Young Edward had spent the intervening years as a sailor both in the Pacific and on the Great Lakes, and he was ready to settle down.

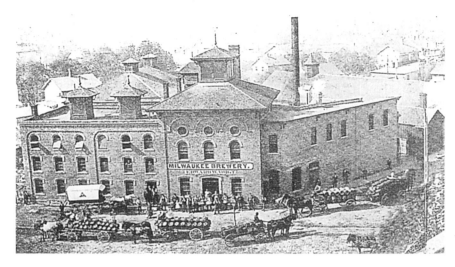

The Voigt brewery about 1880.

FROM ONE HUNDRED YEARS OF BREWING, (CHICAGO: H. S. RICH & CO., 1903).

E. W. Voigt.

FROM ONE HUNDRED YEARS OF BREWING,
(CHICAGO: H. S. RICH & CO., 1903).

E. W. TAKES CHARGE

William Voigt retired in 1871, when sales had climbed to 3,100 barrels. Edward Voigt bought the brewery from him for $30,000 and took over with great enthusiasm. William moved back to Saxony, where he died in 1889. An early lager brand was Boss, with a triangle design that remained as the symbol of his beer. A darker Salvator type was also advertised in the early 1870s. By 1878, E. W. Voigt's Milwaukee Brewery was the largest in Detroit, with sales of 17,500 barrels.

Sometime during the 1880s, the Rheingold name was adopted along with a modified Lorelei theme. Instead of Lorelei sitting on a rock and luring ogling rivermen to a watery grave, a bottle of Rheingold was high on a rock while a bearded dwarf handed glasses of beer to nubile bathers below. This attention-getting scene was on the triangular label and on other promotional items. In later years, a more conservative label was designed for the Rheingold brand ("The Lager Beer of Old"). Another brand was the tonic Maduro, described as "of heavy body, of a mild but extremely rich flavor and of great age" and "of highly nutritive qualities." When malt tonics became popular in the 1890s, Maduro was replaced by the more descriptive Nurishin' ("Gives Strength and Vigor"). A dark Würzburger and seasonal Bock were other turn-of-the-century brands.

Edward Voigt's brother-in-law Henry Zimmermann joined the brewery in 1870, becoming brewmaster in 1874 and later partner. Robert Paul Kiessel, a brewer from the same town in Saxony and a cousin of E. W., worked for him after his arrival in Detroit

Partner and superintendent Henry Zimmerman, in an 1897 convention brochure.
From The Stroh Brewery Company Archive.

in 1876 and was brewmaster for a time in the 1880s. Voigt was interested in storage (aging) cellar design and patented improvements on the existing Davis patent in this field. This caused a disagreement with Kiessel, who felt that his input had been slighted. Kiessel left to become brewmaster at the Westphalia Brewing Company

Under the Union Jack

In 1883, E. W. Voigt changed the name from Milwaukee Brewery to Voigt Brewery Company. When English investors—the so-called British syndicate—went on a buying spree of U.S. breweries six years later, Voigt sold his brewery, as did Goebel, Endriss, Mann, and Michenfelder. The Voigt brewery remained very active, and Voigt Brewery Company, Ltd., declared annual dividends at fall stockholder meetings in London. Major plant expansions occurred in 1890 and 1891; in 1892 mechanical refrigeration was installed. The Chicago architects Charles Koestner & Company and Wilhelm Griesser were retained to design a fully equipped new brewhouse and a new storage cellar, respectively. The new kettle had a volume of 360 barrels, which gave Voigt an annual capacity of 100,000 barrels. The brewery employed more than sixty workers, and twenty wagons called on local outlets. After a few years, the brewing business showed a decline. In 1893, the chairman reported a falling-off in trade because of competition and the generally depressed state of busi-

Voigt workers pose with glasses of Rheingold beer, tools, and signs, perhaps before a holiday. Superintendent Zimmerman is behind barrel at right. Six-pointed stars are medieval beer hospitality symbols.   FROM THE COLLECTION OF JAMES KAISER.

ness. Voigt had yielded first place to Stroh, which in those years claimed a capacity of 300,000 barrels.

There was further bad news the next year. The directors announced that after provisions for depreciation, bad and doubtful debts, and payments for administrative expenses, the accounts showed a deficit of 17,194 pounds, approximately $85,000, and no dividends were declared. Voigt wished to buy back his brewery and negotiated a purchase price of 2 pounds per share on the 10 pounds (approximately $50) par value of the stock. This was consummated in 1896. Voigt strengthened his position and was practically sole owner, although title rested with the corporation.

The final chapter in the British acquisition occurred in the spring of 1900. Voigt Brewery was sold at public auction on February 8 to satisfy a foreclosure claim of $464,700, representing principal and interest on mortgage bonds. E. W. Voigt was the only bidder. He bought his own mortgage for $200,000 and reclaimed the brewery in his own name.

E. W. VOIGT, TYCOON

In spite of this shrewd financial move, the brewery failed to grow after the turn of the century at a rate required for a competitive position. At least part of the problem was Voigt's many other interests. His business investments ranged from the Edison Illuminating Company, where the young Henry Ford worked as engineer for nine years, to a railroad, a sulfite fiber business in Port Huron, and the Grosse Ile Bridge. He also owned large real estate tracts in Detroit, including very valuable land downtown. A dynamic man of many facets, he also was a founding mem-

The former unfinished Voigt/Oakman brewery of 1937 in Pleasant Ridge.
COURTESY PHOTOGRAPHER RICHARD HUNT, FOR AN ARTICLE BY STEVEN FINDLAY
IN THE ROYAL OAK DAILY TRIBUNE, DECEMBER 4, 1982.

ber of the Detroit Art Museum, now the Detroit Institute of Arts. It is not surprising that the brewery did not receive the full attention it probably required, and even that would not have ensured success. Beer sales in 1914 were estimated at only 25,000 barrels. The brewery closed with Prohibition in 1917, three years before E. W.'s death at age eighty-six.

Edward Voigt had been a part of the early days of brewing, and he led his brewery to first place in the city. After a while, this no longer seemed to challenge him enough, with so many other opportunities available in an expanding society.

VOIGT-PROS'T

Repeal brought new interest in reviving the Voigt name for a brewery. Voigt-Pros't came into existence in March 1936 from the merger of two firms. The Voigt part started as the Oakman Brewing Company, organized in July 1933 by Charles G. Oakman and a group of investors that included William F. Voigt, son of E. W. Voigt. Oakman was head of the Saginaw Motor Coach Company and the Oakman Land and Mortgage Company. The group authorized 1,250,000 shares at one dollar par and was raising funds through the sale of stock to build a new brewery.

The new corporation paid $90,000 for a site in Pleasant Ridge at 404 East Ten Mile Road, just east of the Grand Trunk railroad tracks. The site contained a 90-by-250-foot one-story building that had been a dairy and was about ten years old, suitable for offices, packaging, and aging. Detroit architect G. A. Mueller designed a 95-foot-tall brewhouse for a capacity of 360,000 barrels to be built behind the existing structure. The brewhouse was estimated to cost $700,000, a very large sum at that time. A brewmaster named William Stempel was hired.

Kling brewmaster Nickolas Frank, shown in the Sept. 26, 1910, issue of *Michigan Volksblatt*, purchased the Kling Products Company in 1921 and became president of Pros't Liquid Malt Company.

From The Stroh Brewery Company Archive.

However, funding fell far short of expectations, and Oakman left in 1934. By that time, construction costs had been scaled back to $200,000 and capacity to 200,000 barrels. William Voigt assumed leadership for a time and tried his best to complete construction and installation of equipment.

A Complex Deal

The Pros't part was the Pros't Liquid Malt Company, which was the successor to the Frank Malt Products Company. Pros't was originally a Kling brand, and better known. Frank Malt Products had been founded by Nicholas Frank, Kling's last brewmaster, who had bought the name and nonalcoholic beverage business from Kurt Kling in 1921. Repeal had activated Nick Frank's desire to operate a legitimate brewery again and produce real beer. His break came early in 1936, when the Independent Brewing Company abandoned plans to open a brewery for lack of capital. Pros't acquired Independent's assets by a stock swap—one share of Pros't for two and a half shares of Independent. The assets were probably brewing equipment such as tanks that had been purchased and not installed.

With the ink barely dry, Pros't and Voigt merged on March 18, 1936, to form the Voigt-Pros't Brewing Company with an authorized capital of one million shares at one dollar par. The Voigt name was purchased in May 1936 to give greater credence to the venture. In April, Voigt and Pros't transferred their assets to the new entity, which assumed all liabilities. The basis of exchange was one share of Voigt or six-tenths share of Pros't for one of Voigt-Pros't. Stockholders of Independent ended up with a quarter share of Voigt-Pros't for each of their shares.

The original Pros't malt extract plant at Knodell and Milner avenues near the Detroit City Airport became plant number two of Voigt-Pros't. This brewery had been refurbished since repeal for a capacity of 60,000 to 75,000 barrels and was in good shape. A fleet of sixteen trucks was available for sales in Wayne County, and there were distributors for Michigan. Members of the Frank family now assumed control of the operation. They had done business during hard times making and selling liquid malt and did not need grand schemes.

A Race against Time

It all now depended on cash flow from beer and stock sales for completion of plant number one at Ten Mile. The tall building was up, and half of the machinery had been installed. Acceptance of the product from the second plant was essential, but 1936 sales of Pros't beer reached only 17,000 barrels. The following year brought a sluggish economy and excess beer production capacity in Detroit. By spring it was obvious that the brewery could not be completed.

In June, stockholders voted to sell assets for $150,000 cash to an Eastern brewery syndicate, which then sold off the equipment. Brewing of beer was suspended in September, and sales were halted in December. Efforts of the Voigt family to reenter the brewing industry ended with an empty building and stock of greatly reduced value. The structure has been used by the Walmet Corporation for the manufacture of cemented carbides. Brewmaster-to-be Stempel found another opportunity in 1937, when the Regal brewery opened near Mack Avenue, but there, too, tenure proved elusive.

Voigt-Pros't is another case of overestimating the demand for beer and underestimating major competitors after repeal. One of the ironies in this instance was that Pleasant Ridge was a dry community, and there was opposition to locating a brewery there. It was the prospect of jobs for local residents that permitted construction to proceed. Even if the building could have been finished and beer produced, it is doubtful that the Voigt name was strong enough after the long absence to generate sufficient sales for survival.

MEMORABILIA

Voigt is remembered by collectors of brewery advertising for the most beautiful promotional item of any Detroit brewery: the rare Rheingold tray. A colorful lithograph of the brewery and seasonal activities is in a local collection. Voigt was also one of the few U.S. brewers to use ashtrays for advertising, a common practice in Canada. A rare poster shows a sitting Otto von Bismarck looking favorably at a bottle of Rheingold beer, with the caption *"Das lob' ich mir"* ("This I praise"). It is very doubtful that the Prussian chancellor was aware of his endorsement. No artifacts from the post-repeal period seem to have survived, if indeed any were ordered.

MANAGEMENT

1903: Edward W. Voigt, Henry Zimmerman, William F. Voigt, incorporators.

1904: Edward W. Voigt, president and treasurer; Henry Zimmerman, vice president and superintendent; Emil C. P. Landsberg, secretary; William F. Voigt, assistant treasurer.

1914: Edward W. Voigt, president and manager; Henry Zimmerman, vice president, superintendent, and brewmaster; Otto Reinvaldt, treasurer; Emil Landsberg, secretary.

1918: Otto Reinvaldt, president and treasurer; Emil Landsberg, secretary; William Voigt, assistant secretary-treasurer.

1922: Nicholas Frank, president; Anthony J. Lambrecht, vice president; Herman Engel, treasurer.

1934: William F. Voigt, president; J. T. Wivo, secretary; George A. Mueller (architect), Charles G. Oakman, Edward W. Voigt II, and Allan V. Pownall, advisory committee.

1935: J. M. Wettlaufer, president; William F. Voigt, vice president; John F. Wise, secretary-treasurer; G. A. Mueller, Henry and Morris Leavitt, Al Kleiner, Harry Trattner, directors.

1937: Harold V. Mason, president; Nicholas Frank, Sr., vice president and brewmaster; Harry R. Trattner, secretary; Carl J. Frank, treasurer; George L. Frank, assistant brewmaster.

Voigt Family

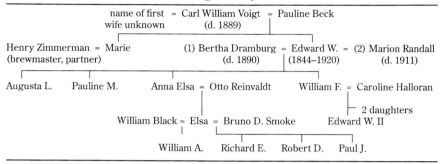

Advertising card promoting Rheingold Export and the new bottle shop.

10

FIVE THAT
SURVIVED THE WAR

All five breweries whose histories are told here were successful and proud firms, of a size that would leave no doubt about reopening after repeal or survival during the war years. Yet families once prominent saw their businesses erode as competition sharpened or there was dissention among stockholders.

Four of the five breweries were started by German brewers, and three of those were situated at or near the Eastern Market. The Martz family operated the Detroit Brewing Company from 1868; Ekhardt & Becker, later E&B, was nearby; Kaiser and Schmidt went back to 1873 and became the Schmidt Brewing Company just north of the market; and there was Koppitz-Melchers, originally on Gratiot, and later Koppitz at the river. The lone ethnic exception in this group was Tivoli, called Altes, which was started with Belgian expertise and capital.

The years after World War II proved treacherous, because there had been such a seller's market during the war. Suddenly, it was a free-for-all, with nationally advertised brands adding their pressure to those of local competitors.

These brands were a part of Detroit and are still alive in the memories of its people. A few of the buildings are still standing, reminders of a time when there were half a dozen good local beers competing for attention.

DETROIT

KLING, MARTZ & WEBER, 1856–1863
JEFFERSON NEAR BELLE ISLE BRIDGE
PENINSULAR BREWING COMPANY, 1863–1868
FRANK MARTZ & COMPANY, CONTINENTAL BREWERY, 1868–1874,
MARTZ BROTHERS, 1874–1886
DETROIT BREWING COMPANY, 1886–1948
ORLEANS AND BRONSON, LATER 2536 ORLEANS AT ADELAIDE

The three Martz brothers—Frank, Michael, and John—were natives of Bavaria who arrived in Detroit in 1839, at ages twenty-one, eighteen, and fifteen, respectively. They reached ownership of the Detroit Brewing Company from two directions. Michael learned to be a shoemaker, and after some travels, he became successful at that trade in Detroit.

The German community must have brought him and Philip Kling together, because in 1856 he joined Kling and Henry Weber in purchasing property near the Belle Isle bridge to either establish a brewery there or own an existing small brewery. Six years later, in 1863, the three partners were proprietors of the Peninsular brewery. Going from boots to beer seems an odd career move, but he must have had ambitions to be a brewery owner, and his younger brother John worked there. Even so, he hedged his investment and continued his shoe business for seven more years.

THE MARTZ BROTHERS JOIN FORCES

In 1868, Michael's brothers, Frank and John, started a brewery at the corner of Orleans and Bronson with John Steiner. The firm was officially called Frank Martz & Company and was promoted as the Continental Brewery. It was successful from the start. In 1875, Michael, then fifty-four years old, sold his interest in the Peninsular Brewery to Philip Kling and bought out the equity of John Steiner. This brought the three brothers together in the Martz Brothers brewery. Michael and Frank managed the business side, and John was the first brewmaster.

The brewhouse consisted of three floors and a cellar. It was not large in area, 40 by 50 feet, and was dwarfed by a 35,000-bushel, four-story malthouse of 45 by 120 feet and a large icehouse and beer storage cellar, 68 by 150 feet, with enough tanks to store 4,000 barrels. A two-story bottling house, 20 by 40 feet, completed the plant. The yearly capacity was given at 16,500 barrels in 1880, but sales were 6,000 barrels in 1879.

MARTZ ON THE MARCH

Ten years after the brothers joined forces, they incorporated the firm under its final name, Detroit Brewing Company, with a capitalization of $150,000. It continued to be very much a Martz family operation. There certainly was no lack of male descendants. When president Michael died in 1897 at the age of seventy-six, he was succeeded by his son George, who had been secretary-treasurer. Frank was still vice president, and his son Charles and Michael's other son Albert divided the position of secretary-treasurer.

The main brand was pale Bohemian in competition with Stroh. Other brands were Erlanger and Extra. Erlanger, named after the Bavarian town of Erlangen, was a light amber beer, also brewed by Schlitz in those years. The beers were well accepted. Already in 1892, production was 30,000 barrels and climbing. The Martz fam-

Brewmaster Herman Kleiner in an 1897 convention brochure.
FROM THE STROH BREWERY COMPANY ARCHIVE.

ily committed itself to a major expansion and had a six-story brewhouse constructed the following year, next to the original brewery. A two-story, 40-by-50-foot bottling facility, a keg wash house, and a boiler house were also built. The expansion was designed by noted brewery architects Fred Wolf and Louis Lehle. The malthouse was large enough to supply the brewery's demand. By 1895, Martz management was claiming a capacity of 100,000 barrels.

A further major upgrading occurred in 1898, when brewmaster Herman Kleiner oversaw the installation of glass-lined steel tanks to replace the original wooden vessels. Metal tanks were a radical departure from cedar or cypress, which were lined with a rosin and had to be relined annually. Manufactured by Pfaudler of Hoboken, New Jersey, steel tanks had an interior glass surface which was sprayed on while the steel was red hot and formed a sanitary permanent bond. After Prohibition, Pfaudler technology permitted the lining of a large tank as a single unit and became the standard of the industry until the use of stainless steel after World War II. Martz also adopted closed steel fermenting tanks, which permitted recovery of carbon dioxide.

Pfaudler's claims for better sanitation and avoiding the annual relining were true, but there was another side: wooden tanks had a traditional appearance, and even the odor of hot rosin during the annual relining was

Brewhouse interior, Detroit Brewing Company. A combination mash-lauter tun is mounted in I-beams at the right, above a six-tap grant (the round horizontal vessel). The brewkettle is at the left. FROM WESTERN BREWER, AUGUST 1897, THROUGH CARLSON'S BREWERY RESEARCH.

part of the romance and tradition of brewing. Change did not come quickly or easily in an industry that relies as much on tradition as brewing.

An Oldbru label joined the Bohemian and was developed into the dominant brand. The label shape for both brands was very distinctive—a rounded diamond with a pointed bottom. When Frank and John Martz both died in 1902, the family was well established as a strong presence on the local beer scene. Annual production was estimated at 130,000 barrels in 1914. This gave the Detroit Brewing Company fifth place out of twenty brewers in the city.

A MODEST REVIVAL

The brewery remained closed during Prohibition, with the Martz family maintaining ownership. When they reopened the brewery in 1934, George resumed the presidency, his brother Albert moved up to vice president, and their cousin Charles took the position of treasurer. George's other brother, Edward, was represented by his son Oscar as secretary. Nonfamily management consisted of brewmaster Andrew Freimann and sales manager Frank C. Bette. The Oldbru name was revived. After the initial pipeline-filling year of 1934, when 184,000 barrels were produced, sales settled at around 125,000 barrels. This was enough to support the Martz families.

Workers toiled for long hours, but life had its pleasant moments. The workers formed a baseball team which played weekends on Belle Isle.

The spartan general office of the Detroit Brewing Company in 1897. From left: G. Varrelmann of Pfaudler, a manufacturer of brewery equipment; George H. Martz, president; Albert A. Martz, treasurer; and Charles A. Martz, secretary.

FROM WESTERN BREWER, AUGUST 1897, THROUGH CARLSON'S BREWERY RESEARCH.

Each summer, there was picnic at the Martz farm in Willis near Belleville, where catered German-type food was served and kegs of Oldbru were tapped.

A MARKETING MALAISE

On the negative side, Oldbru did not receive any noteworthy advertising or develop a memorable personality, and it did not take off as a brand. This was in spite of Martz having hired the experienced sales manager Arthur J. Anderson in 1938. The characteristic die-cut diamond label shape used before Prohibition no doubt presented technical difficulties for fast machine labeling and was replaced by a standard rectangular label, unfortunately dull in color and graphics. Later, a more colorful label for Oldbru Bavarian Type Lager appeared. The text indicated it was Extra Dry, somewhat at odds with the Bavarian type. A special Martz Select Beer failed to catch on.

Sales had gradually declined to 100,000 barrels by 1940. Five Martz men were still running the business, headed by chairman Louis Peter. Brewmaster Freimann retired in 1938, and William F. Stegmeyer, who joined the year before, succeeded him. Like his brewmaster father Matthews, he was trained in brewing science and technology at the Siebel Institute in Chicago. Ale had never been a major segment in Detroit, but Detroit Premium Ale was launched in 1941 with as much publicity as the Frank W. Atherton Agency could generate, including radio and outdoor

Detroit brewery workers posing with a new truck at a time when these vehicles aroused great interest. FROM THE COLLECTION OF JAMES L. KAISER.

ads. The introduction was deemed successful, but the brand could not be maintained during wartime restrictions.

The war years were good for business. In the three years 1944, 1945, and 1946, between 199,000 and 211,000 barrels were sold annually. This doubling of production was surely at some cost to quality, because the amount of traditional raw materials was fixed at prewar levels. With the return to a buyer's market in 1947, sales fell back to 110,000 barrels, and kept on falling. The last year of full production was 1948, when 71,000 barrels were sold. Efforts to sell the brewery failed, and it was closed early in 1949 after eighty years of Martz family ownership, the first of the postwar casualties. President Oscar Martz blamed "terrific expansion of larger Detroit competitors."

This sudden failure probably had its roots in Detroit Brewing's modest efforts between 1935 and 1942. Reopening the plant after repeal must have involved a major capital outlay, but then the business was not or could not be developed. The third Martz generation seemed comfortable being Detroit brewers of reputation. In retrospect, they had a false sense of security. The firm remained a second-tier brewer and became increasingly vulnerable. The buildings still stand in the Eastern Market

The Detroit brewery in 1933.

Chairman Louis Peter Martz with his brewmaster, William F. Stegmeyer, checking wort in front of the brewkettle, about 1950. COURTESY JANICE A. BEAL AND ANN F. STEGMEYER.

area next to those of the E&B Brewing Company, where they serve as refrigerated meat storage and warehouses.

MEMORABILIA

There were some attractive merchandising items before Prohibition, such as special glasses and stock serving trays featuring illustrations of attractive women, but little after repeal seems memorable.

MANAGEMENT

1893: Michael Martz, president; John G. Martz, vice president; George H. Martz, secretary-treasurer; Herman Kleiner, brewmaster.

1904: George H. Martz, president; Albert A. Martz, vice president and treasurer; Charles A. Martz, secretary; Herman Kleiner, brewmaster.

1943–1948: Louis Peter Martz, chairman, manager, and purchasing agent; Albert A. Martz, president; Alfred F. Martz and F. G. Scully, vice presidents; Oscar A. Martz, secretary; Charles W. Martz, treasurer; William F. Stegmeyer, brewmaster.

Martz Family

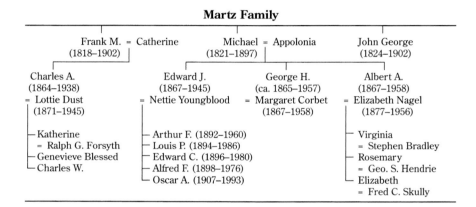

E&B

EKHARDT & BECKER BREWING COMPANY, 1883–1919
244 RUSSELL, 1883–1890
ORLEANS AND WINDER, 1891–1919
E&B BREWING COMPANY, INC., 1933–1962
2437 (ORIGINALLY 475) ORLEANS

Ekhardt & Becker, later E&B, was one of the few Detroit breweries to survive until well after World War II. It finally dropped out of competition in 1962. A brewery with a capacity of 300,000 barrels was just too small, and it was too small even to survive as a branch plant. What had kept E&B viable for so long was savvy marketing, innovative packaging, decent beer, the ability to exploit market niches, and probably also its catchy name.

John Koch's Ulmer Brewery

While E&B cited 1873 as its founding year, August Ekhardt and Herman Becker came on the scene a decade later. It was John Koch who started his Ulmer Brewery on Russell Street in 1873. He brewed 4,000 barrels of lager per year in the late 1870s and also had his own bottling facilities. This placed him in the median range of local brewers. In 1883, he sold his brewery to Ekhardt and Becker. August Ekhardt knew brewing; he had been foreman at Philip Kling's brewery and also had worked for Bernhard Stroh. Herman Becker seems to have been the partner in charge of business and financial affairs.

Ekhardt & Becker's brewmaster Anton Hiller, in an 1897 convention brochure.

FROM THE STROH BREWERY COMPANY ARCHIVE.

An illustration shows the plant to be an undistinguished pair of adjoining two-story buildings, 50 by 140 and 40 by 120 feet, which the artist could render neither imposing nor attractive. Ekhardt's brother-in-law Anton Hiller was taken on as brewmaster to oversee a crew of fifteen men. The new owners named the plant, which had a capacity of 15,000 to 18,000 barrels, Michigan Brewery.

Growth by Merger

In 1891, August Ekhardt and Herman Becker took a giant step to enlarge their operation by merging with the Fulda and Bommer brewery on Winder Street in the Eastern Market area. Fred Fulda and his partner Anthony Kaiser took over the two top positions, Becker became secretary, and Ekhardt supervised the plant. His brother-in-law Anton Hiller was brewmaster. The firm moved all operations to the Fulda brewery, which was larger and had potential for expansion, and closed the Koch brewery. The new plant was located just north of the historic German community. Martz's Detroit Brewing Company was across the street, farther north was Kaiser & Schmidt, and a half-mile south were Stroh and Goebel.

In 1895, Ekhardt & Becker continued its acquisition policy with the Westphalia Brewery on Clinton Street, with the purpose of absorbing the trade and closing the brewery. Sales were estimated at 60,000 barrels in 1914. At that time, Ekhardt's son, thirty-eight-year-old August H. Jr., was

Papke's saloon in Dearborn, with three "corner" signs for Ekhardt & Becker's Lager Beer. The signs, almost certainly "gold" on black, show the brewery with a smoking stack and are decorated with hop vines and barley awns. The boy at left is holding a sign for a September 1885 fair in Plymouth. COURTESY DEARBORN HISTORICAL MUSEUM.

brewmaster; he held that position until 1918. He had been educated at the German-American Academy and joined the brewery in a clerical capacity in 1894. Two years later, he completed a technical course in brewing in New York.

NEW OWNERS AND EQUIPMENT

The owners closed and sold the plant during Prohibition, and dissolved the original company. In 1933, a new firm was organized with some new names as major investors, but initially the sons of the founders, August Ekhardt and William Becker, were president and brewmaster, and vice president, respectively. So much work was required to restore the brewery to an operating condition that production did not begin until 1935. Although only fifty-nine, Ekhardt was not in good health, and he was forced to retire that summer. He did not recover from an operation in January 1936.

William Breitmeier was brought in as general manager; his family had been the initial backers of Conrad Pfeiffer, and he was Pfeiffer's treasurer before Prohibition and the brewery's president after repeal. He took along Pfeiffer brewmaster Betzwieser and hired Edward Hurley from the Peter Fox brewery in Chicago as assistant manager. Sales quickly climbed to 145,000 barrels. In February 1937, Ekhardt & Becker acquired the Regal Brewing Company on Bellevue near Mack Avenue. Regal had been in the liquid malt business and started brewing when Raymond Irion invested in a new brewery. The purchase price was

The office and brewhouse of the former Ekhardt & Becker brewery at the corner of Winder and Orleans in the Eastern Market area, photographed by the author in the late 1970s.

$110,000 for inventories and receivables, plus $490,000 including rentals already paid. Combined sales rose to 244,000 barrels, but fell to 164,000 in 1938. Breitmeier left to join Kurt Kling's brewery in Flint as president.

NIMBLY INTO NICHES

Ekhardt & Becker's management was not afraid to try new marketing ideas. Already in 1936, the new shorter and lighter 12-ounce "Steinie" bottle was used, and the product was promoted as "Steinie Beer." Another slogan was "Flavored with Age." The war and postwar years under the leadership of LeRoy Payne were hectic, as Ekhardt & Becker—E&B since 1944—looked for marketing opportunities in an industry increasingly dominated by large producers. E&B pioneered the 16-ounce bottle in Detroit and was early and heavily into can production. The Schmidt brewery was absorbed in 1952, and that label was brewed along with E&B Beer and E&B Golden Ale.

The brewmaster for most of the 1940s was Otto Noissinger, who was succeeded by assistant John Newell from 1949 to 1962. Continuity of business and technical management no doubt contributed to E&B's relative longevity. The position of plant chemist is not a critical one, but it is a case in point. The chemist from 1942 until the brewery closed twenty years later was a slight-built man named Fred Sturmer. He had started as chemist in Frankenmuth, where his duties included not only the analysis of beer, brewing ingredients, and fuel but also the care of dachshunds. These were the brewery's mascots and a marketing tool, and there was a whole kennel to feed and water. Eventually, Fred tired of having his weekends restricted by dachshund duty and found in E&B a canine-free brewery. After E&B closed, he worked in the Stroh lab until his retirement in 1971. Among his coworkers were Harold Chere, formerly chief chemist at Pfeiffer, and former Goebel chemist Howard Noffze.

In 1963, Pfeiffer acquired E&B and formed a new corporate entity, the Associated Brewing Company, and brewed the brand in its much larger facility. The E&B buildings still stand in the Eastern Market area; the storage building is used for cold storage, and other buildings are also at least partially occupied. When one of the many storage rooms was opened in the early 1970s, a large supply of cone-top cans was found in mint condition. What was at one time a great rarity became a $25 can within a year. The property was purchased in the summer of 1980 by two men associated with J. L. Hirt & Company.

Ekhardt & Becker grew from a small beginning by the very modern technique of acquisition and merging, and the company was innovative to the end. It outlasted its neighbors and almost outlasted Goebel and Pfeiffer. But it was not in the same league as the major Detroit brewers; it had the savvy but not the size.

MEMORABILIA

Attractive merchandising items were used during the years before Prohibition, including trays and glasses. A large variety of items is available from the E&B period.

MANAGEMENT

1897: Fred Fulda, president; Anthony Kaiser, vice president; Herman Becker, secretary-treasurer; August Ekhardt, superintendent; Anton Hiller, brewmaster.

1903: August Ekhardt, Sr., president; Herman Becker, secretary-treasurer.

1938: David I. Huber, chairman; William D. Bradley, president; Edward Yentsch, secretary-treasurer; William G. Breitmeyer, general manager; William M. Betzweiser, brewmaster.

1950: LeRoy Payne, president, manager, and purchasing agent; L. T. Ransom, vice president, sales; E. E. Rothman, secretary; Edward Yentsch, treasurer; John Newell, brewmaster.

1960: LeRoy Payne, president, general manager, treasurer, and purchasing agent; Charles Nicholas, vice president; John Newell, brewmaster.

KOPPITZ

KOPPITZ-MELCHERS, 1890–1918
1125 GRATIOT AT SUPERIOR
KOPPITZ-MELCHERS, INC., 1935–1947
GOEBEL BREWING COMPANY PLANT NO. 3, 1947–1958
DUBOIS AT THE RIVER

Konrad Koppitz, holding a horse, is surrounded by his workers in front of the brewery on Gratiot Avenue. COURTESY HERMAN KONRAD ROSENBUSCH.

When Konrad Emil Koppitz and Arthur C. Melchers established their brewery late in 1890 with some partners, it was the beginning of a great period for the brewing industry but also a successful one for the Anti-Saloon League. The new brewery experienced a good quarter-century before the dry movement throttled and then closed the industry.

ARRIVAL AND DEPARTURE

Konrad Koppitz was born in the Silesia region of Austria in 1854. At age fourteen, he started a three-year apprenticeship in the brewer's trade, and after working in a Viennese brewery, he emigrated to Chicago at age nineteen. He attended the local Wahl-Henius Brewing Institute and found employment at the Schoenhofen and Conrad Seipp breweries. After a year of additional brewing studies in Germany, he returned to Chicago to work for the McAvoy brewery, where he became first cellar man. He was married in May of 1881. Three years later, he moved to Detroit with his wife, Emilie, and their two-year-old son, Benjamin, to become brewmaster at Stroh.

There he met Arthur Melchers, who was the cashier and a relative of Julius Stroh by marriage. Although he was promoted to superintend-

Konrad Koppitz, in an 1897 convention brochure.
FROM THE STROH BREWERY COMPANY ARCHIVE.

ent—the equivalent of today's plant manager—he and Melchers left in December 1890 to found the Koppitz-Melchers Brewing Company. The other partners were his brother-in-law Herman Sachse, who had been associated with the National Brewery in Saginaw, and Charles F. Zielke.

THE CASTLE ON GRATIOT AVENUE

The partners were able to finance a 60,000-barrel brewery on a block-long frontage on Gratiot Avenue. The plant's exterior design lacked only a moat and drawbridge in its effort to imitate a castle. The four-story brewhouse combined the Romanesque arches of the past decades with a massive crennelated tower. This housed grain storage and the malt mill. Below was a 180-barrel kettle, and the brewhouse could turn out three brews per day. The main brand was Pale Select Lager; other brands were Silver Brew, Porter, and a Malt Tonic, as well as Bock in season.

John A. Preston, the secretary and treasurer of the Howard-Northwood Malting Company in Detroit, acquired an interest in Koppitz-Melchers when Howard-Northwood was bought out by the American Malting Company in 1899. When Arthur Melchers retired from the presidency in 1902 because of persistent ill health, Preston was elected president. Koppitz succeeded Preston after his death in 1907.

Members of Detroit's German brewing fraternity knew each other well and met frequently, and thus it came about that Konrad Koppitz's daughter Rose Caroline was married to Herman Albert Rosenbusch, the son of Konrad's successor as Stroh's brewmaster, Otto Rosenbusch. The marriage of Herman and Rose was to last fifty years. But the world was smaller still. The May 1911 wedding was performed by Pastor Otto C. Haass, one of whose sons was an attorney named Walter. Later he was a senior law partner in Race, Haass & Allen. A group led by Walter Haass had bought the closed Goebel brewery during Prohibition as an investment, and he ended up as president of the new Goebel Brewing Company. And whom would Haass select as Goebel's first brewmaster in 1934 but sixty-five-year-old retired Otto Rosenbusch?

The Koppitz-Melchers brewery, on a rainy day in 1919.

The Koppitz plant did not remain open during Prohibition, which seeemed to have caught management by surprise because Konrad's grandson Kenneth Koppitz recalled 12,000 barrels of unfinished beer being poured into sewers. The firm was liquidated in 1920, one year after Konrad's death at age sixty-four.

BEN KOPPITZ

A new corporation was organized in 1935 by two colleagues of the old Koppitz-Melchers, Konrad's son Ben Koppitz and Fred Goettman. Ben had entered the family business in 1898 at age sixteen, and he was superintendent when the brewery closed. He then spent the Prohibition years in Detroit as president of the Brake Equipment Company. Fred Goettman had been hired by the brewery in 1894, when he was twenty-five, to be cashier. He was soon promoted to secretary and became treasurer in 1899. With Ben Koppitz's brewing background and his respected name and Fred Goettman's experience in financial management, raising capital by a stock issue proved relatively easy.

A 2.25-acre property was acquired in 1935 on the Detroit River at the foot of Dubois for the construction of a 200,000-barrel brewery. Aided by a stock issue, construction was started the same year. Detroit architects Mildner & Eisen designed a modernistic plant with strong vertical lines softened by some art deco touches. The centerpiece was a 110-foot

GMC trucks advertising Pale Select line up in 1916.

brewhouse of six floors, capable of four brews per day of 300 barrels each. The brewery was furnished with state-of-the-art equipment, and construction was completed in October 1936.

Gustav Goob, an experienced older brewmaster, was placed in charge of brewing. His tenure at Koppitz was short, and the reason for his departure could not be learned. He was replaced in October 1936 by John A. W. Hartung, who had laboratory and brewing experience at the Jacob Ruppert brewery in New York. Hartung's tenure lasted six years and ended tragically when he fell to his death from the brewery's roof. It was widely believed that business problems brought about a self-inflicted death. He was succeeded by John S. Merkt.

Koppitz Pale Select, the brand name before Prohibition, was placed on the market early in 1937. Sales that year were 86,000 barrels and decreased to 70,000 barrels in 1938. The brand was facing strongly established competition and failed to meet the company's expectations. It was replaced by Koppitz Silver Star, the pre-Prohibition symbol which the advertising agency McCann-Erickson had advised the company to keep. Early in 1941, Ben Koppitz could announce that sales in 1940 were 97,500 barrels, a significant improvement over 1939, and that a strong newspaper campaign was planned through the Livingston Porter Hicks advertising agency. Little did Ben Koppitz realize then that L. P. Hicks, chief executive of that agency, would replace him within eighteen months.

THE HICKS WHIRLWIND

Hicks made such a good impression that he was brought in as sales manager. Unlike the conservative Ben Koppitz, Hicks was an enthusiastic promoter who wanted Koppitz beer to be noted and remembered. The onset of the war provided Hicks with opportunities to show his flair for marketing. He heard about a supply of 20,000 half-gallon crocks that were glazed on the inside, and launched the "Little Brown Jug" beer package for home use. The crocks did not require scarce materials, and

A case delivery cart, with a horse in a leather shoulder pad decorated with brass knobs and initials.   COURTESY WILLIAM A. BARBER.

The new Koppitz brewery on Atwater Street, shown on the April 1937 cover of *Modern Brewer*.
FROM THE STROH BREWERY COMPANY ARCHIVE.

Ben A. Koppitz and Fred P. Goettman, in *Modern Brewer*, April 1937.

he found manufacturers for them. A Bavarian brand was also added to the product line.

It was obvious that Koppitz and Hicks were too far apart in temperament to make a good team. In July 1942, Ben Koppitz resigned, and Hicks was elected president. This also terminated the positions of treasurer George Auch and secretary Earl Graef. Although Koppitz, Auch, and Graef were reelected to the board, Hicks brought in E. A. Houvener of Millenbach Motor Sales as treasurer and A. W. Taylor of Packard as secretary to create a Hicks-oriented management.

A major shakeup occurred in 1943, when dissident stockholders, led by Hicks, ousted Koppitz. Hicks sued Koppitz for fraud, which was supported on May 2, 1944, by Judge Guy A. Miller. He ruled that Ben Koppitz had received five thousand shares in 1934 as secret profit for negotiating the purchase of the brewery site from the Michigan Central Railroad. Judge Miller also determined that Koppitz's ten-year contract, set to expire in 1947, had been terminated legally already in 1942. Goettman was not implicated in any questionable dealings and remained with the new management.

The flamboyant Hicks continued to make news and an occasional wave for the brewery. He launched Victory Beer and the dark Black-Out during 1943 and 1944. There were one hundred different labels for Victory Beer, featuring combat planes, ships, and armament, a fairly blatant effort to piggyback on the war effort. A 50-50 blend of Victory and Black-Out beers was also promoted. This was an early attempt to market what is now called an amber or red beer.

With the war over in 1945, a new Koppitz Beer was introduced with a Hicksian gimmick. Bottles were packed in red tubes with make-believe fuses, to look like giant firecrackers. Although it had been announced that a new beer was coming which was "hotter 'n a firecracker," police

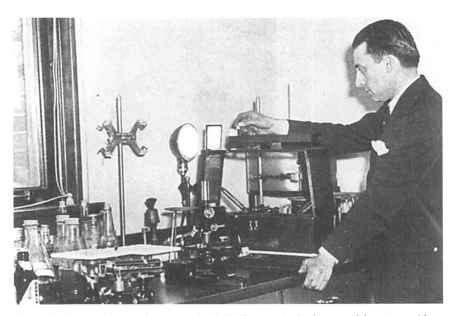

Superintendent and master brewer John A. W. Hartung in the brewery laboratory, with an instrument for measuring beer color by comparison against known standards, in *Modern Brewer*, April 1937. FROM THE STROH BREWERY COMPANY ARCHIVE.

were inundated with calls about dynamite. Hicks had outdone himself, and sales rose 4.5 percent that year to 162,000 barrels, the highest level in the history of the company.

THE END OF KOPPITZ

It was another story in 1946, as sales fell 10 percent. The era of gimmicks may have been over; the new brand also had a tiny label which only a minimalist could appreciate. Management had a chance to purchase the first postwar canner from American Can to be offered locally but elected to go with one-way bottles instead, a choice which undoubtedly placed Koppitz at a disadvantage. A Black Velvet Porter was tried without enough success. Koppitz fell to eighth and last place among city breweries. When the opportunity arose in 1947 to sell the plant to Goebel, stockholders grabbed it. Fred Goettman, who had spent his entire life at Koppitz, may have been very reluctant to see a competitor win out, but he was nearing retirement. Hicks returned full-time to his advertising agency.

Goebel operated the brewery for sixteen years with brewmaster John Merkt until Goebel's fortunes turned. Stroh bought the failing Goebel Brewing Company in 1964, and both it and the twenty-nine-year-old Koppitz plants were razed. The brewhouse equipment was all crated and shipped to Israel; it survives as a bit of Detroit history far from home.

Koppitz-Melchers had a very good name before Prohibition, but that did not go very far in the late 1930s. The brewery hung on until the war years, when staffing and materials were the problem, not sales. The

President Livingston P. Hicks shaking hands with vice president Fred Goettman amidst Christmas cheer in the "Bierstube" (hospitality room), 1940s.   COURTESY WILLIAM A. BARBER.

future for Koppitz was questionable once the war was over, given its second-tier position before the war and the management dispute. The stockholders were able to sell the plant because it was the only large new brewery in the area.

MEMORABILIA

Koppitz-Melchers distributed very attractive trays before Prohibition, notably a horizontal oval tray showing dwarves around a brewkettle and a round tray divided into four seasonal scenes. Gnomes or dwarves were often shown in print ads. Small etched glasses are in many collections. Point-of-purchase ads for saloons and stores of the 1930s are largely uninspired. It was not until the wartime Hicks phase that labels and ads became interesting.

MANAGEMENT

1890–1899: Arthur C. Melchers, president and business manager; Konrad E. Koppitz, vice president and superintendent; B. H. Rothwell, secretary; F. P. Goettman, treasurer.

1904: J. A. Preston, president; Konrad E. Koppitz, Vice president; F. P. Goettman, secretary-treasurer.

1917: Arthur C. Melchers, president; Konrad E. Koppitz, Vice president and superintendent; Herman Sachse, assistant superintendent.

1937: Ben A. Koppitz, president (until 1942); Fred P. Goettman, vice president and general sales manager; J. Arthur Hoffman, secretary-treasurer; John A. W. Hartung, master brewer and chemist (1936–1943).

1942–1947: Livingstone P. Hicks, president, manager, and purchasing agent; Fred P. Goettman, vice president; Albert W. Taylor, secretary; E. A. Houvener, treasurer; John S. Merkt, master brewer.

Koppitz Family

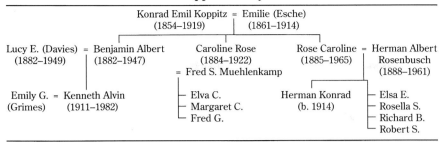

Konrad Emil Koppitz = Emilie (Esche)
(1854–1919) | (1861–1914)

Lucy E. (Davies) = Benjamin Albert | Caroline Rose | Rose Caroline = Herman Albert
(1882–1949) | (1882–1947) | (1884–1922) | (1885–1965) | Rosenbusch
| | = Fred S. Muehlenkamp | | (1888–1961)

Emily G. = Kenneth Alvin | ⌐ Elva C. | Herman Konrad | ⌐ Elsa E.
(Grimes) | (1911–1982) | ⊢ Margaret C. | (b. 1914) | ⊢ Rosella S.
| | ⌐ Fred G. | | ⊢ Richard B.
| | | | ⌐ Robert S.

TIVOLI

FRANTZ BROGNIEZ, 1897
TIVOLI BREWING COMPANY, 1897–1948
ALTES BREWING COMPANY, 1948–1954
NATIONAL BREWING COMPANY OF MICHIGAN, 1954–1967
NATIONAL BREWING COMPANY, 1967–1973
1549–75 MACK (1897–1919), 10205 MACK (1933–1948),
3765 HURLBUT (1967–1973) (SAME LOCATION)

In 1897, a Belgian brewing scientist and civil engineer, Frantz Hector Brogniez, was instrumental in starting a small brewery at the corner of Mack and Hurlbut avenues. Frantz or Franz Brogniez was born on October 26, 1860, in the Belgian province of Hainaut and educated at the University of Louvain. His father had purchased an estate that included a small operating brewery. Brogniez thus learned the trade at home, and he went on to found the first Belgian school for brewing in Lichtervelde. He emigrated in August 1896 with Alida Grymonprez, his second-wife-to-be, after his first marriage ended in divorce. They were married in Windsor, Canada, the following February.

THE BELGIAN CONNECTION

A Brogniez brewery letterhead with a "B" trademark indicates that he started his own brewery. However, he evidently needed capital. Brogniez went into partnership with Bernard Verstein and Louis Schimmel, members of Detroit's well-established Belgian community. Verstein was an older man who had been a prominent lumber dealer in Pennsylvania and was probably the main financial backer. Schimmel had been bookkeeper with Ekhardt & Becker's brewery for ten years after a varied business career. In 1890, thirty-year-old Schimmel had married Julia Kling, the oldest daughter of brewer Philip Kling. This may explain his having venture capital for the new Tivoli brewery. James Singelyn was taken into partnership in 1900.

GOOD-BYE, BROGNIEZ

In 1899, Brogniez traveled to Belgium to be with his dying father. On his return to Detroit nearly a year later, he could reestablish neither

RETURN TO

Frantz Brogniez

BREWERY.

TRADE **B** MARK.

1553 MACK AVE.
DETROIT, MICH.

Letterhead for Frantz Brogniez's Brewery, 1897, which became the Tivoli Brewing Company after refinancing with new partners. According to Frantz Brogniez's son Raymond H. Brogniez, the circles surrounding the B were in the Belgian national colors of black, yellow, and red.

COURTESY DONN E. BROOKS.

his position as brewmaster nor his equity in Tivoli, and he was in effect frozen out. It is known that he felt cheated by his former partners. It is likely that Brogniez failed to protect his equity formally during his long absence, and his partners took advantage of this as the months went by without him. Years later, Altes beer bottles by Tivoli had a neck label referring to Louis Schimmel as the founder, but Brogniez was given credit by contemporary sources.

A SOUTHERN CAREER

Brogniez's expertise in brewing got him an assignment to clear up a quality problem at the Walkerville brewery owned by Hiram Walker. According to family oral history, Walker reneged on his fee, nor did he help Brogniez with his problem with Schimmel. Brogniez left Detroit in 1904 and had a successful career as brewmaster, first at the People's Brewery in Terre Haute, then with a long tenure at the Houston Ice & Brewing Company, where he became a vice president and brewmaster of its Magnolia brewery. An accomplished musician, he was a cofounder of the Houston Symphony. One cannot help thinking that Brogniez could have been a great asset to the business and cultural life of Detroit.

THE TIVOLI BREWERY

Tivoli was the last brewery to be founded in Detroit that prospered for decades both before and after Prohibition. The original plant built by

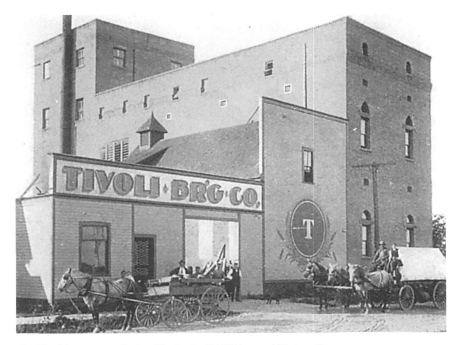

The Tivoli brewery as depicted in the April 1898 issue of *Western Brewer*.
CARLSON'S BREWERY RESEARCH.

Brogniez and Schimmel in March of 1897 soon outgrew its capacity. With Verstein's support, a much larger brewery was erected in 1898, which was described in the trade press. The plant consisted of three- and four-floor buildings, 65 by 122 feet, of a design that was simple and modern in a period when castle-like decorations were favored. Pfaudler representatives had sold new glass-lined tanks to the Detroit Brewing Company and also supplied Tivoli with glass-lined fermenting and storage cellars.

The brewery was greatly expanded in the years before Prohibition. All the buildings were raised an additional floor. The original simple architectural style was no longer deemed impressive enough; small turrets sprouted along the roof line, simulating the look of a feudal castle. A new office building was added a short distance away to provide a courtyard. The plant capacity was now rated at 75,000 barrels. Two compressors provided 35 tons of refrigeration; many older breweries that had converted from ice to mechanical refrigeration to cool beer going into storage were satisfied with 20-ton machines.

PROHIBITION PROJECTS

Louis Schimmel was president when Prohibition became law, and he stayed with Tivoli until January 1, 1921. The plant was kept open with carbonated beverages and liquid malt. An attractive Tivoli soda bottle with a stippled texture is probably now the only reminder of this period. There is strong anecdotal evidence that Tivoli sold real beer during the first year of Prohibition, when enforcement was relatively lax. Charles

Tivoli management posing with a representative of Pfaudler, a manufacturer of brewhouse and stock house vessels, in 1897. Seated: Louis Schimmel, secretary and treasurer, and B. Verstein, president. Standing: G. Varrellmann of Pfaudler, and Frantz Brogniez.

FROM THE APRIL 1898 ISSUE OF WESTERN BREWER. CARLSON'S BREWERY RESEARCH.

Rose was employed in local delivery from 1900 to 1946; he was barn boss when Prohibition became law, and retired as traffic manager when horses were long gone. His son Bernard recalls his father Charles telling about the first wagon of illegal beer to be delivered: "Everybody was afraid to drive the team, so I finally did it myself." It was a big event at the time, and his father's story stuck in young Bernie's memory.

The vertical Pfaudler tanks did not survive Prohibition, as the years of inactivity took their toll. Also, early glass-lined tanks consisted of sections bolted together; later technology permitted an entire 600-barrel tank to be heated until glowing and to be sprayed with molten glass, leaving a smooth interior finish. But the new management opted for tradition, and when the brewery reopened in 1934, fermentation in open wooden casks was promoted.

Tivoli was in better shape to start marketing beer than plants that had to be refitted. Former brewmaster Adolph Wandrei, assisted by his brother Walter, returned for a few years before retiring. The top management team was new and consisted of Howard H. Colby and Elwood M. Bayne. Colby was the attorney who arranged the acquisition of the assets by the new owners, and Bayne had married Schimmel's daughter Clara. Capital was raised by selling stock at one-dollar par ($608,000) and 5 percent debenture notes ($302,000).

ON A ROLL

Demand started very strong, with sales of 154,000 barrels in 1934. Management decided to build a new 500-barrel brewhouse. The new building was designed by the local firm Mildner & Eisen to be eight floors tall. It had the clean vertical lines and ample window space characteristic of commercial buildings erected between 1930 and 1950. The brewhouse opened in March 1935 after five hectic months of construction.

The new facility placed Tivoli among the six largest brewers in Detroit. The 500-barrel kettle ensured a capacity of 400,000 barrels annually with four brews per day, which was then considered the maximum for twenty-four-hour operation. In 1935, sales increased by 41 percent to 218,000 barrels, and there was another huge increase to 357,000 barrels in 1936 before sales leveled off. Tivoli had arrived as a challenger to Stroh, Goebel, and Pfeiffer.

Tivoli Pilsener was the first brand to be brewed. In August 1936, Altes Lager was reintroduced in a green bottle and became the most popular beer brewed by Tivoli. The green bottle was complemented by an attractive green label. Two line extensions were tried briefly—an Altes Draft joined the Lager, and about 1942, there was an Altes Imperial. A Skyball brand was also launched at that time. None of these succeeded, but the Altes Lager proved such a durable seller that in 1949, the brewery's name was changed from Tivoli to Altes Brewing Company. Tivoli was a good name at the turn of the century, when many beer drinkers

The beer that bewitches

ALTES LAGER BIER

Newspaper ad, 1910.

were first-generation residents familiar with the famous Copenhagen amusement park. Tivoli connoted fun and a pleasant time, similar to what Coney Island or Luna Park once represented in this country.

BIG FISH EAT LITTLE FISH

In that year of 1949, the company tried to tap the growing population on the West Coast and acquired the Aztec brewery in San Diego. This venture had to be abandoned in 1953, and Altes itself was purchased in 1955 by the National Brewing Company of Baltimore. This was an old-line brewery owned by the Hoffberger family and brewers of National Bohemian. The Altes brewery was renamed National Brewing Company of Michigan. Advertising for the Altes brand was reduced in order to introduce the new corporate brand, "National Boh."

Oral history has it that Altes became difficult to find, while National Bohemian was everywhere. Detroit beer quaffers, to whom Baltimore was not necessarily a role model for good beer, resented being pushed to drink the new brand. Also, Altes had a no-nonsense blue-collar image—it was a man's beer—and "Mr. Boh", the symbol of National, may have

A very fancy beer truck for home deliveries.
FROM THE NATIONAL AUTOMOTIVE HISTORY COLLECTION, DETROIT PUBLIC LIBRARY.

seemed foppish. National Boh just did not sell. By the time Altes was revived, consumers had switched to other brands.

The Detroit brewery, facing sagging sales, produced the popular Colt 45 malt liquor and developed the flavored Malt Duck beer. Unfortunately for the Detroit operation, the National home brewery in Baltimore also showed declining sales, and it became necessary to combine production in Baltimore.

The plant on Hurlbut near Mack Avenue was closed in 1973, much to the disappointment of the local staff, which deserved a better fate and had hopes of going it alone. A decade later, when specialty beers were being brewed under franchise, financing might have been possible. The last brewmaster was Karl Seidl; he ended his career with Stroh as head of the grain-unloading and yeast-drying operation.

The Altes brand survived the brewery. With continuing consolidation, a bigger fish gobbled up the one that had swallowed the minnow. It came to pass that the former Carling brewery in Frankenmuth was acquired by G. Heileman of LaCrosse. Among Carling's assets was the Altes brand. By this roundabout way, Altes was again being brewed in Michigan, an hour and a half up I-75 and much farther away in corporate culture from the old days on Hurlbut Street. The brewing of Altes in Michigan ceased with the closing of the Frankenmuth brewery in 1991.

Tivoli management photographed in 1933. *From left:* Howard H. Colby, chairman; Elwood M. Bayne, president; Adolph Wandrei, brewmaster. FROM THE STROH BREWERY COMPANY ARCHIVE.

MEMORABILIA

Interesting advertising pieces of both the pre-Prohibition and later Altes period are known; early items are scarce. Tivoli was the only Detroit brewery to have hanging globe lamps; two have survived and are among the rarest of local brewery collectibles.

MANAGEMENT

1898: Bernard Verstein, president; Frantz Brogniez, vice president and superintendent; Louis Schimmel, secretary and treasurer.

1908: Bernard Verstine, president; Louis W. Schimmel, secretary and general manager; James Singelyn, vice president and treasurer; Adolph Wandrei, brewmaster.

1937: Howard H. Colby, chairman; Elwood M. Bayne, president; Hugh Martin, vice president; John F. Hillenbrand, secretary and director of sales; Frank C. Flumerfelt, treasurer; Otto Schmidt, brewmaster.

1949: Howard H. Colby, president and manager; John F. Hillenbrand, S. Taylor Creighton, and Hugh Martin, vice presidents; Marion F. Zindler, secretary-treasurer; Oscar Teeg, master brewer (1944–1953; formerly chemist); Fred Studer, chief engineer (1940–1966).

1955: Jerold C. Hoffberger, president (also president of National Brewing Company in Baltimore); Dawson L. Farber, Warren Carroll (also general manager), and John F. Hillebrand, vice presidents; John A. Billstone, secretary-treasurer (1965–1967); John Balconi, master brewer (1954–1970); Harold Rothchild, chemist.

SCHMIDT

GEORGE HAUCK & COMPANY, 1873–1892
REUTER & KAISER, 1892–1895
KAISER & SCHMIDT, CHAMPION BREWERY, 1895–1919
SCHMIDT PRODUCTS COMPANY, 1919–1933
SCHMIDT BREWING COMPANY, 1933–1951
400 (RENUMBERED 1995) WILKINS

The Schmidt brewery in 1933, looking east on Wilkins Street.

FROM THE STROH BREWERY COMPANY ARCHIVE.

George Hauck and Christian Bauer were partners in a brewery on the near northeast side, a few blocks east and north of the Stroh brewery. Hauck was a Bavarian by birth who arrived in Detroit about 1858. His early history is unknown, as is how he met Bauer, who came to this country in 1854 at age fifteen from Mecklenburg in Northern Germany. Initially, the small brewery had an address next door to the Hauck residence. George Hauck's brother Matthew also boarded and worked there; later, he brewed with William Moloney.

HAUCK TO KAISER TO SCHMIDT

In the early 1880s, the property consisted of two adjoining buildings of three and four floors standing on a 90-by-100-foot property. The small brewery had a capacity of 3,500 barrels. Over the years, Hauck had a number of partners after Bauer, including Joseph Peter Kaiser. After Hauck's death in 1882, his widow, Margaret, sold the brewery to the Kaiser family. In 1895, Frank A. Schmidt became associated with the operation and ended up being joint owner with Kaiser. The firm Kaiser & Schmidt operated successfully until 1919 under the name Champion Brewery. Its main brand was Old Fashion Beer. The brewing capacity was listed as 30,000 barrels in 1897; additions in 1900 and 1901 increased this to an estimated 100,000 barrels.

Clearly, major construction had occurred. Photographs taken during Prohibition and right after repeal show a modern five-story structure along Wilkins Street north of Eastern Market. Nothing can be seen of

Partners in the Kaiser & Schmidt Brewing Company, in an 1897 convention brochure. *From left:* Joseph Kaiser; Julius Kaiser. FROM THE STROH BREWERY COMPANY ARCHIVE.

Hauck's original buildings. Peter Kaiser, who had purchased the brewery with his wife, Catherine, in 1882, died in 1929, and with him ended the last Kaiser connection. During Prohibition, the renamed Schmidt Products Company leased the plant to the Acme Beverage Company for production of hop-flavored malt syrup under the Campfire and Oh Boy! labels.

In December 1932, a new corporation was formed, headed by Frank Schmidt's sons George S. and Frank A. Jr., who had been treasurer of the Michigan State Bank of Detroit. Veteran brewmaster John Kleiner was placed in charge. New building additions for beer aging and packaging were designed by Detroit architect George A. Mueller and completed in January 1934. The brewery now stretched a whole block from St. Aubin to Dequindre. Because syrup had been manufactured all along during Prohibition, startup time was greatly reduced. The new beer, Schmidt's Famous, was on the market in June 1933, very shortly after the return of legal beer.

A STRONG START

Business got off to an excellent start with 1934 sales of 229,000 barrels. While there was a drop to 168,000 barrels in 1935, sales recovered to 198,000 in 1937 and 213,000 in 1938. These volumes were more than the 1934 packaging facilities could handle adequately. A 70-by-200-foot packaging center was erected at a cost of $300,000, which occupied the entire block from Wilkins to Brewster on the eastern side of the Grand Trunk Railway.

In addition to the Famous brand, Schmidt also revived the dark Würzburger and a Bock in spring. After a couple of years, the Famous brand was replaced, first by Sparkling Beer, "made from the finest malt,

George Schmidt, from *Michigan Volksblatt*, Sept. 26, 1910.

selected rice and the bud of choice hops," and then by a very contemporary approach, the Natural Brew. Schmidt's label also proclaimed, "No sugar, no glucose added." This claim for ingredient purity was meant to stress the nonfattening quality of Schmidt beer. In any case, these are natural substances and were not used for lager but only in ale brewing to increase the alcohol content. Production during the war years averaged around 300,000 barrels. It seemed that Schmidt was well positioned to grow after the war. Frank Schmidt, Jr., died in 1944 at age fifty-six. His place as treasurer was taken by Conrad Leppek, husband of Frank's sister Anna. The management team of George and Frank Schmidt, Fred Rieg, and Bill Fredericks had been in charge since repeal and had performed well. Now only Fred Rieg, another brother-in-law who was married to Frank's sister Margaret, was left from the old team. The new management had less than two years left before the business climate changed drastically and very serious competition began. Adequate marketing preparation for the coming selling climate would have to be taken well ahead of time.

POSTWAR LETDOWN

This evidently did not happen, because sales volumes fell back after the war to levels of the mid-1930s. The major Detroit brewers all showed gains in the late 1940s. By 1950, sales of Schmidt beer were down to 105,000 barrels. That year, assistant brewmaster Max Walsdorf finally was promoted. In a last-ditch effort for new business, he brewed a Jolly Ale. Production ceased in 1951. The E&B Brewing Company, which had excess capacity, acquired the label. Former brewmaster Walsdorf, a jovial and popular man, stayed in the area and represented a firm of brewery suppliers.

Schmidt was the second major casualty of the postwar era, after the Detroit Brewing Company a few blocks farther south closed in 1948. A lot of beer was sold during the war, and a lot of money must have been made by and for the Schmidt family. It seems that when the time came to choose between expanding and competing hard or coasting, management was conservative. Perhaps there was little choice against the strong marketing efforts of Goebel and Pfeiffer during this period. Hindsight indicates that caution was indeed the better strategy, given the fate of other local competitors.

One of the buildings has survived to the present time. The refrigerated storage cellar, where beer was aged in tanks, is now used for meat storage.

MEMORABILIA

Collectibles from the Kaiser & Schmidt era are scarce. The best-known piece is a large oval stock tray showing the head of a pretty woman with a soulful expression advertising Champion Beer. Schmidt was one of the very few firms to have a Prohibition serving tray, for "malt, hops and brewery supplies"; it promoted the Campfire brand malt syrup. Prewar tin-over-cardboard and glass signs are known.

MANAGEMENT

1882: Margaret Hauck, Peter Kaiser, Catherine Kaiser.

1914: Joseph P. Kaiser and Frank A. Schmidt, proprietors; Fred A. Kaiser, brewmaster.

1937: George Schmidt, president; Frank A. Schmidt, Jr., vice president and treasurer; William W. Fredericks, secretary; John H. Kleiner, brewmaster.

1947–1951: George Schmidt, president; Frederick A. Rieg, first vice president; William W. Fredericks, second vice president; Conrad E. Leppek, treasurer; Gustav Weymar (1948–1949) and Max Walsdorf (1950–1951), master brewers; William Thieme, chief engineer (1941–48).

Schmidt Family

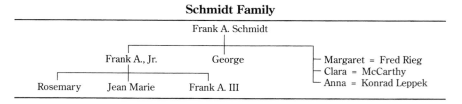

11

GOEBEL: THE COMPETITOR ACROSS THE STREET

Of all the brewers who settled in Detroit and competed, only two gave Stroh cause to worry at a time when mistakes could and did have very serious consequences. During the early years, Stroh was far from being the dominant brewer it became after the turn of the century. This did not matter then; it was a more forgiving time.

Goebel was a relative latecomer and one of many minor competitors. That all changed in 1889, when Goebel, with English capital, built an imposing brewhouse. Stroh and Goebel now faced each other across Gratiot Avenue, friendly competitors to be sure, but each determined to be on top. Goebel kept challenging Stroh with a good product and innovative packaging, but Stroh always managed to stay in front. Then came the crucial period after World War II, and suddenly Stroh was struggling in third place.

A. GOEBEL & COMPANY, 1873–1889
GOEBEL BREWING COMPANY, LTD., 1889–1897
GOEBEL BREWING COMPANY, 1897–1964
ACQUIRED BY THE STROH BREWERY COMPANY, 1964
RIVARD AND MAPLE (351 RIVARD, LATER 2001 RIVARD)

The Goebel brewery started modestly and gave no indication that it would become a factor on the regional scene for decades and nationally

217

August Goebel. From the 50th anniversary edition of *Michigan Volksblatt*, 1903.

in the 1950s. August Goebel and Theodore Gorenflo opened a 4,000-barrel lager brewery in 1873–74. Both had been born in Germany, Goebel in 1839 in Munstermaifeld, Rhenish Prussia, and Gorenflo seven years later. Goebel was seventeen when he arrived in Detroit. Like Bernhard Stroh, he was heading for Chicago but ran out of funds. He became an apprentice at Elwood's bookbinding shop, and when the Civil War broke out, he enlisted in Company A, 2nd Michigan Infantry, as a private. The regiment saw much action, and Goebel gradually rose to the rank of captain. His colonelcy was probably awarded much later.

Colonel Goebel, VIP

Goebel became very interested in politics; in 1870, he served as superintendent of public works in Detroit, and he was a representative from Wayne County in the state legislature for the term 1879–1880. He "was not particularly distinguished as a legislator, but his colleagues liked him for his generosity and good nature." He was more of a lobbyist against Prohibition, and as a joke he had bock beer signs printed with the legend "Drink Mosher Bock Beer—the best beer made," referring to a fellow legislator and prominent prohibitionist, Charles Mosher of Hillsdale. Goebel's jovial personality prevented any ill feelings. In 1885, Goebel was elected to the board of councilmen and was chosen as presiding officer when Marvin H. Chamberlain was elected mayor. He ran unsuccessfully as Wayne County sheriff and aspired to be collector of internal revenue, but being a brewer disqualified him. His last office was an appointment to the water board for the fiscal year 1888–89.

Goebel was twenty-eight when Gorenflo settled in Detroit in 1867. When and how the two men met has not been recorded, but in 1873 they were partners in the newly formed A. Goebel & Company. The beer was well received. Five years later they were selling 8,000 to 9,000 barrels; this doubled during the 1880s. Goebel became the third-largest Detroit brewer after Voigt and Kling. A detailed description of Goebel's brewery was recorded in 1880. The plant stood on a corner lot 93 by 105 feet with

August Goebel.

FROM OUR MICHIGAN FRIENDS "AS WE SEE 'EM," C. O. YOUNGSTRAND, ED., 1905.

a 35-by-60-foot brewhouse, two stories above two cellars 18 by 40 and 9 by 30. The malthouse was 40 by 57 with three stories ending in the typical pyramidal kiln tower. In the back was a two-story icehouse, 34 by 70, and fermenting cellars, with a 16-by-70 subcellar for aging. The brewmaster was probably Albert Maas, who represented Goebel at the first convention of the U.S. Brewmasters Association in Chicago in 1887. Stroh's brewmaster Ben Koppitz also attended.

BACKED BY THE BRITISH

In 1889, a British syndicate was looking for investment opportunities in the American brewing industry. Through the efforts of August

The Goebel office building was erected at the corner of Rivard and Maple, where Jacob Mann's home once stood. The building to the left of the office lasted until the brewery closed in 1964.

Goebel, this syndicate acquired three Detroit breweries in addition to his own, with a total capacity of 50,000 barrels. These were the Bavarian Brewing Company of Anton Michenfelder, the Charles Endriss brewery, and Jacob Mann's plant at Rivard and Maple. Both the Endriss and Mann breweries were near the Goebel property. The Michenfelder and Mann plants were closed almost immediately. The Goebel Brewing Company, Ltd., was incorporated with capital stock of $600,000 and August Goebel as president and manager in 1890. Four years later, the Endriss brewery was also closed. Goebel continued operating as resident manager under the British ownership.

A major investment was undertaken in 1897 with the construction

The Goebel crew knocked off work one afternoon about three o'clock and posed during a party in 1888, creating one of the great group photographs of brewery workers, foremen, and bosses. Maltsters fill the back row except for a fermentation man holding a yeast skimmer, used for Goebel's porter. Teamsters are next in leather aprons, which had chest pockets for holding route books. Colonel August Goebel, then forty-two, is fourth from the left in the front row; to his right is brewmaster Joseph Aiple. The small boy at left is Walter Wacker, sitting on the knee of his father, John, a cooper with a nearby shop. Walter became a Goebel employee, and rejoining the brewery in 1934 as bottling superintendent, he recalled the afternoon. A pair of saloon corner signs featured the winged G trademark.

FROM THE STROH BREWERY COMPANY ARCHIVE.

of a large new plant next to the Mann site on Rivard. The five-story brewhouse contained two 400-barrel steam kettles and rivaled the nearby much older Stroh brewery in size. There was ample refrigeration for the claimed capacity of 350,000 barrels. A group photograph taken in 1888— a child in the photo, Walter Wacker, had a long career at Goebel and knew the details—shows six men with malt shovels, indicating the plant also included a malthouse.

Brewmaster Aiple offered the top-of-the-line Blue Label Extra Pale Export, regular Export, a Pilsener, and the dark and full-bodied Würzburger. A malt tonic, wrapped in paper and fluted at the neck, was advertised "for the sick and convalescent" or as "Nourishing, Strengthening and Exhilarating, but not intoxicating." The alcohol content was less than 2 percent. A fine porcelain tray set in a brass ring attests to the brewing of Porter. A small change in the product name from "Goebel's" to

A Packard truck, ready to roll about 1914, was loaded with kegs exactly as horse-drawn wagons had been, including suspending four barrels from the bed.

FROM THE NATIONAL AUTOMOTIVE HISTORY COLLECTION, DETROIT PUBLIC LIBRARY.

"Goebel" occurred during this time. Goebel was a major part of the golden age of brewing in Detroit.

THE LAST OF THE GOEBELS

The turn of the century brought significant changes in management as the founders grew older. August Jr. was brought into the firm in 1891 as secretary-treasurer. Gorenflo retired in 1896; at one time vice president, he was last listed in 1894 as bookkeeper. When August Goebel died in 1905 at age sixty-six after a brief illness, his position was taken by Fred Brede, who had joined the brewery in 1888 as secretary-treasurer, and August Jr. became general manager. The younger son Fritz took over as brewmaster when Aiple left to manage the new Union Brewing Company in 1898.

In 1912, Stroh started construction of its eight-story brewhouse and won the contest for plant size, if not always for sales. But the Goebel plant had been built big enough to more than double the initial capacity. Another personnel shift occurred in 1914, probably based on the shares held by the Goebel family. August Jr. moved up to become president, his brother Fritz became vice president and superintendent, and Brede returned to his initial function as treasurer.

UNDER NEW OWNERSHIP

Prohibition forced Goebel to close. British capital no doubt had been invested well, but the investors were not interested in a marginal operation. A family group headed by Detroit attorney Walter F. Haass, a senior partner in the prominent law firm Race, Haass & Allen, purchased the property as a real estate investment. The brewery was

The Goebel brewhouse at the southeast corner of Rivard and Maple, when it was closed during Prohibition. Space was rented to various businesses.

FROM THE MANNING BROTHERS HISTORIC PHOTOGRAPHIC COLLECTION.

August Goebel, Jr., in 1911.
FROM THE STROH BREWERY COMPANY ARCHIVE.

renamed Detroit Industries Building and space was rented to various light manufacturing and similar tenants. After repeal, the principal owners, Walter Haass and his sisters Elsa and Hermine and their spouses, set about to activate the brewery. Walter assumed the presidency, Hermine's husband, Charles F. Clippert of the Clippert Brick Company, became vice president, and Elsa's husband, attorney C. Redman Moon, was secretary. Hermine's son-in-law Hugh Nesbitt, owner of the very successful Nesbitt Company in California, served for several years as vice president in charge of sales.

The Goebel family was represented only by purchasing agent Ted E. Goebel, a grandson of the colonel. August Jr. had died in 1932. His brother Fritz was part of a group that invested in plans for the Fort Dearborn brewery. When this failed to materialize, he moved to Saginaw in 1937 to become president and general manager of the Banner Brewing Company. He died tragically in 1939 from a gunshot accident while on a hunting trip.

The new company was incorporated November 16, 1932, to gather investment capital for the expected reopening. The final capitalization in May 1933 was for 1,400,000 shares at one-dollar par. The issue was completely subscribed, but Philip Moon, Redman's son, recalled that "Walter (Haass) had a rough time selling almost 1.5 million shares."

Goebel had to catch up with Stroh, located just across Gratiot Avenue. Stroh had managed to keep its plant open with near beer and did not face the

Fritz Goebel, with granddaughter Susan, about 1936. COURTESY SUSAN TYLER.

Goebel secretary Charles Redman Moon, Sr., in 1935.

startup problem after a fourteen-year shutdown. Haass decided not to rush into production with makeshift equipment. It was not until September 1933 that capital was in place for a new brewhouse and other equipment, costing half a million dollars. The old corner office building was razed and replaced with a new boiler and engine building to supply both steam for brewing and refrigeration for aging. The brewhouse received a new modern facade, and the entire plant was painted white.

Everything was ready for production in the spring of 1934. Haass hit upon the idea of hiring Otto Rosenbusch, the retired pre-Prohibition brewmaster from Stroh. The fact that Otto was also the father of Stroh's current brewmaster, Herman A. Rosenbusch, must have added an edge to the competition between the two neighbors. He seemed to have welcomed the position and hired Anthony Hahn, the former brewmaster at Kolb in Bay City, to be his assistant. He also hired Howard Noffze, a young chemist, to set up the first brewing laboratory in Detroit. Howard would work almost thirty years at Goebel, and another decade in the Stroh lab. A new corporate logo was chosen to replace the winged locomotive front: a very Germanic-looking eagle in a circle.

The first sales occurred in April 1934. Two products

Goebel vice president Charles F. Clippert, in 1935.

New 1934 Dodge Brothers delivery trucks with the Germanic eagle emblem are lined up along the north side of Maple in front of freshly painted buildings. A new engine building had been erected on the corner lot across from the brewhouse, where the office once stood. The adjoining structure with three narrow windows dates back to Jacob Mann's brewery.
FROM THE MANNING BROTHERS HISTORIC PHOTOGRAPHIC COLLECTION.

were brewed by Otto, a Goebel and a Munchener Dark. A Bock was added after a few years. Initial Goebel beer sales were strong and reached an impressive 367,000 barrels in 1935, then fell back into the range of 250,000. Otto Rosenbusch retired for good in 1936, knowing that he had completed his last assignment successfully. About that time, Stroh was planning a new office building, and Herman A. Rosenbusch, not to be outdone by his father, laid out a larger lab on the second floor. The analysis of brewing quality criteria, once part of the brewmaster's duties, had expanded to become a full-time position for at least one chemist.

Otto Rosenbusch was succeeded by Herman Zerweck, a distinguished-looking brewmaster of the old school. From the fourth generation of a brewing family in Germany, he had served his apprenticeship there and had been brewmaster of a large New York brewery.

Walter Haass had become friendly with August Busch, and Zerweck copied the paler and lighter Budweiser. His product became

The Goebel brewery was photographed from the Stroh brewhouse in the 1940s. The emblem had been modified to an American bald eagle.

FROM THE MANNING BROTHERS HISTORIC PHOTOGRAPHIC COLLECTION.

The two 430-barrel copper brewkettles of Goebel were among the largest in Detroit. The three handles in sleeves at the left operated valves below the kettle. The pipe sticking up next to the vertical beam at the left is a floating level indicator; the projecting rod is calibrated in barrels.

FROM THE MANNING BROTHERS HISTORIC PHOTOGRAPHIC COLLECTION.

The Bock beer sign on the back bar of the Goebel hospitality room indicates it was spring of 1935. Seated in the middle is Otto Rosenbusch, Stroh's brewmaster for thirty-nine years, who was brought back from retirement at age sixty-seven to start up brewing at Goebel.

FROM THE MANNING BROTHERS HISTORIC PHOTOGRAPHIC COLLECTION.

increasingly popular. Goebel used its cypress tanks as an advertising vehicle. "From the cypress casks of Goebel" was the slogan until wartime made advertising unnecessary. Goebel also launched an ale, but the product languished. The lion's share of Michigan's small ale business belonged to the Frankenmuth Brewing Company.

ADMAN ANDERSON

Walter Haass was looking for a general sales manager, and in February 1938, he appointed Edwin J. Anderson, who had held a similar position with Hiram Walker. Anderson became a vice president after Nesbitt retired, and he worked closely with distributors at the annual Rally of Distributors and the advertising agency Brooke, Smith, French, and Dorrance. Anderson also made good use of Goebel's pre-Prohibition tradition of using a matched team of Clydesdales to promote the product. In the late 1930s Goebel assembled a great eight-horse hitch of champion Clydesdales which traveled from New York to Florida and as far west as Wisconsin. Wartime restrictions closed this showpiece, and it was not revived after the war. Goebel also replaced the angular-winged German eagle with an American bald eagle above five stars.

In late 1941 and early 1942, within a matter of months, Walter Haass, Charles Clippert, and Redman Moon all died. With nobody of the Haass team left but widows, Anderson requested and was given the presidency. Anderson's personality was different from that of the conservative Walter Haass. He saw opportunities for changes and expansion. One of the first visible marketing changes was to package beer in 7-ounce

The first anniversary of the Gold Label brand was celebrated with a company banquet in 1940. President Walter F. Haass, behind the cake, is flanked by treasurer Frank Bishop at the left and sales manager Edwin J. Anderson and brewmaster Herman Zerweck at the right. Identification by Howard Noffze.   PRESS PHOTO SERVICE, FROM THE STROH BREWERY COMPANY ARCHIVE.

painted-label bottles under the Bantam name, using a small rooster as emblem. This 7-ounce package found a market niche, and the rooster became identified with Goebel. The other new brand was Gold Label.

After the war, Anderson pushed a successful expansion program, which culminated in Goebel selling over 1 million barrels in 1948. In 1947, the Muskegon brewery of the Grand Rapids Brewing Company was acquired and became Plant No. 2. Sales, pushing capacity, were still climbing with the popular Bantam line. Goebel's sponsorship of the Detroit Lions football team kept the brand in front of a large beer market. In the following year, Koppitz-Melchers closed its fourteen-year old brewery, and Goebel had its Plant No. 3. Frank Bauer was hired as assistant master brewer; he took over two years later when Zerweck retired. The Gold Label brand was replaced in favor of Extra Dry in 1949, some forty years before this name became popular as a new beer type. In 1951, Private Stock 22 became a second brand.

AMBUSH IN THE WEST

With Goebel on a roll, Anderson took a gamble and went west. The Golden West Brewing Company in Oakland, California, became a wholly owned subsidiary in 1950. During this period, several major brewers wanted to tap into the market created by the growing California population. These ventures all failed; neither Pabst, Falstaff, nor Goebel could transfer their successes to the West Coast. Probably the marketing effort and approach required to enter that market successfully was underestimated. Even when a native brewery was in difficulties and welcomed a buyer, many loyal customers rejected the new brand. There also were

The Goebel brewery viewed from the south, about 1960. The large packaging building in the foreground blocked Rivard Street. The Stroh stock houses are in the left background. The tall structures in the far right background are the Rickel grain silos.

PHOTO BY RANSIER-ANDERSON FOR THE STROH BREWERY COMPANY.

small regional flavor differences, and the Midwestern beers may have seemed bitter.

The growing popularity of Coors on the West Coast added a serious obstacle. Coors was brewed far enough west not to be perceived as an Eastern beer, and its mild flavor was different enough to create a unique image. When Goebel's military sales of canned beer destined for Korea ceased in 1954, the fate of the Goebel brewery in Oakland was just a matter of time. The plant was closed in late 1956.

MEANWHILE, BACK HOME . . .

Back in Michigan, things still seemed to be going well. Anderson was an ardent sports fan. Goebel sponsored telecasts of the Tigers and the Lions, of which he was also president. Goebel was selling more than a million barrels annually in a period when such a volume placed a firm in the top 10 percent of the industry. On the technical side, former assistant brewmaster Frank Bauer was appointed vice president and supervising master brewer in 1954, with two assistants in addition to the brewmasters at the other three plants.

In retrospect, there were signs of future difficulties. Sales volume peaked in 1953 at 1.3 million barrels. The Extra Dry brand was discon-

Outdoor posters from the 1950s. FROM THE STROH BREWERY COMPANY ARCHIVE.

tinued in 1955 after six years, a short time then for a beer brand. Stroh was suddenly hot, exceeding 1 million barrels for the first time in 1953 and 2 million in 1955. Goebel sales had stabilized at 810,000 barrels in 1956–57, still very respectable but at the level of a decade earlier.

The year 1958 was a watershed for all operating Detroit brewers, when a strike that began April 1 was not settled until May 20. The proportion of out-of-state beer rose from 33.2 percent in 1957 to 42.2 percent in 1958, and shippers into Michigan gained a strong and irreversible hold.

DEFEAT ON GRATIOT AVENUE

By 1960, it was obvious that Goebel was on a downward slide. Anderson was replaced as president by Leroy J. Wallace. He had been treasurer since 1950 and executive vice president for two years. Wallace estimated a sales loss of $4 million and an income loss of half a million from the strike, but he presented an upbeat forecast. However, the lost revenue further limited Goebel's options and renewed the declining sales trend.

It was also Frank Bauer's last year. Director of quality control Thomas R. Montgomery was promoted to vice president of production and master brewer. Howard Noffze left to work in the Stroh laboratory. His position was taken by Elton Pomaville, who was promoted to assistant brewmaster in 1964. This proved to be Goebel's last full year of operation. Pomaville, who had acquired a good reputation, found employment as assistant brewmaster at Falstaff in St. Louis.

In retrospect, it is obvious that the franchise had suffered from too many changes in personnel and marketing slogans. Erwin H. Haass, the son of Walter's older brother Otto, took over as president, and he tried to salvage something of the family's equity.

The end was not pretty, as Goebel's management tried desperately to come up with a new marketing plan. The rooster was literally killed off on television to loud squawks. The beer business had become very unforgiving. In addition, certain work rules limited productivity. The number of cases that could be delivered by one worker per eight-hour day was pegged at 125. Drewrys, a popular beer from Ft. Wayne, could be delivered in Detroit at lower cost than Goebel. Across the street was Stroh, now a 2-million-barrel brewery with essentially the same old-fashioned label as in the 1930s, a consistent product, and the cost advantage of economies of scale. Unable to lower the cost of production or raise the price, Goebel closed its doors in 1964, nine years shy of its centennial.

A NAME REMEMBERED

The entire Goebel property was acquired by Stroh. The brewhouse, cellars, and powerplant were razed and became parking lots for an expanded hospitality center. Some garage buildings were kept, and what was the packaging building later became a can plant.

Then an odd thing happened to the Goebel brand. Stroh management decided to brew it with the Goebel yeast on a very small scale, with a different hop blend and without firebrewing, but with the same care and quality control as Stroh's Bohemian brand. Raymond J. Kowalski, the last Goebel sales and advertising manager, was given the Goebel brand to sell. There was no advertising except for a lower price. Slowly, the brand recovered and became recognized as a good, reliable local product. Ten years after Goebel folded, the brand accounted for a quarter-million barrels in annual sales. Old-time comedian George Goebel was retained for commercials and print ads. Goebel was alive and quite well again.

The Goebel case illustrates just how critical the balance is between the marketing function, with its necessary innovative and expansion-oriented outlook, and conservatism, which is also needed for a brewery's image with consumers. Goebel expanded greatly but let its image and quality base shrink to the point where it could no longer support the franchise.

MEMORABILIA

Goebel had a variety of merchandising items in the years before Prohibition, which are greatly outnumbered by collectors and therefore much in demand. One exception is a set of three attractive Delft blue trays in both the regular and small sizes, which are relatively common. An ivory-colored ceramic mug is also frequently seen. Attractive etched glasses and lithographs are known. A wide range of post-Prohibition items makes Goebel an easy entry-level specialty for Michigan-oriented breweriana collectors. Goebel cans go back to the "German" eagle design with a flat top. The rarest Goebel can is the olive-drab wartime issue.

MANAGEMENT

1893: William B. Moran, president; Joseph B. Moore, treasurer; August Goebel, manager; Theodore Gorenflo, superintendent; Ralph Phelps, Jr., counsel; Fred W. Brede, secretary.

1897: August Goebel, president and manager; Fred W. Brede, assistant manager; Joseph B. Moore, treasurer; Ralph Phelps, Jr., counsel; August Goebel, Jr., secretary.

1938: Walter F. Haass, president and general manager; Charles F. Clippert, vice president; Edwin A. Anderson, general sales manager; C. Redman Moon, secretary; Frank C. Bishop, treasurer; Theodore E. Goebel, assistant secretary; Charles Elich, general superintendent; Herman Zerweck, master brewer; Romeo Samson, chief engineer; Walter Wacker, bottling superintendent; Howard Noffze, chemist; Charles E. Carey, sales and advertising manager.

1948: Edwin J. Anderson, president; Fred. W. Prichard, vice president and treasurer; Charles E. Carey, vice president, sales; Harry Allen, secretary; Theodore E. Goebel, purchasing agent; technical staff unchanged except for Frank M. Bauer, assistant brewer; Barnum P. Coolidge, advertising manager.

1954: E. J. Anderson, president and general manager; C. E. Carey, vice president, sales and advertising (Percy A. Rheaume and B. Coolidge, assistants); Fritz C. Hyde, Jr., vice president; Charles E. Dawson, vice president and treasurer; H. Allen, secretary; T. E. Goebel, purchasing; F. M. Bauer, supervising master brewer; Al Gruner and Robert Flugfelder, assistant brewers; John Merkt, master brewer Plant No. 3 (formerly Koppitz); John Geyer, assistant brewer Plant No. 3; other technical staff unchanged.

1960: E. J. Anderson, chairman; Leroy J. Wallace, executive vice president and general manager; Robert A. Schiffer, vice president; Harold O. Olson, secretary; N. W. Calkins, marketing dir.; F. M. Bauer, vice president and supervising master brewer; Carl W. Wrede, master brewer; Thomas R. Montgomery, director of quality control; Howard H. Noffze, chemist; Frank V. Hamilton, bottling superintendent.

1964; Erwin H. Haass, president (1961–65); Ernst F. Kern, vice president; H. O. Olson, secretary; J. L. Chadwick, treasurer; Donald Kirkham, controller; Raymond J. Kowalski, sales and advertising manager; Albert Gruner, master brewer; Elton Pomaville, assistant brewer; H. Dunn, purchasing agent; Donald Beebe, chemist; Lee Lundy, engineer; Walter R. Butson, bottling superintendent.

12

PFEIFFER: THE GIANT THAT SCARED STROH

Like Colonel Goebel, Conrad Pfeiffer arrived in Detroit from Germany and faced an entrenched Stroh brewery already in its second generation. Like Goebel, he entered the industry successfully and established himself in the community. Pfeiffer did not require English capital to grow. His partners were the Breitmeyers, a local family that was active in the business.

What turned Pfeiffer from a provincial and somewhat sleepy firm into an aggressive giant in the 1940s and 1950s was the arrival of Alfred Epstein. He was "another country heard from," the rare Jewish brewer among the many Teutonic and a few Slavic owners plying their trade after Prohibition. Epstein gained control of Pfeiffer by competence and energy. After the war he was able to assemble a team which put Pfeiffer beer on the regional map in capital letters. The rise and fall of Pfeiffer is as interesting a story as the Detroit brewing industry has to offer.

CONRAD PFEIFFER, 1889–1892
CONRAD PFEIFFER & COMPANY, 1892–1902
C. PFEIFFER BREWING COMPANY, 1902–1920
PFEIFFER BREWING COMPANY, 1933–1962
ASSOCIATED BREWING COMPANY, 1962–1972
ARMADA CORPORATION, 1972
912 BEAUFAIT, 1889–1918
3740 BELLEVUE, 1933–1972

Conrad Pfeiffer. From Our Michigan Friends "As We See 'Em," C. O. Youngstrand, ed., 1905.

When Conrad Pfeiffer emigrated from the German province of Hessen in 1871 at age seventeen, few would have predicted that he would become head of a large firm. His education was very limited, and he started out as a farmhand. Later, he was apprenticed to a locksmith, and then he worked at the Riverside Iron Works, where he became a foreman. In 1881, at age twenty-seven, Pfeiffer began his career in brewing as a worker at Phillip Kling's brewery. This led to his becoming a foreman at the brewery of Charles Endriss. After eight years, he felt confident enough to start a brewery with his nephew Martin Breitmeyer, whose family backed the venture.

Pfeiffer's Famous Lager

The business was incorporated in 1892 as Conrad Pfeiffer & Company. Soon people along Mack Avenue heard about the Famous Lager

The stake truck changed the way kegs were loaded, about 1912.
FROM THE NATIONAL AUTOMOTIVE HISTORY COLLECTION, DETROIT PUBLIC LIBRARY.

and the dark Würzburger brands. The brewery prospered and expanded. In 1902, John C. Beutler, Frank Breitmeyer, Martin Breitmeyer, Henry C. Dietz, and Conrad Pfeiffer reincorporated the firm as the C. Pfeiffer Brewing Company with $150,000 in capital stock. An elaborate hospitality center was added near the brewery, with a glass-enclosed palm court and an outdoor beer garden with fountain and bandshell. Pfeiffer had become a significant part of the local beer industry.

Pfeiffer and his wife, the former Luisa Cramer, had two daughters and three sons, but none of the boys survived to adulthood. When Pfeiffer died in 1911 at age fifty-seven, his widow took his place as president, and their daughter Lillian became vice president. Three members of the Breitmeyer family—William, Martin, and Frank—were also active in management. Sales in 1914 were estimated near 100,000 barrels, placing Pfeiffer eighth out of twenty brewers.

ENTER ALFRED EPSTEIN

No production took place during the Prohibition years. In 1926, the State Products Company was organized to acquire the assets of the former C. Pfeiffer Brewing Company in preparation for the eventual repeal. A new firm was incorporated in June 1933 under the name of Pfeiffer Brewing Company. The former general manager and treasurer, William G. Breitmeyer, became president, and newcomer Alfred Epstein was vice president. Canadian-born Albert T. Montreuil served the first three years as chairman.

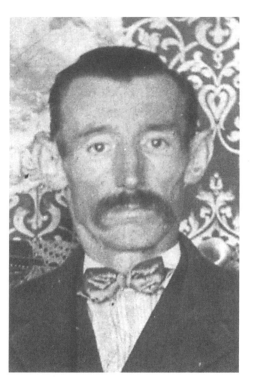

Herman Ortwein, Pfeiffer brewmaster during the first decades, photographed in 1900 after he retired.

Epstein was born in the small Austrian town of Teschen in 1894 and emigrated to the United States in 1922, following his brother Elias, who had arrived before the war. Alfred had no background in brewing, but he saw an opportunity to be useful and obviously understood what needed to be done to get a dormant plant in operation. It was Alfred Epstein who called on suppliers for malt, bottles, and other needed items; arranged for the necessary credit; and promoted a stock offering under a five-year contract.

Management used the funds from the stock sale to finance new construction and better equipment. By the summer of 1934, Pfeiffer's management was optimistic enough to reintroduce the dark Würzburger. And 1935 was a banner year; volume of beer sold almost doubled from 200,000 barrels. The stock was traded both locally and in New York. Epstein was on a fast track, and this must have caused friction with William Breitmeyer. The upshot was that Breitmeyer left and joined E&B, and then Kurt Kling's efforts to revitalize his family tradition with a brewery in Flint. Montreuil also resigned and became chairman of the Mundus Brewing Company on Detroit's west side. Epstein took over as president and general manager, and by 1937, he was very much in control of Pfeiffer.

The human chemistry and the product were right, and Pfeiffer's Famous sold well. Income went to increase plant capacity, particularly for a new stock house and refrigeration and packaging facilities. Sales ranged from about 250,000 to 400,000 barrels during the decade, placing Pfeiffer among the very successful revival brewers. Epstein was also instrumental in organizing Drewerys Ltd. USA, and became its board chairman.

JOHNNY PFEIFFER (SAY "FIFER")

In 1940, the mascot "Johnny Pfeiffer" made his first appearance. Before Prohibition, most people knew that Pfeiffer meant "piper" in German, and they knew how to pronounce it. Johnny Pfeiffer was an inspired

Rear view of the Pfeiffer plant in October 1918, already showing faded signs. The building at the left was occupied by the American Linseed Company. Pfeiffer expanded greatly on both sides of the railroad tracks after repeal of Prohibition in 1933.

FROM THE MANNING BROTHERS HISTORIC PHOTOGRAPHIC COLLECTION.

creation, a cheerful and readily identifiable symbol who also taught people how to say the name. In no small measure, Johnny Pfeiffer orchestrated the growth of the brewery.

Pfeiffer's sales volume grew to slightly more than half a million barrels during the war. An embarrassing episode occurred when the books were audited in 1942, and it was discovered that treasurer Lloyd H. Buhs and office manager Charles K. Wright had withdrawn $216,000 and transferred it to a firm controlled by Buhs. This company, Engineering Specialties Corporation, had a Navy propeller contract. This was taken over by Pfeiffer, but the poor performance on the contract caused additional losses.

HITTING THE JACKPOT

Beginning with 1947, the firm experienced an unprecedented growth that saw sales reach two million barrels in five years. Plant capacity had to be expanded almost continually. It started with the purchase of the former Dailey brewery in Flint in 1947, which Kling had acquired and

The Pfeiffer Brewery complex in the mid-1940s. New stock houses (K, J), packaging and case storage buildings (C, O) and an office building (B) were added.

IN PFEIFFER ANNUAL REPORT, 1946. FROM THE COLLECTION OF JAMES JOSWIAK.

Left, brewmaster August Thies checking wort at a modern grant, where a single large pipe replaces numerous small pipes ending in valves called "taps." Right, railroad sidings greatly simplified material supply and shipping, compared with other Detroit breweries, which required a truck transfer.

IN PFEIFFER ANNUAL REPORT, 1949. FROM THE COLLECTION OF JAMES JOSWIAK.

The Pfeiffer board of directors pose for the *Annual Report* in the peak year of 1950. Seated, from left: Homer C. Fritsch, Sr., William M. Packer, Louis A. DeHayes, president Alfred Epstein, T. Mel Rinehart. Standing: general counsel W. Henry Gallagher, vice president and treasurer Merle A. Yockey, vice president of sales Harold L. Richeson.

FROM THE COLLECTION OF JAMES JOSWIAK.

modernized in the 1930s. Pfeiffer used this brewery solely for draft beer; by 1949, its capacity had been doubled to 250,000 barrels.

During those heady years, Pfeiffer could do no wrong; the brand was hot, and the only problem was how to brew enough. At the same time, Stroh saw its sales shrink to make it a weakened No. 3 brewer behind Pfeiffer and Goebel. Stroh's reluctance to place beer in cans certainly must have helped its competitors in the postwar years.

Pfeiffer management probably did not know exactly what it was doing right, and when sales started to fall off in the middle fifties, the reason was an even greater puzzle. The meteoric rise resulted in a three-year peak and was followed by a decade-long slow erosion.

The strike in 1958 probably hurt Pfeiffer more than any other Detroit brewer. Pfeiffer had borrowed heavily to finance its expansion, and funds that had to service a debt could not be used for marketing.

Alfred's son Herbert joined the brewery as advertising manager in 1952 at age twenty-six, and he became marketing vice president the following year. The prominence of the Epstein family in the local brewing scene was not unacknowledged among competing beer salesmen. An ethnic joke making the rounds in bars asked for the difference between Stroh's and Pfeiffer's beer. The answer was that one is fire-brewed, the other heb-brewed.

Herbert Epstein stayed in marketing until 1958, then assisted his father as executive vice president. Alfred Epstein remained president and chief stockholder until 1959, when he retired from active manage-

It's for Swing-Shifter's and late Stayer-Upper's
'THE JOHNNY FIFER SHOW'
ALL NIGHT - EVERY NIGHT
12 MIDNIGHT 'TIL 6 A.M.
RICHARD JOHN III (DICK) HALLWOOD
(Sunday Musical Program 10 p.m. to 12 Midnight)
W B B C
1330 ON YOUR DIAL

Pfeiffer advertising from the 1950s.

ment but continued to serve as board chairman. Herbert Epstein took over as president.

THE END OF THE WINNING STREAK

Slight increases in barrels were noted in the years 1960 to 1962, and dividends were paid in 1960 and 1961. However, labor costs and competition kept going up. The Michigan State Legislature added an additional burden by increasing the state excise tax from $1.25 to $6.61 per barrel, by far the highest levy in the Midwest.

A DARING GAMBLE

In 1962, Pfeiffer took a bold step, changed the corporate title to Associated Brewing Company, and embarked on an ambitious acquisition program to broaden the brand base. It acquired the E&B Brewing Company on November 15, 1962, for 300,000 shares of common stock valued at almost $800,000. On June 30, 1964, Sterling Brewers, Inc., of Evansville, Indiana, was purchased for $6.5 million plus 122,000 shares with a value of slightly under half a million. The last merger was with Drewrys, Ltd., USA at the end of 1965. George K. Bissell, chairman and president of Drewrys, became chairman of Pfeiffer, with Herbert Epstein as president.

Associated now had five brands: Pfeiffer, Schmidt in St. Paul, Piels in the East, and Drewrys and Sterling in Indiana. The concept was to have strong regional brands. In 1969, Associated ranked tenth in size nationally, with almost four million barrels sold. The firm generated earnings, but none of the five brands showed any growth, and all were vulnerable to competition. The great home brewery on Beaufait had already been closed in 1966; sales of the Pfeiffer brand were insufficient to keep the big plant open, as it could be brewed more economically in Indiana.

SELLING THE PIECES

Innovations in 1970 such as the "Big Mouth" bottle opening or Mickeys Malt Liquor were no substitute for a strong national brand. Discussions with G. Heileman about selling the St. Paul and Indiana breweries started in 1971. The Indiana operations lost slightly more than half a million dollars that year. This sale was consummated June 30, 1972. In addition, the company, now called Armada Corporation, sold the remaining breweries in Brooklyn, New York, and Willimansett, Massachusetts, to Rheingold Breweries in 1973. The post-Prohibition phase of Pfeiffer, so proudly described in the early 1950s, ended with $9 million.

Alfred Epstein died in 1976 at age eighty-one. He worked as hard as anybody in the industry to get a moribund brewery on-stream and took over the business when he was convinced that he could do better. There are people still alive who remember those early years and admire him for his energy and ethics.

The case history of Pfeiffer illustrates the inherent weakness of even a strong and savvy regional brewer in an era of national brand marketing and expansion. Very few regional breweries, whether in Detroit or elsewhere, had good prospects as independent entities. Pfeiffer was not alone in following a strategy of acquiring local brands. Falstaff in St. Louis and Goebel had taken similar actions, with essentially similar negative outcomes. G. Heileman, which took over more breweries than anybody else in an effort to upgrade the size of acquired plants, eventually closed all the breweries it had obtained from Associated. The large Pfeiffer plant still stands, a huge ghost that probably will take a century to crumble. The sad part is that nobody seems to miss the brand; it was hot in the 1950s, and that was so long ago.

After the brewery closed, some of the workers found employment at Stroh. Former chief chemist Harold Chere accepted a position in the Stroh laboratory, maintaining a cheerful disposition, then retired to Florida. Herbert Epstein moved to Atlanta and started a luggage manufacturing business. Connections to the old Conrad Pfeiffer family could not be established. Some years ago, a descendant of secretary Henry Dietz moved to Florida from Detroit, but the trail ends there, and it has been sixty-five years since a Breitmeyer was active in the firm.

MEMORABILIA

Early Pfeiffer memorabilia are hard to find, except for embossed bottles. Signs from the 1930s are scarce. There is a wealth of material from the postwar era showing Johnny Pfeiffer in a variety of media.

MANAGEMENT

1905–1910: Conrad Pfeiffer, president; Martin Breitmeyer, vice president and treasurer; Henry C. Dietz, secretary; Herman Ortwein, brewmaster.

1914: Louisa Pfeiffer, president; Lillian Pfeiffer, vice president; William G. Breitmeyer, treasurer and general manager; Martin Breitmeyer, secretary; Andrew Freimann, brewmaster.

1935: Albert T. Montreuil, chairman; William G. Breitmeyer, president; Alfred Epstein, vice president and general manager; L. H. Buhs, secretary and treasurer; C. W. Hinz, assistant treasurer; Fred G. Haas, brewmaster.

1938: Alfred Epstein, president and general manager; H. L. Richeson, vice president, sales (until 1953); L. H. Buhs, secretary-treasurer; C. W. Hinz, assistant secretary-treasurer.

1952: Alfred Epstein, president and manager; H. L. Richeson, vice president, sales; M. J. Boyd, vice president, purchasing; M. A. Yockey, vice president and treasurer; G. E. Delaney, secretary; August Thies, master brewer (1943–1954); Edward Maerkl (later brewmaster), R. Breitmeyer, I. Bandl, assistant brewers; Harold L. Chere, chief chemist; Herbert S. Epstein, advertising manager.

1963 (Associated): Alfred Epstein, chairman (1960–1965); Herbert S. Epstein, president; Henry Protzman, executive vice president (1960–1967); Roy C. Trudeau, vice president, finance (1960–1967).

Pfeiffer Family

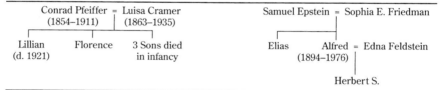

Conrad Pfeiffer = Luisa Cramer
(1854–1911)   (1863–1935)

Lillian   Florence   3 Sons died
(d. 1921)   in infancy

Samuel Epstein = Sophia E. Friedman

Elias   Alfred = Edna Feldstein
             (1894–1976)

                       Herbert S.

"A Good Drink Makes Old Young" was the German slogan on a bottle label for the amber Würzburger style, ca. 1936.   FROM THE STROH BREWERY COMPANY ARCHIVE.

13

MICROBREWERIES
AND BREWPUBS

T he brewpub and microbrewery movement started on the West Coast in the early 1970s and slowly spread throughout the nation. It reversed a century-old trend for increasingly larger plant size and greater difficulty of entering the industry. The historic cycle started all over again: the modern brewpub is an adaptation of the tavern where home-brewed beer, home-baked bread, and home-cooked food were served long ago.

DETROIT MICROBREWERIES AND BREWPUBS

THE DETROIT AND MACKINAC BREWING COMPANY, 1992–1994
MOTOR CITY BREWING WORKS, 1995–
470 WEST CANFIELD

Tom Burns, Jr., son of a State of Michigan Court of Appeals judge, was a part of this early movement. He worked for the Cartright Brewing Company in Portland, Oregon, while he was a student at Lewis & Clark Northwestern School of Law. His passion was brewing, and after obtaining a law degree and passing the bar examination, he went to work for the Boulder Brewing Company in Colorado.

Burns returned to Michigan in 1984 and engaged in legal work toward changing Michigan's law prohibiting brewpubs at the request of Ben Edwards, president of the Traffic Jam & Snug restaurant. Edwards's

Tom Burns, Jr., the first of the area's microbrewers, seated before his brewing vessels in 1992.
COURTESY DETROIT FREE PRESS.

restaurant served homemade breads and cheeses and also wanted to add home-brewed beers. Edwards had a 10-barrel brewery built at the rear of the restaurant's parking lot in preparation for the expected license.

The resulting law permitted a small on-premise brewpub, but did not permit the owner of a retail liquor license also to hold a brewer's license. Ben Edwards had to divest himself of ownership of the brewery so that Burns could rent the facility.

A "Blessing of the Brewery" celebration on June 28, 1992, kicked off the revival of brewing in Detroit, seven years after the closing of the Stroh brewery. Canfield Ale, a nicely balanced amber brew, became the most popular brand. Burns produced draft beer only, feeling that the more costly bottling operation could come later. The break-even point was said to be selling 50 half-barrel kegs per week.

Sadly, Tom Burns never reached his goal. He succumbed to cancer on May 1, 1994, at age thirty-nine, leaving a wife and three small children, and memories of shared amber brews.

Two of Burns's brewers, John Linardos and Steve Rouse, reopened the Canfield Street brewery in January 1995 as the Motor City Brewing Works. Four brands are brewed on a regular basis: Pale Ale, similar to the former Canfield Ale, Nut Brown Ale, a mild ale called Ghetto Blaster, and a black Honey Porter. John and his former partner have eliminated filtration and chill-proofing, so the beers have the slight haze typical of traditional processing. A small bottling line has been installed to fill both 12-ounce and the newer 22-ounce bottles.

TRAFFIC JAM & SNUG, INC., BREWPUB, 1994–
511 W. CANFIELD

The Traffic Jam & Snug, more commonly known as "TJ's," has been a well-known institution near the Wayne State University campus for thirty years. It evolved from a burger-and-beer bar of the 1960s to an eclectic, full-service restaurant seating more than two hundred. Long known for its homemade breads, desserts, and blue-ribbon cheeses, president Ben Edwards also acquired Michigan's first brewpub license.

The Traffic Jam operates almost certainly the only microbrewery using cheese-making equipment and owns the "Dairy-Brewed Beer" trademark. The practice of producing bread, cheese, and beer with the same equipment began with Belgian monks and probably led to the development of lambic-style beers.

While TJ's equipment is used interchangeably, it is sanitized to keep lactic cultures out of the brewing process. The milk pasteurizer doubles as brewkettle, and open stainless whey-fermenting vessels were adapted to the lower fermenting temperature of brewer's wort. The green beer is either keg-conditioned or aged in seven-barrel stainless tanks.

The Traffic Jam features unfiltered all-grain brews, of which three are available on tap. These are currently a pale Bikini Wheat, a Red Pale Mild ("lively hopped yet subtly strawberry hued"), and an India Pale Ale ("golden hued with a strong tang of hops"). Two ales, porter, and a very strong barley wine from the nearby Motor City Brewing Works are available in bottles. The dairy-brewery may be observed from a windowed balcony.

ATWATER BLOCK BREWING COMPANY, 1997–
JOSEPH CAMPAU AT ATWATER

Atwater Block, the largest microbrewery in the Detroit metropolitan area, is located in a former warehouse in the revitalized area between Jefferson Avenue and the Detroit River. It is across the street from Stroh River Place, the former corporate headquarters of The Stroh Brewery Company and a complex of apartments, townhouses, and the Rattlesnake restaurant. Joseph Campau is becoming a hotbed of hops and hockey; Andrews to the south and Dunleavyz closer to Jefferson provide meals, refreshment, and buses for Red Wing games.

This microbrewery is the culmination of years of hopes and effort by Scott Henderson. Former president Henderson returned from Boston to his native Detroit, assembled a group of investors headed by Chris Lawson, and convinced them to finance a $3-million microbrewery. The finished establishment is well designed, spacious, and shows professional attention to detail. Period brewery photographs and collectibles add to the atmosphere. A long bar seats forty-two, and there is table seating for more than a hundred, in addition to a lounge area. With high ceilings and a certain noise level, it seems destined to be a lively place.

Atwater Block has a consulting agreement with a German brewery and malting plant, so the brewing unit is from Germany. The original head brewer on contract from Germany, Tom Majorosi, developed the three main brands: pale ("hell"), an amber ("rost"), and a dark ("dunkel"). Other types have also been brewed more recently, and bottled beer is available in many locations and in Tiger Stadium. The kitchen prepares a full range of lunches and dinners.

SUBURBAN MICROBREWERIES AND BREWPUBS

A number of suburban Detroit establishments have opened in the last few years, and the trend for additional suburban brewpubs is expected to continue. The initials "RH" in parentheses indicate that substantial information was provided by Rex Halfpenny, editor of the *Michigan Beer Guide*.

BIG ROCK CHOP & BREW HOUSE, 1997–
245 SOUTH EATON, BIRMINGHAM

The former Birmingham train station was remodeled by Norman LePage into the popular Eaton Street Station restaurant in 1984. After thirteen years, LePage and his wife Bonnie reopened it with partners Ray and Mary Nicholson as a very upscale brewpub for intimate dining. With tableside service from an à la carte menu, extensive martini selections, and a cigar lounge upstairs, "brewpub" seems largely a legal term. Brewer Dean Jones produces six honest craft brews in a 15-barrel unit, ranging from a popular pale ale to an award-winning Scottish ale and an oatmeal stout. (RH)

CJ'S BREWING COMPANY, 1997–
8115 RICHARDSON, BETWEEN HAGGARTY AND UNION LAKE, COMMERCE TOWNSHIP

Cary Moore, who grew up in the area, has a background in both construction and the pizza business, which helped in building a new family-oriented dining room. Five beers are brewed by Dan Scarsella on a 7-barrel scale: CJ's Gold, American Wheat, Vat33 India Pale Ale, a Red Ale, and a Stout. (RH)

COPPER CANYON BREWERY, 1998–
27522 NORTHWESTERN, SOUTHFIELD

Owner Ed Miri has planned for a casual upscale interior with copper accents. The brewer of the 15-barrel unit, which is located east of Telegraph and north of I-696, is Matt Allyn. The regular beer is a mild ale, and Matt brews four others as well as seasonal specials. (RH)

DETROIT BREW FACTORY, 1997–
18065 EAST EIGHT MILE, EASTPOINTE

Pat Scanlon and Doug Beedy operate a small, one-barrel microbrewery with an added attraction: six half-barrel units where patrons can be brewers for the day, selecting formulas and returning later to condition and bottle. Because it is illegal to operate a brew-on-premise in Michigan, all beers are bottled with the approved bottle labels and can be purchased. Thus at any given time there are two to three dozen beers available. The facility is a renovated storefront and is casual and friendly. (RH)

DRAGONMEAD MICROBREWERY, 1998–
14600 EAST 11 MILE, WARREN

Larry Channell, Bill Wrobel, and Earl Scherbarth acquired a new building on the I-696 service drive just west of Groesbeck and installed a 3-barrel microbrewery. The objective of the partners is to supply restaurants with special brews and to offer products and services to home brewers. A variety of house-brewed beers can be sampled in the taproom.

FIRE ACADEMY BREWERY AND GRILL, 1997–
6677 NORTH WAYNE ROAD, BETWEEN WARREN AND FORT, WESTLAND

Owners George Riley and Michael Reddy are retired from the fire service, and the brewpub is awash in fire-fighting memorabilia, including two fire trucks, with booths in the back of one. There are also hourly fire drills, with flashing lights, siren, and a mannequin sliding down a pole. Russ Beattie produces six thirst quenchers on a 10-barrel scale; the brews are named after the house theme—Axe Ale, for example. The Fire Academy has become a popular restaurant. (RH)

LOCAL COLOR BREWING COMPANY, 1998–
42705 GRAND RIVER, NOVI

Local Color is a serious, professional investment by Peter Paisley, comprising an ambitious restaurant and state of the art, automated, 25-barrel brewery in a large, three-story building. Designer Ron Rea incorporated the brewery into the decor, creating a dramatic, modern, industrial interior. The ales, Smooth Talker Pilsener and Tomboy Red, were highly rated in a *Detroit Free Press* article by John Tanasychuk, who found the place swarming with younger people. Kendrick Belau is head brewer. (RH)

O'MARA'S RESTAURANT & BREWPUB, 1994–
2555 TWELVE MILE ROAD, BERKLEY

Kevin O'Mara's cozy Irish restaurant, done in forest green with dark oak paneling, is popular with an older crowd that also likes mixed drinks. A range of extract brews is prepared on a 2-barrel scale by Harry Sawyer. (RH)

ROYAL OAK BREWERY, 1995–
215 EAST FOURTH, ROYAL OAK

This large brewpub is operated by partners Drew Ciora, who had experience in California brewpub operations, and Michael Plesz. The pub is a block from Main Street and 11 Mile in downtown Royal Oak. The 14-barrel brewing unit and bright beer tanks are right behind the bar, without any partition. This gives a feeling of intimacy with the brewery, although it places brewer Tim Selewski always onstage.

The beer menu lists seven types, from a very pale ale and wheat to a porter, with five usually on tap. A dry-hopped ("India") pale ale tasted in the spring of 1998 recalled the very best of New York City's dry-hopped beers of fifty years ago. The menu is extensive and features fresh ingredients.

WOODWARD AVENUE BREWERS, 1997–
22646 WOODWARD, FERNDALE

Located near Nine Mile, brewer and partner Grant Johnson's pub serves good food and brews, from Blonde to Bronze to Porter, as well as a Hefe-Weizen. Beers from the 15-barrel unit were highly rated by *Metro Times* readers.

14

Detroit Maltsters

The earliest brewers had no choice but to malt their own barley or have bags of malt shipped from a Great Lakes port such as Buffalo. Both sources were probably used. The name of Detroit's first brewery, Owen & Scott's Farmers Brewery, strongly suggests that local barley growers were investors. As Owen & Scott also advertised in Essex County, Ontario, farmers on both sides of the river probably were backers, suppliers, and customers. Ads for barley appeared as early as 1831 in the *Detroit Free Press and Advocate:* "The subscribers will pay fifty cents per bushel for Barley, delivered at their Brewery opposite the Mansion-House, commonly called the Farmer's Brewery of Detroit."

By the 1850s, there was a lively commerce by local malting brewers to sell surplus malt to other brewers and distillers. These competed with early maltsters such as Williams (1840) and George Langdon (1850). Twenty years later, the ale brewer W. C. Duncan, whose sales were declining, switched to malting exclusively.

Most of the local malting barley was grown near Chatham, Ontario, judging by the presence of several malthouses there. W. J. Howard and William Northwood founded a small malting business there in 1870, which grew so rapidly that by 1880, they could claim to be the largest maltsters in Canada. With much of the business being export to the United States and with duties increasing, a plant was erected at One Lafayette Avenue to supply the local breweries.

Five Detroit malthouses were listed in *Tovey's Official Brewers' and Maltster's Directory* for 1884: Howard & Northwood, One Lafayette Avenue, 400,000 bushels; Williams & Company, opposite Michigan Central Railroad Depot, 200,000 bushels; George C. Langdon, 37 Wood-bridge East, 80,000 bushels; William S. Duncan & Company, Lafayette and Beaubien, 65,000 bushels; Canada Malt Company, 623 Fort Street, 150,000 bushels (1 bushel = 48 lbs. barley).

After Howard's death in 1895, Northwood became president and J. A. Preston was appointed secretary-treasurer. At that time, the Canada Malt Company and Rickel & Company were the only other maltsters in Detroit.

RICKEL

H. W. RICKEL & COMPANY, 1876–1971
FLEISCHMAN MALTING COMPANY, CHICAGO, 1971–1976
ARCHER-DANIELS-MIDLAND, 1976–1985
1824 ADELAIDE

The Ontario malthouse, Rickel's first plant. The small office building to the right lists "H. W. Rickel, Prop., Dealer in Barley, Malt & Hops."   COURTESY JOHN M. RICKEL.

The original malthouse at Adelaide, which offered the great advantage of a Grand Trunk Railroad siding. The two brick buildings at the left survived until recent decades.

COURTESY JOHN M. RICKEL.

The person who rose to dominate the local malting sector was Henry W. Rickel. His firm stayed in business until 1971, and the plant was active until the mid-1980s. Rickel's life had many elements of a Horatio Alger story. He was born in Kassel, Germany, in 1833 and emigrated alone at age seventeen. He arrived in Detroit in 1854, and the young man must have held many menial jobs before becoming a hotel manager. Striking out on his own, he bought a grocery store at the corner of Riopelle and Monroe. Rickel was forty-three when he bought the Mueller malthouse on Antoine Street in 1876, late in life to be making a career move in those days.

The following year, he had his own 65,000-bushel malthouse built at the corner of Clinton and Hastings. He called it the Ontario Malt House, probably because Ontario barley was used and had a good reputation. The timing was right, because it was a period of population growth and increasing beer consumption. One year later, he leased the Hawley malthouse at First and Congress, while the capacity of his own plant was dou-

The Rickel malthouse complex about 1940, with Adelaide now passing over the excavated railroad tracks. The small building and the former dry kiln house had become dwarfed by concrete grain silos and a very tall head house, where grain elevating, cleaning, and grading machinery was located. Demolition of the Rickel complex started at the old office building at far left in the spring of 1995.   COURTESY JOHN M. RICKEL.

bled. The enlarged maltings employed twelve men during the cool weather and three men in the summer when shipping was the only activity. Rickel also obtained control of the Duncan malthouse at Champlain and Beaubien, and later he also operated the Goebel malthouse.

In 1903, Rickel, then seventy, made his biggest and final move with the help of his sons Harry and Armin. They had a 300,000-bushel drum house erected near Eastern Market, where Adelaide Street crosses the tracks of the Grand Trunk Railroad, which then ran at street level. Three years later, the firm was incorporated, and Henry Rickel retired. He died in 1910 at age seventy-seven. Harry became president, but ten years later, in 1913, he sold his interest to his brother Armin. The plant was rated at half a million bushels when Prohibition all but shut down the domestic malt business.

The plant capacity was more than doubled after repeal by several additions, including the purchase of ten malting drums ordered from Hiram Walker & Sons in Walkerville. While the industry was competitive, the profit margin was sufficient for major maltsters from Milwaukee and Chicago to maintain local representatives. Armin and his son John H. had many good years supplying Rickel malt to Detroit breweries, as personal relationships were important and had existed with some breweries for three generations.

The reduction in the number of breweries after the war changed the malting industry also; competition became sharp, and the margin shrank to the point where Rickel no longer could be profitable. Several very large malting companies in Wisconsin and Minnesota grew to dominate the industry, with the advantage of proximity to the malting barley crop and economies of scale. In 1971, Rickel was acquired by the Fleischman Malting Company, a large maltster headquartered in Chicago, which in turn was later bought by the mega grain processor Archer-Daniels-Midland. The old Rickel plant continued to supply Stroh with a certain percentage of malt. When Stroh closed its brewery in 1985, the fate of the Rickel malthouse was sealed. Archer-Daniels-Midland closed the plant and began razing buildings in 1994 in preparation for selling the land. The last remaining building, the 175-foot-tall elevator and headhouse holding grain cleaning and grading machinery, was toppled in a spectacular demolition in June 1996.

The Rickels, like the Strohs, had lived on the east side for generations, and still do. When John H. Rickel's son John M. was in high school, it was still expected that he could continue the family tradition. As he grew up, the economic facts increasingly pointed elsewhere. John M. Rickel now is an established attorney, accountant, and lecturer. All that is left from more than 125 years of malting tradition are old photographs on his office walls, stories told by his father and grandfather, and the memory of the aroma of barley sprouting—like freshly sliced cucumber—and hot malt fresh from the kiln.

MANAGEMENT

1970: John H. Rickel, president; John F. Longe, executive vice president; Richard H. Bonner, vice president, production; Raymond E. Spahn, vice president, laboratory director; John M. Rickel, treasurer; Lewis A. Rockwell, secretary; Alan R. Graff, technical director.

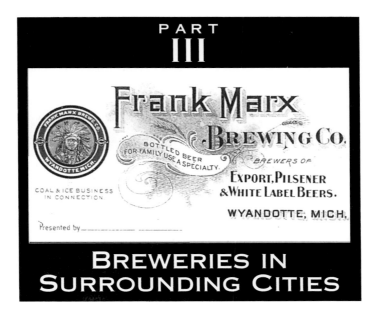

BREWERIES IN
SURROUNDING CITIES

15

ANN ARBOR

The brewing history of Ann Arbor is like a microcosm of Detroit's and shows the same cultural and economic forces at work. First there were a couple of early English ale and porter brewers, and then the German lager brewers moved in and took over. With one exception, Ann Arbor breweries were very small. The total number of firms is believed to be six. Unlike in Detroit, where German brewers congregated in a certain area, those in Ann Arbor tended to give each other room and stake out a territory. Three chose geographic names: Central, Western, and Northern Brewery.

Only one firm was able to outgrow its humble beginning and construct a typical small-town brewery. It started as the Western Brewery in 1861. Not only did the plant survive up to and through Prohibition, but it continued through World War II as the Ann Arbor Brewing Company, closing in 1949. If Ann Arbor breweries were small, it also permitted almost all buildings to be adapted to other uses.

A city like contemporary Ann Arbor, with a large university and a busy downtown dining and entertainment district, proved a natural choice for brewpubs. Thus forty-six years after brewing ceased, new brewers restarted the craft.

BAVARIAN

BAVARIAN BREWERY, LISTED 1860–1872
FULLER, BETWEEN ELIZABETH AND STATE

An envelope postmarked in Ann Arbor on Aug. 28, 1862, with a scalloped rubber stamping for R. Hooper & Son, manufacturer of ale & porter. FROM THE STROH BREWERY COMPANY ARCHIVE.

Frederick Ruoff operated a brewery on his home property in the late 1850s and early 1870s, first as the Bavarian Brewery, later under his own name. He was already listed as brewery proprietor in the first Ann Arbor city directory of 1860. No details of his operation could be found. Ruoff is an unusual name, and it is quite likely that Fred Ruoff was related to August Ruoff, who immigrated during the same period, settled in Detroit, and later brewed on Gratiot Avenue.

HOOPER

R. HOOPER & SON, CA. 1858–1866
ANN ARBOR BREWERY, 1866–1868
STATE AND FULLER (LATER HIGH)

The Hooper Brewery was first listed in 1860 at the corner of State and Fuller, now High Street. It is on record that Hooper bought the land in 1856, and no directory was issued prior to 1860. He lived nearby, at the corner of State and Ann streets, later 712 East Ann, and may well have brewed at home. Hooper's partner in the brewery was his son Frederick.

It was the chance purchase of a philatelic cover—a stamped envelope—that provided interesting evidence of the earlier period of that brewery. The stamp is lightly canceled with the date August 26, 1862, plainly visible.

The most interesting part of the cover is the sender's rubber stamp at the top left corner: "R. Hooper & Son, Manufacturers of ALE, & Porter, and dealer in MALT & HOPS, Ann Arbor, Mich." City directories and real estate records outlined the history of this brewer.

Hooper died in 1866, leaving a widow, three sons, and a daughter. Two years later, the brewery was being operated by his sons Frederick and Charles as the Ann Arbor Brewery. The next directory was issued in 1872. The brewery is no longer listed, probably a victim of the changing demand from ale to lager.

The Hooper family brewed for about a decade, long enough to be a part of the life of a very small Ann Arbor, but almost nothing of them has survived. Brewers in the 1860s sold kegs and draft only, as bottles were still too expensive to be used for beer. Unfortunately, all we have are some directory entries and an envelope.

CENTRAL

CENTRAL BREWERY, CA. 1865–1875
524 (NOW 724) NORTH FIFTH AT SUMMIT

About 1865, John Adam Polk erected a very small brewery next door to his residence. The brewery probably had a capacity of 5,000 barrels. It had the customary underground storage area of limestone walls to

The Central brewery on North Fifth Avenue after it was converted to apartments.
COURTESY PETER YATES, FOR THE DEC. 1979 ANN ARBOR OBSERVER.

The corner lot where the City brewery once stood, photographed about 1900, when a flour mill occupied a new brick building. Only the caves remained from the original structure.

COURTESY BENTLEY HISTORICAL LIBRARY, UNIVERSITY OF MICHIGAN.

shoulder height, then brick and an arched brick ceiling. At one time, a tunnel led from the vault in the direction of the Huron River. This would permit the transport of river ice for cooling, and it carried the runoff in the right direction. A spring on Polk's adjoining property supplied clean water for the tiny and primitive brewery.

The business did not prosper, and by 1875, Polk had moved to the west side of town and taken up carpentry. The brewery became a residence for various immigrants. In the 1970s, the owners, Robert Harrington and landscape architect John Hollowell, created six contemporary apartments in the building and called it "The Brewery."

It is quite possible that Polk brewed at home for several years before he erected a brewery, and that he was one of the customers of Hooper's malt and hops.

CITY

CITY BREWERY, G. F. HAUSER & COMPANY, LISTED 1860–1868
CITY BREWERY (JOHN REYER), CA. 1868–1886
FIRST NEAR BROADWAY, LATER NUMBERED 210 SOUTH FIRST

G. F. Hauser opened a brewery in "lower town" before the first directory of 1860 was printed. He advertised "Beer and Lager Beer," the latter very likely being heavier and aged longer. By 1868, the brewery belonged to John Reyer. The brewery was constructed on a sloping corner lot. One could therefore enter the basement caves from the rear at ground level. This greatly facilitated the hauling of ice and the rolling out of barrels. These caves are the only surviving part of the City Brewery, but they are a good example of the E-shaped tunnel layout.

In spite of its central location and advantageous site, the City Brewery failed to grow out of its original size. It had a life span of twenty years at most. A flour mill, the Ann Arbor Central Mill, occupied the brewery after 1886. The existing brick building was erected about 1900. The flour mill failed during the depression, and in 1932 Lohr's Ann Arbor Implement Company moved into the premises. In recent decades, the caves were filled with garden tractors and snowmobiles and could be viewed on request. The property is now owned by Michael "Mick" Easton, who operates an antique mall on the premises.

No information on John Reyer's products could be located, and no collectibles are known.

NORTHERN

NORTHERN BREWERY, 1872–1892

ANN ARBOR BREWING COMPANY, 1892–1902

ANN ARBOR CITY BREWERY, 1902–1908

1037 JONES DRIVE (FORMERLY MILL STREET)

Brewmaster Ernest Rehberg of the Northern brewery, in an 1897 convention brochure.

FROM THE STROH BREWERY COMPANY ARCHIVE.

This small brewery was erected in 1872 by George Krause on what was then Mill Street. It was sold almost immediately to brothers John and Fred Frey. Sometime during the next two years, John sold his interest to Fred. According to county records, Fred Frey produced "about 2,400 barrels of beer" in 1881 and "consumed about 5,000 bushels of grain and 4,000 pounds of hops in the manufacture of this beverage." Based on materials usage after World War II, Frey's lager must have had a very strong body and the bitterness to match.

During 1880, Frey's Northern Brewery laid in "about

A Northern brewery beer wagon in front of Binder's saloon, 6 West Liberty Street.

The Northern brewery after architects Richard Fry and David Peters renovated it for their offices.

1,000 tons of ice." There were good springs under the Broadway hill for brewing water, and a pond was formed by damming Traver Creek to harvest ice. A barn-like building in an engraving published in 1894 was presumably an ice house.

In 1884 or 1885, Herman Hardinghaus bought the brewery from Frey, and he operated it until his death in 1904. Hardinghaus was a trained brewer who had worked in the trade for eight years in Cincinnati and St. Louis. Afterward, he operated his own brewery in Ypsilanti until 1884. In 1886, Hardinghaus had the substantial two-story structure erected, which still serves as the core of the present building. He also brewed ale and had facilities for bottling.

The foreman of the Northern Brewery since 1884, Ernest Rehberg, was born in Detroit and had worked in Jacob Mann's brewery there. Rehberg was also active in local Ann Arbor politics. He prospered and became quite prominent. When the Northern Brewery was reorganized in 1892 as the Ann Arbor Brewing Company, Rehberg became president with Hardinghaus taking the vice presidency.

In 1902, Rehberg left the brewery, but he rejoined it after the death of Hardinghaus and took former bookkeeper Lewis Roberts as partner. They changed the firm's name to Ann Arbor City Brewery. The new name did not help to overcome increasing competition. The plant was closed in 1908. Rehberg, with his son Carl, went into the ice business, which had been a sideline for many years and now became their living.

A number of firms used the building, before it became a foundry in 1922. The Ann Arbor Foundry Company occupied the premises for fifty years. In 1972, architects Richard Fry and David Peters purchased the building and completely renovated it into offices, including their own.

The Northern Brewery was an entry-level business for four brewers. It was not until Hardinghaus built a proper brick building that the company had a chance to expand, but it never grew large enough to compete successfully at the turn of the century.

MEMORABILIA

No merchandising items are known from this brewery. The Stroh collection has a single bottle, embossed "George Hardinghaus/Northern Brewery" in a slug plate. No doubt, other bottles are in specialized collections, but they are very rare.

MANAGEMENT

1894: Ernest Rehberg, president; Herman Hardinghaus, vice president; Gustave Brehm, secretary-treasurer.

ANN ARBOR

WESTERN BREWERY, 1861–1902
MICHIGAN UNION BREWING COMPANY, 1902–1920
ANN ARBOR BREWING COMPANY, 1933–1949
416 SOUTH FOURTH

A Western brewery wagon in front of Louis Kurtz's saloon at 120 West Liberty Street. The stag sign in the window is from Toledo's Buckeye brewery.

FROM THE SAM STURGIS COLLECTION, BOX 2, A232.8,
BENTLEY HISTORICAL LIBRARY, UNIVERSITY OF MICHIGAN.

Ann Arbor's most successful brewery was started by Peter Brehm and John Reyer, who built a lager brewery on South Fourth, between Liberty and West Madison streets. Reyer soon sold out to Brehm and purchased the City Brewery. In the late 1870s, after Franz or Frank Ruck had bought the brewery from Brehm's widow, sales were about 1,400 barrels. The main building consisted of two stories and a basement and occupied an area of 60 by 30 feet. The plant was acquired in 1880 by Chris Martin and Matt Fischer. It was under their ownership that the brewery grew from 3,000 barrels of production in 1880 to 35,000 barrels in 1906.

In 1902, new brick buildings were erected, including an impressive four-story brewhouse. The name was changed to Michigan Union Brewing Company in honor of the local Bartenders and Brewers Union. Both owners worked in the plant, Martin as brewmaster and Fischer as bottle shop foreman. It took twelve hours to carry a brew from mash tub to fermenter, and the day started at five in the morning. Former employees have reminisced about an informally run business where everybody knew and relied on one another, and sons came to work alongside their fathers.

Distribution was mostly to local saloons and households. The driver made weekly trips by wagon to Dexter and Saline. When the brewery bought a locally made Star truck in 1915, Milan and Whitmore Lake were added to the delivery route.

An attempt to remain open during Prohibition by selling near beer

MICHIGAN
UNION BREWING CO.

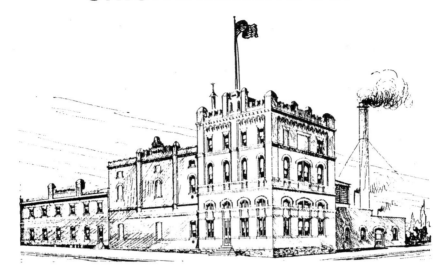

A drawing of the Michigan Union brewery in the 1903 Ann Arbor directory.
COURTESY BENTLEY HISTORICAL LIBRARY, UNIVERSITY OF MICHIGAN.

failed early. The property was rented to the C. A. Connor Ice Cream Company from 1920 to 1933. New ownership headed by Charles Ackerman took over brewing in 1932. The plant was refitted with new equipment and packaging machinery and renamed Ann Arbor Brewing Company. Ackermann wore many hats—he was chairman, president, manager, purchasing agent, and sales and advertising manager. In the spring of 1938, Albert Bek, formerly with Hudepohl in Cincinnati, was engaged to be a one-man technical staff—brewmaster, chemist, and bottle shop superintendent. The brands were Ann Arbor Old Tyme and Cream Top Old Style Lager. Capacity was rated optimistically for publication at 50,000 barrels.

Ann Arbor in those years was a relatively small and friendly town with many saloons. In the old days, beer could be had by any young man of fourteen as long as he behaved, and some of that German right-to-drink-beer attitude lingered. The Ann Arbor brewery had a door on the hill end that led to a room with a tap in the wall. On the other side was a keg, always tapped, and anybody was welcome to walk in and help himself to a beer or two.

The Ann Arbor Brewing Company hung on until 1941, when the war changed beer to a very desirable commodity. There would be a myriad headaches about equipment, supplies, and manpower, but finding customers was not a problem. In 1943, Philip J. Halm replaced Bek, and the Town Club brand was added. Martin Cunea took over the supervision in 1946, but it was not a position with a future. Facing postwar competition, the Ackerman management put the brewery up for sale in 1947.

With good hindsight, it is surprising that the brewery found a buyer. The era of marketing on television was beginning. Pabst advertised highly popular boxing matches, Stroh sponsored Red Wings hockey, and Goebel had the Lions, yet Milton and Cerna Johnson invested in and operated the brewery for a couple of years. Milton Johnson wore even more hats than Ackerman—he was also treasurer in addition to the other offices, although he had the good sense not to appoint himself chairman. Fred Heusel was the brewmaster, and Van Dyke beer and ale was the product line. The brewery was, of course, too large to be a hobby and too small for a competitive business. It closed in 1949, and with it brewing in Ann Arbor ceased for the next forty-five years.

Argus Optics took over the building sometime after the brewing equipment was sold and removed. In 1963, the property was acquired by the University of Michigan for a film library and audio-visual center. The Mathematical Society now publishes *Mathematical Reviews* in the former

The Michigan Union brewery after it was converted to the University of Michigan's Audio-Visual Library, University of Michigan.

COURTESY PETER YATES, FOR THE DEC. 1979 ANN ARBOR OBSERVER.

brewery. The basement is a large and well-lit room. Far in the back is a door, on the uphill side toward the building, which is one floor lower in height. When the door is opened, steps lead down to a dirt floor, stretching into the distance. Suddenly, one is taken a century back in time. The walls are field stone to shoulder height, and there is the typical brick vaulted ceiling of nineteenth-century brewery cellars. Here is where beer was aged even before Michigan Union had mechanical refrigeration.

MEMORABILIA

Michigan Union's bottles were attractively embossed with an eagle and shield, a very common symbol and trademark feature of the times. While not rare, these bottles in fine condition are very desirable. A small etched glass showing the brewery is known. The Ann Arbor Brewing Company also used typical merchandising items such as tin-over-cardboard signs; enlarged reproductions can be seen in the Grizzly Peak brewpub.

MANAGEMENT

1902: George E. Apfel, president; Louis Kurtz, vice president; William A. Gwinner, secretary; Christian Martin, treasurer.

1903: Louis Kurtz, president; John Koch, vice president; William Gwinner, secretary; Chris. Martin, treasurer.

1941: Charles Ackermann, chairman, president, and manager; Theodore R. Ziefle, vice president and treasurer; James K. O'Donnell, secretary; master brewers Albert R. Bek (1941–1942), Philip J. Halm (1943–1945), Martin Gunia (1946–1947).

1948: Milton Johnson, president, treasurer, and sales manager; Cerna W. Johnson, vice president; Fred Heusel, brewmaster.

BREWPUBS
AND MICROBREWERIES

GRIZZLY PEAK, 1995–
120 WEST WASHINGTON

For decades, Bud Metzger owned and operated the famed Old German restaurant in downtown Ann Arbor. When he retired in 1995, his collection of steins, which had decorated the venerable local landmark, were auctioned off. The restaurant was completely refurbished, with two open areas flanking a central taproom. The "Schwarzwald" German decor has been replaced by enlarged Ann Arbor breweriana decoration, and the German dishes also have given way to a broad and very contemporary menu. "Grizzly Peak" is meant to evoke the California origin of owners Jon Carlson and Chet Czlapeka.

It is a well-planned venture. Schelde Enterprises of Grand Rapids, which has experience in brewpub management, has been retained to operate the 7-barrel brewery. The head brewer is Casey Burke. The five beers range from two ales, a red and a dark, to a strong stout. Grizzly Peak also offers about thirty-five bottled beers from near and far and has a good choice of domestic wines.

Matt and Rene Greff, backed by lots of enthusiasm and a seventeen-member group of relatives and friends, opened a pub in downtown Ann Arbor less than two blocks from Grizzly Peak. The atmosphere and food are very informal, with probably the best fish and chips in Michigan. Matt Greff was assisted by Bonnie Day in the 7-barrel brewery during the crucial start-up months. The six house taps range from a dark wheat to a stout and are described in lengthy paragraphs on the beer list. The purist may object to equating Maerzen with Oktoberfest—Maerz means "March" and was historically brewed for summer consumption—but one goes to a brewpub not to criticize the text but to socialize. There are six guest taps and about twenty bottled beers from which to choose, and socializing comes easily.

Brewbakers is located next to the Ann Arbor Farmer's Market in the basement of historic Kerrytown, which features indoor specialty shops. It is a takeout place for interesting freshly brewed beer and bread. The 15-barrel brewery is on one side, and the bakery on the other. The brewer is Derek Foster; the cask-conditioned ale is popular, and he also produces sodas. Owners Barry Seifer and Sarah Minor hope to clone the concept. Because they hold a brewer's license, there is no taproom or restaurant. (RH)

16

MOUNT CLEMENS

At one time widely known for its baths and as a health and resort town about twenty miles northeast of Detroit, Mount Clemens was never really known for its locally brewed beers. The clientele who came to take the cure or to relax were not primarily beer drinkers. They did, however, cause the town to grow to a size that could support breweries in the years before Prohibition.

There were three breweries in Mount Clemens of which there are records or at least a listing. In addition, census records indicate that two additional families were supported by brewing in the early decades. In the 1860 census appears Nelson Stein from France, a brewer of age fifty, together with his family. The 1870 census lists the thirty-five-year-old Prussian brewer Joseph Buechel, his wife Sophia, and three small children, and a Baltus Whitmayer, who worked in the brewery. Neither name reappears in a subsequent census, nor are there any records of their activities. While brewing could not be established as a continuing industry this early in Macomb County, probably because of the small market and fluid population, there definitely was a very early interest in malt beverages.

The last brewery closed in 1935 after failed attempts to entice investors into an obviously unwise venture. Sixty years were to pass before beer was again brewed in Macomb County, in a brewpub and on a small scale.

MILLER

WILLIAM MILLER, 1860–1884
FRONT STREET

Only fragments of information are available from this very early and small brewing operation. William Miller was listed under "saloon keepers" on an 1859 map of Mount Clemens, which also included a small business directory. The following year he was listed as a brewer, age twenty-two, in the 1860 census that also showed Mary Miller, age sixty-two, probably his mother. A business directory appeared in 1868, which showed him to be a brewer of lager beer.

Sales in 1878 and 1879 were given by Salem at 300 and only 180 barrels, respectively; perhaps the competition from August Biewer, the other brewer in town at that time, had an adverse effect. A brief notation in the 1884 edition of *Tovey's Handbook* lists Miller as a brewer of Weiss ("white," in this sense "wheat") beer. The year of the brewery's closing is not known.

August Biewer. From *Past and Present in Macomb County*, by Robert Eldridge, 1905.
Courtesy Macomb County Historical Society.

BIEWER

August Biewer, Clinton River Brewery, 1873–1919
22 Pine

August Biewer had immigrated from Germany in 1867 when he was twenty-five years old, and he arrived in Mount Clemens four years later by way of Chicago and Detroit. His background must have included training in a brewery. Once situated in Mount Clemens, he started his own small brewing operation on Front Street near the Clinton River, in competition with William Miller. A description of the nine-year-old Clinton River Brewery in 1882 lists the annual capacity at 1,000 barrels; sales in 1879 were 860 barrels. The brewery proper had an area of 90 by 45 feet, with an icehouse of 20 by 24 and a storage area of 20 by 28. At some later time, Biewer moved five blocks to larger quarters on Pine Street. There he had space to install bottling facilities.

By the turn of the century, Biewer was a large man whose appearance indicated the period's custom of not stinting on food and drink. He owned two saloons, one at Court Street near Macomb, and the Biewer

Standing at the side of Biewer's brewery with cigars, wagon, and flags, the Biewer staff is ready for a July 4th parade. COURTESY MACOMB COUNTY HISTORICAL SOCIETY.

Gardens on South Gratiot near the Medea Bath House. The Gardens had a long life as a hotel after Biewer sold it in 1900. He brought his son and namesake into the business, and in 1912, August Jr. became owner and manager. The brewery operated until Prohibition. No drawing or photo showing the complete brewery has surfaced so far.

MEMORABILIA

Very little in the way of merchandising items has survived. Shell glasses and mugs advertising Biewer's beer are known, and must have been common during the time of his beer garden, but are now rarely seen. Embossed bottles are in several collections. A pre-1890 bottle with a partial label shows that the brand was simply August Biewer's Lager. His claim to fame: "The only beer in town."

MOUNT CLEMENS

MOUNT CLEMENS BREWING COMPANY, 1890–1935
37 SOUTH FRONT (LATER BROADWAY)

The Mount Clemens Brewing Company was the most successful brewery in town, at least on a relative basis. Its Pearl Foam beer is known from ads and promotional items, and the recollections of an owner's relative are on file in the local library. Like many small breweries, it had a brief fling after repeal of Prohibition.

Joseph Oberstadt, who was trained as a brewer in Westphalia, Germany, immigrated in 1871, and worked for twelve years as a brewery foreman in Fred Dittmer's brewery before coming to Mount Clemens in 1889.

The Mount Clemens brewery, with the brewery saloon at left.

COURTESY MACOMB COUNTY HISTORICAL SOCIETY.

He opened his own brewery the following year on Front Street near the Clinton River; the street is now northbound Gratiot Avenue. Mount Clemens had a small Belgian community already from earlier decades, and many of the Belgian men went to work for the new brewery. This occupied a frontage of 300 feet and included a saloon. A tunnel for aging beer underground had an exit to the Clinton riverbank, and a portion still exists about 100 feet south of the Cass-Crocker Street bridge. The capacity was given as 6,000 barrels in 1897.

Oberstadt was joined by secretary and treasurer Paul Lefevre. Lefevre had learned brewing in his native Belgium, and at the time of Oberstadt's venture, he was city treasurer. In 1896, Lefevre was listed as president, and Oberstadt assumed the other offices. Another investor was Joseph J. Noecker, treasurer of the Westphalia Brewing Company in Detroit, who was listed as president in 1892. The presidency seems to have rotated among Oberstadt's backers.

This arrangement did not work out to everybody's satisfaction. In 1905, Oberstadt left the brewery and accepted a position as manager of a beer depot to be established by the Goebel Brewing Company on South Front Street. That same year, August Schulte was named president of the Mount Clemens Brewery.

In 1912, John G. Freimann, also originally from Germany and a former brewmaster at Ruppert, bought the brewery. Freimann hired Carl Boike as brewmaster and superintendent. Freimann's brother Konrad also worked in the brewery. Freimann tried to remain open during Prohibition as the Mount Clemens Beverage Company, manufacturing soft drinks, near beer, and cider. This venture failed, and the production ceased for a year in 1925. After Freimann's death in 1928, his brother Konrad rented the brewery for the manufacture of liquid malt. His son Conrad also worked with him. Later "Connie" Freimann found employment for many years at Stroh.

John Freimann's son Leonard, his widow, and his stepson Ervin Egle reopened the brewery in 1933. Albert Martins was brought in and placed in charge of sales; his father had been associated with John Freimann's other brother in the Upper Sandusky Brewing Company. Beer sales amounted to 23,000 barrels in 1934, not a bad beginning but too small to sustain a competitive brewing operation.

Brewmaster Joseph Oberstadt in an 1897 convention brochure.
FROM THE STROH BREWERY COMPANY ARCHIVE.

Shortly afterward, the brewmaster accepted a position with the larger Wolverine Brewery in Pontiac. With increasing competition and no brewmaster, operations were suspended, and the brewery went into bankruptcy. The property was purchased the following summer by two investors, David Rott and George Spetzor, for $5,800 subject to a $13,000 mortgage. Their financing was inadequate, but Rott surfaced again in 1942, when he bought or leased the failing Kling brewery in Flint. James Singelyn, a director and officer of the Tivoli Brewery before Prohibition, tried unsuccessfully to reopen the plant under his own name in 1934. Singelyn had operated the Burns Hotel on Cadillac Square during Prohibition and was evidently very interested in returning to brewing. He tried one more time in 1938 to reopen the brewery as the Health City Brewing Company by a stock sale, but that also failed. Fortunately for investors, all proceeds were held in escrow and were refunded when the entire $165,000 stock issue could not be sold.

MEMORABILIA

Mementos of the Mount Clemens Brewing Company are very scarce. A stag stock tray inscribed for Pearl Foam Beer and small etched glasses are known. Embossed bottles turn up occasionally. A beer coaster advertising Pearl Foam in gothic letters gives the phone number 1504. No

Master brewers posed during a visit at the Mt. Clemens brewery. Oberstadt is standing between the left door and the window. The man with a white hat in the center is E. W. Voigt.

COURTESY MACOMB COUNTY HISTORICAL SOCIETY.

merchandising items from the brief reopening in 1933–34 have been located so far, if indeed any were ordered.

MANAGEMENT
1897: Paul Lefevre, Joseph Oberstadt, owners.
1913–1914: John Freimann, president and manager; John R. Murphy, vice president; August Henkel, secretary-treasurer.
1933: Leonard Freimann, president; Bertha Freimann, vice president; Ervin W. Egle, treasurer and bottling superintendant.

BREWPUBS
AND MICROBREWERIES

GREAT BARABOO BREWING COMPANY, 1995–
35905 UTICA ROAD AT MORAVIAN, CLINTON TOWNSHIP

Louis Dricolas, who owns a couple of popular restaurants in St. Clair Shores, proceeded with plans for a brewpub after Michigan laws changed in 1992. He found a suitable location on Utica Road between 15 and 16 Mile Roads for a spacious restaurant that includes an impressive 14-barrel brewing unit. The brewhouse is visible behind glass. Two copper-clad conical fermenters are in the dining area, and the chill tanks are in the kitchen.

Baraboo is primarily an informal and comfortable full-service restaurant in which the brewpub is an added attraction. Thus there are several domestic and imported beers available in bottles, in addition to the four types brewed on the premises: golden and red ales, a wheat beer, and a porter. A seasonal brew may also be on tap. The Great Baraboo Brewing Company is Macomb County's first brewpub and is a fine addition to the local restaurant and growing brewpub roster.

17

PONTIAC

Brewing in Pontiac goes back to the 1850s, but it was only an intermittent local industry until repeal of Prohibition, when the new Wolverine Brewing Company distributed throughout the surrounding counties. Wolverine produced beer until wartime restrictions proved too difficult for the small operation.

Information is limited to city directories (the Oakland County Pioneer and Historical Society has probably the most complete set) and the holdings of collector Paul Rothrock. Only one snapshot could be located, other than reproductions of newspaper articles from the 1930s.

The chances of brewing returning to Pontiac were nil for decades. But after a hiatus of more than fifty years, Pontiac offered the right building at the right price to two young men looking for a microbrewery site, and then a brewpub opened downtown in the revived South Saginaw section. When Chrysler opened its technical center in Auburn Hills, I-75 north of Pontiac became a growth corridor. It was not long before a branch of Gaylord's Big Buck Brewery opened in Auburn Hills. Brewing in Oakland County is in full swing.

DAWSON

ROBERT DAWSON, 1856–1886
SAGINAW STREET

Robert Dawson was already listed as a brewer living in Pontiac in 1856. By 1860, his address was given as the west side of Saginaw Street, near the railroad depot. He seems to have been typical of the early home brewers, who established small brewing operations in a part of their residences. Sales in the late 1870s amounted to 300 to 400 barrels annually. Embossed bottles are known, indicating more than just a very limited distribution. The latest directory entry occurs in 1886, when his address was still on Saginaw, now "opp. Dawson's Exchange." The specifics of this business are unknown, but it seems that Dawson was no longer restricted to brewing. Only a few bottles embossed R. Dawson/Pontiac are known.

CARHARRT

ALBANY STEAM BREWERY, 1870–1871
PATTERSON STREET

James Carhartt was one of the pioneer residents of Pontiac, and he is on record as a supplier of groceries and provisions in 1856–57. Just when he branched out into brewing is unknown, as city directories appeared only sporadically. He is shown to have been a brewer in 1870–71 on Patterson Street "near gas house." In addition to James, E. B. and G. Carhartt were also active in the brewery.

PONTIAC

PONTIAC BREWING COMPANY, 1900–1905
PONTIAC BREWERY COMPANY, 1905–1915
36–40 PATTERSON

Pontiac's largest brewery before Prohibition was incorporated in 1900 with a capitalization of $25,000, with local investors as officers. Of interest is the presence of Raymond Clemens, initially as manager and later as secretary and treasurer. He was one of the four Clemens brothers who were associated with the East Side Brewery in Detroit. The firm was reincorporated in October 1905 with a $30,000 capitalization as the Pontiac Brewery Company. Both the president and vice president remained in office, so the change probably represented new financial backing and not a serious business or personnel problem.

A letterhead printed for the 1910s shows that the corporate emblem was Chief Pontiac in full war regalia on a lookout rock. The brands were Pontiac Favorite and Blue Label, and the slogan, neither realistic nor unique, was "The Beer That Made Milwaukee Jealous." In 1912, Raymond Clemens's brother Peter was listed as vice president. As Peter Clemens had been a brewmaster at the East Side Brewery, it can be assumed that his duties also included the brewing operations in Pontiac. The brewery was listed for the last time in the 1915 Pontiac directory.

MEMORABILIA
Only embossed bottles are relatively common. A stock tray showing a stag inscribed "Pontiac Brewery Company," the two brands, and the slogan about Milwaukee's alleged jealousy is in a few local collections.

PONTIAC BREWERY COMPANY

· THE BEER THAT MADE MILWAUKEE JEALOUS

PONTIAC, MICH.,_____ _____191__

Chief Pontiac was featured on the Pontiac brewery stationery.

COURTESY OAKLAND COUNTY PIONEER AND HISTORICAL SOCIETY.

MANAGEMENT

1904: Pierre Buckley, president; Edward Nusbaumer, vice president; M. H. Lillis, secretary; Raymond Clemens, manager, later secretary-treasurer.

1912–1915: Edward Nusbaumer, president; Peter J. Clemens, vice president; Raymond Clemens, secretary-treasurer.

WOLVERINE

WOLVERINE BREWING COMPANY, 1933–1942
555 GOING SREET

This enterprise was incorporated in August 1933 with an authorized capitalization of $300,000, of which about half was issued to pay for the construction of a new brewery. An additional stock issue of $106,500 at one-dollar par was offered early in 1934 to improve the plant and pay for a bottling line, which started operating in May. The capacity was given as 75,000 barrels, but a realistic annual output for the 135-barrel brewhouse would be 50,000 barrels.

Production in 1934 was 39,000 barrels of Wolverine Beer, and there must have been reason for optimism. The package had an oval label with strong graphics, showing a map of Michigan in the center. After a minor slippage to 37,500 barrels in 1935, sales declined to 29,000 when a weakened economy hurt local employment. Frank Drouillard replaced Frank Tobin as president in 1936. A Dark Horse Ale and the special Rhein-Brau— "The Aristocrat," said to be based on a winning formula at the 1893 Chicago World's Fair—were marketed in an effort to boost sales. But it was the introduction of the Chief Pontiac label that improved sales and permitted a raise in wages. At its peak, the Wolverine brewery employed about sixty-five persons and used twelve delivery trucks and twenty-three outstate distributors.

The firm was still in business when war broke out, but by 1943, the

The Wolverine brewery in Nov. 1936. The tall building at the left was the brewhouse. Offices, fermenting and storage cellars, and the packaging plant are at the right.

FROM THE COLLECTION OF ERNEST OEST.

effort to maintain the brewery in the face of wartime restriction proved too difficult. The last brewmaster was John F. Geyer of the Frankenmuth brewing family. The brewery, although dilapidated, is still standing. The building that housed the office and beer tanks for fermenting and storage is used for the repair of automobiles.

MEMORABILIA
Wolverine memorabilia are rare, except for bottle labels.

MANAGEMENT
1934: Frank J. Tobin, president, later director; Joseph G. Schiesel, vice president; Emmons B. Chase, secretary-treasurer; John Teasdale, general manager; Carl Brehm, brewmaster.

1937: Frank Drouillard, president; Joseph G. Schiesel, vice president; Emmons B. Chase, secretary; J. Price Hill, treasurer; John Silhany, brewmaster.

1939: J. Price Hill, president; Joseph G. Schiesel, vice president; Harold Schmidt, secretary; Anthony Miller, treasurer; John Silhany, brewmaster.

1941: Frank Drouillard, president; Edwin A. Brooks, vice president and secretary; J. Paul Shelton, vice president; William Vrooman, treasurer; Jacob Christmas, brewmaster (until May), John F. Geyer (from June).

BREWPUBS
AND MICROBREWERIES

KING BREWING COMPANY, 1995–
895 OAKLAND

When home- and microbrewer Scott King and former partner Jeff Gibbs looked for a location for their planned microbrewery, Pontiac was not on the short list. However, Pontiac turned out to have two essential requirements: a very suitable building at an affordable price, and a minimal bureaucracy to delay turning plans into reality. The location on busy Oakland Avenue is providing additional benefits of visibility and easy access for their taproom.

King and former home brewer Jeff Maier are brewing three ales in a 15-barrel brewhouse—a hoppy King's Pale Ale, a dark Crown Brown Ale, and a smooth Royal Amber Ale—as well as a robust Porter. In addition, seasonal brews rotate throughout the year.

BO'S BREWERY & BISTRO, 1996–
51 N. SAGINAW

Douglas Young combined his restaurant and bartending experience with a strong appreciation for the microbreweries he saw during travels on the West Coast and started a family-owned brewpub. His father, Bo, is president, and his brother Burgess is also a partner. Young operates Bo's primarily as a restaurant, with his beers and a large selection of single malt whiskeys the big attraction. The family found a perfect location near the corner of Huron and Saginaw, in a section that is becoming a local entertainment magnet.

The 15-barrel dual vessel brewing unit is impressively clad in copper for looks. The brewer in charge is Dave Hale, who has a sound brewing education and at least four beers on tap. Furnished in contemporary style, Bo's is spacious and a pleasant place to relax.

BIG BUCK BREWERY & STEAKHOUSE, 1997–
255 TAKATA DRIVE, AUBURN HILLS

A slightly smaller sister microbrewery to the original huge Big Buck in Gaylord, Michigan, the Auburn Hills facility is also visible from Interstate 75, just south of the South University exit, between I-75 and Opdyke. Big Buck is a large and growing operation, and the Auburn Hills site is very large: the dining room seats 450, and there is space for 200 at the bar. The place has the feel of a rustic lodge, and what it lacks in intimacy it makes up in beers produced in top-notch equipment by a highly competent staff.

The Auburn Hills facility is equipped with a 15-barrel brewing unit and 30-barrel Unitanks, in which wort is fermented and the end-fermented beer is chilled prior to filtration. The beers range from light to dark and full-bodied; Buck Naked Light, Raspberry Wheat, Big Buck Beer, Red Bird Ale, and Boyne Amber Ale are also bottled in Gaylord. There is an extensive menu, and much copy is devoted to the steak selections.

Big Buck is unique among area microbreweries and brewpubs in having gone public in 1996 in order to expand to other locations and in its adjacency to and visibility from a major highway. If success continues, Big Buck will be a chain of large restaurants in which on-premise-brewed beer accounts for about 25 percent of restaurant sales.

MANAGEMENT

William F. Rolinski, president; Gary J. Hewett, executive vice president; Anthony P. Dombrowski, chief financial officer; Scott Graham, corporate brewmaster.

ROCHESTER MILLS BEER COMPANY, 1998–
400 WATER STREET, ROCHESTER

The owners of the Royal Oak Brewery, Drew Ciora and Mike Plesz, opened this attractive brewpub in downtown Rochester. Brewer Pat Scanlon offers up to ten beers and ales from his 15-barrel unit, with Lager and Red being popular. (RH)

18

WINDSOR

The inclusion in this book of Windsor and surrounding Ontario communities—La Salle, Riverside, Tecumseh, and Walkerville—is based on the fact that despite the international border and a distinct history, Windsor is and always has been a part of the greater Detroit economic region. Even long ago, there was movement of goods, capital, and people back and forth across the Detroit River. Detroit's first brewery advertised its beers in the *Essex County Immigrant* as early as 1831. The history of the British-American Brewing Company reads like that of a Detroit brewery for the first fifty years, and both of the major Windsor breweries had brewmasters who were trained in the United States. Several Canadians invested in Detroit breweries, and during Prohibition, three breweries were started in the greater Windsor area primarily to supply the illegal U.S. market. In more recent decades, several Canadian brewmasters have found employment and career opportunities in Detroit with Stroh.

A brewery was reported in Windsor as early as 1854. In 1864, Arthur and Henry Kennedy branched out into brewing from selling wine and spirits. A decade later, Robert Shanks brewed ale and porter in his Detroit River Brewery from 1876 to 1879, but it was not until 1885 that locally brewed lager, ale, and porter became a permanent Windsor industry.

Windsor's active downtown district, with its many restaurants and places of entertainment, has also made it a promising city for brewpubs. As this segment of the industry is still very fluid, new ventures may be formed in any given year.

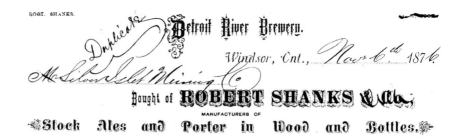

Letterhead, 1876. The name crossed out at top right was former partner A. W. Cook.

FROM THE COLLECTION OF LAWRENCE SHERK.

WINDSOR

WINDSOR BREWERY, 1886–1899
GOYEAU AND WYANDOTTE

J. J. Guittard operated a 5,000-barrel lager brewery in October 1897 at a site where Fredrick Stephen and Robert Dempster first brewed in 1886 and a number of other brewers had failed. Guittard was born in 1862 in Mildmay, Bruce County, Ontario, where his father was proprietor of the Commercial Hotel. J. J. Guittard had acquired the Woodbine Hotel at the corner of Pitt and Goyeau streets in April 1897. He had been connected with hotels for a decade, and he probably wanted to supply his own product to several hotel bars. The brewery staff consisted only of himself, his sister in the office, and an L. Sauer as head brewer. The brewery was closed in January 1899.

HOFER

HOFER BREWING COMPANY, LTD., 1929–1939
136 (LATER 400) FRONT, LA SALLE

A small brewery was incorporated in 1927 and built in an attractive contemporary style during 1928 in the downriver town of La Salle, just north of Amherstberg. The sole reason for this venture was to export beer to the States, where Prohibition created a large demand. In those years, there was nothing illegal in an Ontario brewery manufacturing beer "for export." The fact that somebody was running motorboats with cases of Hofer's Select Lager in the middle of the night to Ecorse or Wyandotte was not a provincial police matter. The location was considered ideal for transporting beer across the Detroit River, which has several large

The former Hofer brewery, photographed by the author in 1995. The two large rectangular areas on either side of the central tower were originally windows.

islands in this area. Brewer Joseph Karl Hofer was financed primarily by La Salle's mayor, Vital Benoit, who invested $40,000 and held 80 percent of the stock.

Hofer remained manager until 1936. His Select Ale had a good reputation. Other brands were Crown Derby and Gold Label. He was replaced by R. A. Vigneux; in 1937, J. P. Masterdon became the last manager of the La Salle brewery as business wound down after repeal of Prohibition. Canadian Breweries, Ltd., acquired the plant in 1939 and closed it. The building still stands on La Salle's main street, as does the tavern-restaurant next door, the Chateau LaSalle, formerly the Wellington. There, according to oral history, Detroit's Purple Gang made its deals for shipments to Detroit. The ground floor of the former brewery houses a shop where wicker items and assorted gifts are sold. Perhaps this is not the proper fate for a brewery of questionable reputation, but the occupancy maintains the building.

Joseph Hofer had one more chance to brew in the area; in the early 1940s he was brewmaster at the Pfeiffer brewery in Flint.

MANAGEMENT
1929: Vital Benoit, president; J. K. Hofer, brewmaster; A. B. Dixon, R. F. L. McCarroll, Nicholas Ballard, E. L. Hyland, directors.

RIVERSIDE

RIVERSIDE BREWING COMPANY, LTD., 1926–1935
5300 RIVERSIDE, RIVERSIDE

The Riverside Brewing Company was founded in 1926, certainly to take advantage of the great demand for Canadian beer during Prohibition. The brewery was situated at the river's edge with a convenient dock for export. Stroh's former brewmaster Otto Rosenbusch was one of the investors. He even called his beer Bohemian Lager, which was the name of Stroh's "near beer" at that time. "The taste that tells" was the slogan. Of course, everybody knew that a Canadian lager contained alcohol. The other brands were Old Derby Ale, Culmbacher, and also a XXX Porter— an ambitious lineup indicating much more than just a quick Prohibition business.

In 1935, Canadian Breweries, Ltd., also bought and closed this brewery and sold the assets for $27,000. The building, which was used by a seed firm at one time, still stands near the river.

Riverside Brewery, Near Tecumseh, Ont., Can.

Postcard of the Riverside brewery.   FROM THE COLLECTION OF LAWRENCE SHERK.

1926–1935: F. J. Kirsch, president; Otto Rosenbusch, brewmaster.

TECUMSEH

TECUMSEH BREWING COMPANY, LTD., 1927-1931
OLD COMRADES BREWING COMPANY, LTD., 1947-1952
CANADIAN BREWERIES, LTD., TECUMSEH BREWERY, 1952-1956
TECUMSEH ROAD AT VICTORIA, TECUMSEH

When the Dominion Cannery was erected in 1912, nobody would have expected that it ever could become a brewery, but that is what happened in 1927. Brewing got off to a somewhat shaky start in 1928. It can be assumed that the driving force behind Tecumseh Beer and Ale was primarily U.S. customers. Operations ceased in 1931 when the cannery required the space for storage.

J. E. MacQueen and a group of World War II veterans planned to revive brewing in the cannery in 1947. They chose the name Old Comrades Brewing, and operations commenced on August 20, 1948, with much better success than with the earlier Tecumseh venture. Joseph Schneider, a brewmaster from Munich, was hired to brew Old Comrades Lager and Ale, but one suspects that his personal favorites were Schneider's Beer and Schneider's Ale.

E. P. Taylor bought the plant for his growing Canadian Breweries, Ltd., empire in 1952. After three years under the CBL umbrella, the small Tecumseh brewery became obsolete as Taylor acquired larger breweries in Windsor. CBL closed the plant in 1956 and announced demolition in September 1963.

Tecumseh, Ontario, Canada.

287

WINDSOR

Postcard of the Tecumseh brewery.

FROM THE COLLECTION OF LAWRENCE SHERK.

Advertisement for the British-American brewery, in an 1897 convention brochure.

CARLING

BRITISH-AMERICAN BREWING COMPANY, 1885–1950
115–121 SANDWICH, CORNER OF BRUCE, WINDSOR
BRADING CINCINNATI CREAM BREWING COMPANY, 1950–1957
CARLING BREWERIES, LTD., 1957–1969
515 RIVERSIDE WEST, WINDSOR

The British-American brewery was founded in 1885 when twenty-six-year-old Louis Griesinger, Jr., relocated from Detroit. He was the son of a brewery architect and contractor, who had built the breweries of Bernhard Stroh, Voigt, Kling, Ruoff, Endriss, and Mann. Louis Griesinger, Sr., put up the capital and had the brewery built. He may have reasoned that with two dozen active breweries in Detroit and none in Windsor, this was a good opportunity for his son to become a brewery owner. Louis Jr. had worked for Kling and Mann and then spent seven years under William Gerst, foreman at Christian Moerlein in Cincinnati. While he supervised the plant, his sister Pauline managed the office.

ALBERT IRION AND SONS

Ida, another sister, married twenty-five-year-old Albert L. Irion in 1883. He was a native of Ottawa, Illinois, and while he had no prior brewing experience, there were evidently good feelings between him and Griesinger, and he was made a partner in 1893. This arrangement lasted until 1898, when Griesinger retired because of ill health, and Irion became sole proprietor. The new brewmaster was Joseph Geiser. He had worked for Lackman in Cincinnati and Kling in Detroit and had been the foreman at Phoenix in Bay City for seven years. He was succeeded by

W. R. Bonds, a graduate of the Chicago Brewers Academy founded by J. E. Siebel.

The brewery produced about 15,000 barrels in 1896, mostly the famous Cincinnati Cream Lager which was introduced in 1887. It was said that the brand name was a spur-of-the-moment suggestion by one of their agents who knew of Griesinger's tenure at Moerlein. The original brand was the Export, which continued to be brewed, along with a Dublin Porter, also introduced in 1887. Other brands were Black Pirate Ale, British Special Ale, Heavy Muenchener Lager, and Half/Half.

British-America became a stock company in 1903. The plant was a four-story building that took up most of the block and at that time had a capacity of 30,000 barrels. The beer was aged three months in enameled steel tanks made by the Detroit Steel Cooperage Company.

Ale brewmaster Joseph Geiser, in an 1897 convention brochure.
FROM THE STROH BREWERY COMPANY ARCHIVE.

Irion retired in 1912 after fourteen years at the helm, because his health also failed. He left the running of the brewery to his two sons Louis A. and Raymond. In 1929, the Irion brothers sold the business to brokers, and the following year, E. P. Taylor of Canadian Breweries, Ltd. ("CBL"), acquired the brewery. Cincinnati Cream Lager remained the main brand. Raymond Irion returned to the brewing industry in 1933 as investor in and president of the Regal Brewing Company in Detroit. This venture, however, failed after a few years (see chapter 8). Louis Irion went to work at the Walkerville Brewing Company, where he was manager until 1955; Raymond joined him there in an administrative capacity until 1954.

E. P. TAYLOR

The British-American name remained until 1950, when Taylor transferred the brewery to the Brading chain of Ottawa as the Brading Cincinnati Cream Brewery Company. Two old-fashioned beers of strong flavor, British XXX Stout and Old Stock Ale, were also brewed. In 1957, Taylor unified the corporate names of his growing empire; it was now the Windsor plant of Carling Breweries, Ltd., a division of Canadian Breweries, Ltd. Black Label, the Carling house lager, was brewed in addition to Cincinnati Cream, and the plant capacity was expanded to a quarter-million barrels. Staff changes were frequent during this period as Taylor rotated executives. A decade later, the CBL group had peaked and was in decline. The Windsor plant hung on until it was closed on September 30, 1969.

FROM BOTTLES TO BETS

The good location near downtown with proximity to the Detroit River saved at least part of the plant from the wrecker's ball. The bottling facility was completely remodeled in 1974 to become Windsor's art museum. The conversion was very successful. In 1993, the site proved even too convenient for art, and the building was converted to the gambling casino that opened in May 1994. The art museum is expected to return to the former brewery building after a permanent casino is built.

MEMORABILIA
Canadian collectors have located a number of items from the British-American period. A tray showing "The Handsome Waiter," his grin a mixture of condescension and willingness to please, is a popular collectible.

MANAGEMENT
1897: Louis Griesinger, Jr., and Albert L. Irion, proprietors; Pauline Griesinger, bookkeeper; Joseph Geiser, brewmaster.
1903: A. L. Irion, president; W. R. Bonds, vice president, secretary, and brewmaster; Pauline Griesinger, treasurer.
1941: C. S. King, president; E. P. Taylor, vice president; W. C. Butler, secretary; Frank Schofield, master brewer.
1946: E. P. Taylor, president; D. E. Betts, vice president; W. C. Butler, secretary; H. A. Cornwall, treasurer; A. F. Fuerth, manager; L. M. Wildman, brewmaster.
1950: C. A. Snowdon, president; A. F. Fuerth, manager; J. R. Cameron, master brewer.
1956: A. F. Fuerth, president; P. A. R. Thompson and J. G. Campbell, vice presidents; W. E. Drewry, secretary; G. R. Hallamore, treasurer.
1959: C. O. Dalton, president; J. M. McLean, manager; T. G. Ramsay, master brewer.
1961–1969: L. Pare, manager; W. T. Barnes, master brewer.

WALKERVILLE

WALKERVILLE BREWERY, LTD., 1890–1945
CARLING BREWERIES (WALKERVILLE), LTD., 1945–1947
O'KEEFE'S BREWERY (WALKERVILLE), LTD., 1947–1951
O'KEEFE'S OLD VIENNA BREWING COMPANY, 1951–1956
FIFTH STREET, WALKERVILLE

Hiram Walker had this lager brewery built in 1890 to expand from distilling, and top-fermenting cellars for John Bull Ale, XXX Porter, and Pure

Malt Stout were added three years later. Walker, being seventy-four years old when the plant opened, soon sold a significant part of the equity to his vice president, S. A. Griggs, whose family had moved from Ohio to Detroit when Griggs was a child. As three of Hiram Walker's sons were on the board of directors and E. C. Walker was president, the Walker family still maintained control. Bernard Michenfelder of the Detroit Michenfelder brewing family was in charge of the lager department and the Superior Lager brand. He left in 1898 and purchased the brewery in Upper Sandusky, Ohio.

Lager brewmaster Bernard Michenfelder, in an 1897 convention brochure.
FROM THE STROH BREWERY COMPANY ARCHIVE.

Hiram Walker's spirits had found favor in Detroit, and it was natural also to export the beer. The firm established a U.S. agency in 1895 at the former Duncan Malt House on 134–146 Beaubien Street. Perhaps the Walker family saw a way to consolidate control, or Griggs wished to move back to Detroit. In any case, he was appointed manager of the agency. The beers were sold under the St. George label in Canada and were distributed as Robin Hood Ale and Extra Stout in Detroit.

Griggs retired in 1925, and by that time, the Walkers also were no longer interested and sold the brewery to a group of Detroit investors. C. Andrich was president until 1931, when Herman Radner assumed that function. Later, the Radner name would become well known through his daughter Gilda's career as a comedian. Louis A. Irion moved over from the British-American Brewing Company as managing director. The capacity was increased to 100,000 barrels for Walkerville Old Style Lager, Rob Roy Ale, Malt Stout, and XXX Porter. The beers were well accepted locally.

INTO THE TAYLOR EMPIRE

The small-town atmosphere ended abruptly in March 1944 with the arrival of brewing empire builder E. P. Taylor, who acquired the Walkerville brewery as part of his campaign to make Carling a national Canadian brand. One year later, he changed its name to Carling Breweries

The British-American brewery in the 1930s.

The Walkerville brewery in the 1930s.

(Windsor), Ltd. The brands now were Carling's Red Cap Ale and Black Label Lager. In 1947, the name was changed again to O'Keefe's Brewery (Windsor) Ltd., to produce O'Keefe's Old Vienna Beer and Old Stock Ale. Irion stayed on as Taylor's manager through these changes until 1955.

On September 13, 1956, Canadian Breweries, Ltd., announced that it had bought Brading's Brewery and would close the O'Keefe brewery and the Tecumseh brewery. The fate of eighty-nine employees of three area breweries absorbed by CBL was not immediately announced, but Carling offered a severance package including one week's pay for each year employed, plus a welfare settlement.

E. P. Taylor at his horse breeding farm Windfield, September 1950.

ARCHIVES OF ONTARIO, GILBERT MILNE COLLECTION. COURTESY DAVID MILNE.

MANAGEMENT

1897: E. C. Walker, president; William Aikman, Jr.,vice president; S. A. Griggs, managing director; J. H. Walker, treasurer; F. H. Walker, director; E. W. Bauslaugh, secretary; Bernard Michenfelder, lager beer brewmaster; A. Brabant, ale brewmaster.

1941: H. J. Mero, chairman; Herman D. Radner, president; S. L. Springsteen, vice president; Louis A. Irion, manager; Raymond E. Irion, advertising manager; William J. Waas, master brewer.

1946: E. P. Taylor, chairman; D. C. Betts, president; H. A. Taylor, vice president; W. C. Butler, secretary; H. A. Cornwall, treasurer; Louis A. Irion, manager; Kai B. Jacobsen, master brewer.

1950: Louis A. Irion, manager; Kai B. Jacobsen, master brewer.

BREWPUBS AND MICROBREWERIES

CHARLY'S BREW PUB, 1986–
4715 TECUMSEH ROAD EAST

Tavern owner Dave Cooper's brewpub has become established as a favorite local meeting place. Mike Dumouchelle brews Time Out, a Pilsener type, now also available in bottles.

WALKERVILLE BREWING COMPANY, 1998–
525 ARGYLE, WALKERVILLE

Karen Bethune and Michael Plunkett purchased the Walkerville Brewing Company name, and after an absence of fifty-four years, Walkerville beer has reappeared in a former Hiram Walker warehouse. A Canadian-made brewing unit was obtained from a defunct Waco, Texas, microbrewery. The brewer is Jason Britton, formerly with Amsterdam Breweries in Toronto. (William Marentette, in *Canadian Brewerianist*)

19

WYANDOTTE

Like Mount Clemens to the northeast, Wyandotte to the southwest was founded independently of Detroit and developed its
own industries and character. Wyandotte is known for its
long riverfront, the chemical industry, and the entrance to Grosse Ile,
but not beer. Yet in the years before Prohibition there were two breweries competing for local business. The histories of the two Wyandotte
breweries are interesting because they show that competitive forces and
the response to them were already active fifty years before they became
a major issue.

MARX

GEORGE MARX, 1863–1884
MARX BROS. BREWING COMPANY, 1884–1891
MARX BROS., 1891–1897
WYANDOTTE BREWING COMPANY, 1897–1904
FRANK MARX BREWING COMPANY, 1904–1909
MARX BREWING COMPANY, 1909–1919
THE MARX COMPANY, 1919–1933
MARX BREWING COMPANY, INC., 1933–1936
WYANDOTTE BREWING COMPANY, 1936–1937
FRONT AND OAK, LATER 2907 VAN ALSTYNE

The downriver city of Wyandotte was a long way from Detroit in 1863,
when George Marx selected the choice corner of Front and Oak streets
near the Detroit River for his modest brewery. Front Street was later
renamed Van Alstyne Boulevard, and it is still the main riverside avenue.

Marx Brewing Co.,
Wyandotte, Michigan.

Workers, trucks, and wagons are lined up for a formal plant photograph, about 1915. Flags and smoke have obviously been added by a retoucher, and the street has been wiped clean.

COURTESY WYANDOTTE MUSEUM.

Marx was the only brewer in town, and about 1,000 barrels a year were enough to supply the local demand and to make a living. He also had a corner saloon across the street from the brewery, where his lager was always fresh.

RIVERSIDE BUSINESS

For twenty years, Marx attended to his business. In 1884, he brought his brothers and his son Frank in as partners. George died in 1886, and Frank Marx assumed control. The brewery was expanded to take up a whole block on Front Street. A dance hall was added to the saloon, where patrons could enjoy an excellent view of the river and the Canadian shore. Marx brands in 1898 were Export, Pilsener, and White Label. These were later replaced by Banner and Gold Star, which was to become the main brand. Frank Marx added a coal and ice business and advertised these products along with beer.

A MERGER MAKES SENSE

In 1890, a competitor, the Eureka Brewing and Ice Company, began brewing farther down on Front Street. Charles Riopelle, Hugo Mehl-hose, and Ferdinand Fickel were associated with that firm. When Eureka started to fail twenty years later, the Marx family offered a merger. Mehlhose sold his interest to the Marxes and retired, as did Frank Marx. Riopelle and Fickel joined a new and larger Marx Brewing Company as president and second vice president, respectively, and the Eureka brewery was closed.

PART III
BREWERIES IN
SURROUNDING
CITIES

The new owners started an expansion program and updated the equipment. A bottling plant capable of packaging 100 bottles per minute was also erected. With a 200-barrel kettle, Marx had the capacity to brew 50,000 barrels. Given the seasonal nature of beer consumption and the size of the market, 25,000 barrels was probably a very good year.

With Prohibition sentiment growing during World War I, Marx launched the non-alcoholic drink Marxie and Malt-Juice. Prohibition closed the brewing operation in 1919, as Marxie could not compete with real beer coming across the river, but the ice business was maintained.

Founder George Marx.
COURTESY WYANDOTTE MUSEUM.

A VERY GOOD FIRST YEAR

The Marx brewery was reopened in November 1933. A highly successful stock offering was held in April 1934, and ambitious plans were announced by president M. F. Nichols. George Marx's grandson Frank A. Marx was vice president, the last of the family to be involved in the brewery. Alois Chronowski, who was also on the board of Auto City Brewing Company, served as treasurer. Albert Schmidt and John L. Brown of Detroit were directors. Sales were an encouraging 43,400 barrels in 1934 and must have started off well the following spring. During the summer of 1935, twenty new trucks were bought, and a second shift was added to the bottling plant. Marx even launched a new ale to complement the lager. However, sales declined in the fall. The total for the year was only 500 barrels above that of 1934, and the early optimism and investments proved to have been misplaced.

TROUBLE ABREWING

The year also brought friction within the board. Herman Wise, leader of twelve dissenting stockholders, petitioned for reorganization under the bankruptcy statutes. He claimed internal dissension and charged that director John Brown received payments for unperformed services. Brown, head of the John L. Brown & Company firm of stockbrokers, had promoted several brewery stock issues. He had been cited in January 1935 for also being a director of the Auto City and C&K brew-

JOHN J. MARX
SECTY.

THEO. HOERSCH
TREAS.

FRANK MARX
PRES. AND GEN'L. MGR.

CHAS. H. RIOPELLE
VICE-PRES.

JEREMIAH DRENNAN
VICE-PRES.

FERDINAND FICKEL
SUP'T.

EDW. HAAS
AUDITOR

Workers pose with Joseph Marx (in bowler), William Marx, and Ferdinand Fickel (to the right of the barrel).   COURTESY WYANDOTTE MUSEUM.

eries in Detroit and Food City of Battle Creek, in violation of the Liquor Control Act which forbade interlocking directorates.

Eldred Bass was appointed trustee, and in May 1936, a new board took over, headed by Bass and Richard J. Lynch. An attempt to raise operating capital by a stock issue failed. The brewery was ordered sold, and on July 8, 1936, it was purchased by Lynch, Bass, and partners for $45,000 and assumption of a secured debt of $114,000. In a last-ditch attempt to revive the firm, the name was changed to Wyandotte Brewing Company, and the brands became Bavarian Lager and Nine Castle Ale. Rumor had it that old beer that had been kept in stock tanks since spring was now bottled under the new labels. Only 8,900 barrels were sold in 1936. The Wyandotte Brewing Company declared bankruptcy in June 1937, and the assets were auctioned off in August. The building remained empty until it was razed in 1941.

Marx never had much business outside nearby downriver communities. The Wahl Brewery in Monroe prevented significant expansion southward. Marx was safe in Wyandotte as long as horses were the mode of transportation. There exists a post-repeal photo of four Marx trucks lined up before Tiger Stadium, then Navin Field. It was a long shot to expect that Marx could compete with Detroit breweries in Detroit; it was far more likely that Detroit beers invaded the downriver market and outspent and outpromoted Marx. Hometown loyalty in the beer business

◄   Frank Marx, surrounded by his officers.   COURTESY WYANDOTTE MUSEUM.

Marx wagons are lined up across from the brewery in 1917. The sign on the first wagon from the left advertises Marx Special Gold Star Beer. The building to the right was the Marx Pavilion.   From the Manning Brothers Historic Photographic Collection.

Four trucks advertising Marx's Bavarian Lager line up at Navin Field in May 1935.
From the Manning Brothers Historic Photographic Collection.

is a very weak foundation on which to build, and stockholder friction has proven to be a sure way for an early failure.

MEMORABILIA

Marx was not known for passing out merchandising items before Prohibition, judging by their paucity. The Wyandotte Museum, the former Biddle House, has a small collection. Round tip trays with stock designs of pretty women's faces are rare. A round tray advertising Marx's Special Gold Star Brew is in the collection of Dr. Karl Schroeder and seems to be the only example known. Embossed bottles for Marx beer are available, as are labels from the 1930s. Marx also provided an attractive tin-over-cardboard sign after repeal.

MANAGEMENT

1910: Frank Marx, president and general manager; Charles Riopelle, vice president; Jeremiah Brennan, vice president; Ferdinand Fickel, superintendent; John J. Marx, secretary, Theodore Hoersch, treasurer.

1912: Charles Riopelle, president; Jeremiah Brennan, first vice president; Ferdinand Fickel, second vice president; John J. Marx, secretary; Theodore Hoersch, treasurer.

1934: M. F. Nichols, president; Frank A. Marx, vice president; Alois Chronowski, treasurer; C. Gaynier, secretary.

1936: Bernard P. Costello, chairman and secretary, Eldred B. Bass, president and general manager; Richard J. Lynch, first vice president; Frank Armstrong, second vice president and assistant secretary; A. C. Milne, treasurer; Leonard B. Burton, brewmaster.

1937: Richard J. Lynch, president; Eldred B. Bass, vice president and general manager; Walter Ebert, vice president; A. C. Milne, secretary-treasurer.

EUREKA

EUREKA BREWING AND ICE COMPANY, 1890–1909
POPLAR AND FRONT

The Eureka brewery got a later start than its larger downriver competitor, Marx, and when it became obvious that the local market could not support two breweries, it merged with Marx, with the latter becoming the surviving firm and plant.

Charles H. Riopelle and Hugo Mehlhose incorporated the firm in 1889, naming it after the Eureka Iron & Steel Company, which had been vital to the beginnings of Wyandotte in the 1850s. Hugo Mehlhose had an ice cream parlor and a river ice business. According to oral history, his brother Louis, besides working in the steel mill, bottled Goebel keg beer for local consumption. Both brothers used river ice. Hugo sold the labor-intensive ice business to his brother, who had four sons to operate it, and invested in the beer business instead.

In the summer of 1890, the new brewery building was completed; it was opened formally on August 21. An excellent photograph of the initial brewery with various staff members is in a local collection. In the center is brewmaster Ferdinand Fickel, a man of stocky build and legendary

The Eureka brewery at the turn of the century. The stocky man in the center is brewmaster and partner Ferdinand Fickel. Courtesy Dr. Karl Schroeder.

A promotional drawing of the Eureka brewery. The malthouse portion at the right was never built. Courtesy Wyandotte Historical Museum.

appetite who, it is still recalled, never met a seidl (stein) of beer or a plate of wurst (sausage) he did not like. The photograph shows a substantial building of three floors at left and four floors in a narrower part at right. In a drawing printed in 1898, the left part has been duplicated to the right of the center portion, giving a balanced structure. The two wings are labeled "EUREKA BREWERY" and "MALTHOUSE," respectively. A malt kiln stack is shown on top of the new wing. This was wishful promotion, as the malthouse wing was never built.

At the turn of the century, Charles Riopelle and Hugo Mehlhose were president and secretary-treasurer, respectively. Eureka's brands were Pilsener and Export Lager, and there must have been sharp competition with the well-established Marx brewery. In January of 1910, agreement was reached to merge with Marx and to close the Eureka brewery. The consolidation centered on Marx acquiring the Mehlhose interests, which consisted of ownership equity of Hugo and Louis Mehlhose and M. P. Zeller. It was understood that Hugo Mehlhose was ready to retire from business. Charles Riopelle and Ferdinand Fickel, the other partners of Eureka, joined Marx.

Ferdinand Fickel, in an 1897 convention brochure.
FROM THE STROH BREWERY COMPANY ARCHIVE.

Merger and consolidation as the result of competition in a flat or declining market is not a modern phenomenon. It was the best solution at the time, as it strengthened the surviving firm. Much of the site of the brewery grounds is now occupied by the Wyandotte filtration plant, but the brewery building proper still stands.

MEMORABILIA

This brewery left little evidence of its nineteen years of existence. Collectibles from the Eureka Brewing and Ice Company are extremely scarce. A large oval stock tray of a Bavarian tavern scene in the style of the genre painter Gruenzer with rim text for the Eureka Brewing Company is in the collection of Dr. Karl Schroeder and is the only one known so far. No other items from Eureka seem to be available, and even bottles embossed for the Eureka Brewing Company are difficult to locate.

MANAGEMENT

1901: Charles H. Riopelle, president; Hugo Mehlhose, secretary-treasurer; Ferdinand Fickel, brewmaster.

BREWPUBS AND MICROBREWERIES

Owner John Grzywa's son John Jr. brews a Blonde, a Wheat Ale, and several others in a 3-barrel unit in Sport's, which opened in 1990 as a 50s bar and grill at the corner of Second and Maple in downtown Wyandotte. (RH)

20

YPSILANTI

Small as Ypsilanti must have been in the early 1860s, there was room for two brewers. A decade later, there was even a malthouse to supply them, and a third brewery opened in town. This was the Grove Brewery of Louis Foerster, which survived until 1940 under a different name and ownership. For its modest size, Ypsilanti was a very friendly town for beer drinkers. With this history and the presence of a university (Eastern Michigan), it should be only a matter of time before a brewpub or a microbrewery opens and brewing in Ypsilanti is resumed.

GROB

JACOB F. GROB, 1861–1915
5 FOREST

Jacob Grob, who was born in Württemberg, Germany, in 1839, is credited with having started the first brewery in Ypsilanti. His parents immigrated in 1851 and first settled in Monroe. It was a busy year in 1861 for twenty-two-year-old Jacob. He came to Ypsilanti, married Sophie Post, and erected a small brewery at his home on the south side of Forest Avenue near the "west end of the bridge." In 1864, he built an extensive icehouse, also a first for the village. In the late 1870s, he operated a saloon from his home as well. Grob produced 190 barrels in 1878 and slightly fewer the following year. He may have brewed once a week on a 4- or 5-barrel scale, as microbrewers who are just starting out do now. It is unlikely that Grob bottled his beer. It seems the sort of place where one drank draft, sent a child over to fill a pitcher for home consumption, or ordered a keg for a group outing.

In the late 1880s, Grob also sold ice. It seems that he gradually shifted from beer to ice as Foerster's brewery grew. No pictures of him or his home are known.

EAGLE

EAGLE BREWERY, 1866–1876
EAST CONGRESS

Another early Ypsilanti brewer was Andrew J. Leech. He was born in New York State in 1830. When he was five, his parents, Andrew C. and Betsy Leech, settled on a farm in Canton, Michigan. The year 1865 found him working as a grocer in Ypsilanti, and the following year, he either erected or acquired the small brewery. Nothing is known about his products, but the name Andrew Leech suggests an ale brewer. The Eagle Brewery operated for ten years. A few years later, it had become a wagon shop.

SWAYNE'S

SWAYNE'S MALT HOUSE, 1870–CA. 1890
FOREST AND RIVER

L. C. Wallington converted a three-story, 50-by-94-foot school building into a malting operation about 1870. The details of this unlikely conversion are left unexplained, nor do we know why a school building became available. In 1872, F. G. Swayne purchased Wallington's interest and set about to enlarge the malthouse. Capacity increased from 11,000 bushels in 1874 to 40,000 bushels in 1880. An undated sepia photograph in the collection of the Ypsilanti Historical Museum shows what is almost certainly the enlarged Swayne malting plant.

FOERSTER

ADAM FOERSTER & BROTHER, GROVE STREET BREWERY, 1870–1878
L. Z. FOERSTER & COMPANY, 1878–1884
LOUIS Z. FOERSTER, 1884–1893
L. Z. FOERSTER BREWING COMPANY, 1893–1914
HOCH BREWING COMPANY, 1914–1916
LIBERTY BREWING COMPANY, 1933–1934
YPSILANTI BREWING COMPANY, 1934–1941
DAWES BREWING COMPANY, 1941–1943
414 SOUTH GROVE

The identity of this brewery's founder is in doubt, as conflicting names are cited. H. Lee and 1866 were mentioned in the 1903 industry history

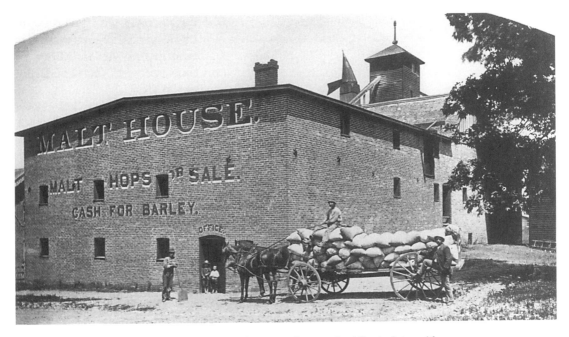

Swayne's malthouse, about 1880. The pointed roof structure is a rotating kiln stack top with a wind vane, which prevents draft interference with the malt-drying process.

COURTESY YPSILANTI HISTORICAL MUSEUM.

One Hundred Years of Brewing, but the local reference, published twenty-two years earlier, cited Taufkirth and Trockenbrod. There is no disagreement that an existing brewery on Grove Street was purchased by the brothers Adam and Louis Ziegler Foerster in 1870. It is likely that when asked thirty years later who founded the brewery, H. Lee was recalled as the seller and was assumed to have been the original owner.

Ludwig and Margaret Foerster had immigrated to Canada from Germany about 1835 and settled in Wellesly Township, Waterloo County, Ontario, where Louis was born in 1836. The family moved to Michigan the following year. Louis learned the trade of carpenter and joiner. He married Margaret Loeffler, and they had one son, Jacob. When Margaret died in 1865, Louis married Rosa Smith. The union was blessed with six children; Jacob and the two oldest, Louis and Leopold, would later become partners with their father.

GROVE BREWERY DAYS

The brothers Adam and Louis Foerster kept the original name of Grove Brewery, which name was later embossed on bottles and signs. In 1874, Adam sold his share to his brother and moved to Lansing. Louis tried to make it alone, but he took a new partner after one year. This was Herman Hardinghaus, an experienced brewer. An 1883 advertisement lists Louis Z. Foerster and Herman Hardinghaus in connection with L. Z. Foerster & Company's Grove Brewery and Bottling Works. Harding-

L. Z. Foerster, from *Past and Present in Washtenaw County, Michigan*. Samuel W. Beakes, 1906.

haus stayed with Foerster for eight years, then moved to nearby Ann Arbor, where he took over the Northern Brewery in 1884.

Sales in the late 1870s were between 2,000 and 2,500 barrels and were estimated at 4,000 to 5,000 barrels in 1881. Demand kept increasing, and in 1887, the original wood building was replaced by a larger brick structure. Louis Foerster incorporated the brewery in 1891, with himself as president and treasurer and his son Louis K. as vice president. The business must have prospered, because an illustration in an 1894 directory shows it to be a group of three three-story buildings and one older and smaller building at the corner of Grove and Prospect streets. The main brewery building measured 115 by 78 feet and had a keystone dated 1887, the year the original frame structure was replaced by brick walls. There is a recognizable malt kiln and a smokestack from an engine house. Beer was bottled in a small structure across the street under the Gold Band Export Beer label, and Bavarian and a Bock were also brewed.

BEER TIME

A photo of ten men and two boys taken about 1912 has survived in the family of one of the boys, Michael Sullivan, who was born in 1900. The only tool visible is an oil lamp being held by a cellarman, but half the men are holding small brass beer mugs. Young Mike Sullivan is holding a large bucket of beer; part of his job was to fetch beer for the gang during the day. After Prohibition, special beer times were written into union contracts, which restricted drinking to a morning and an afternoon break and during lunch. The legal environment of the 1980s caused even this schedule to be abandoned, and all drinking of beer on brewery property was prohibited. But in the early days, the custom of having a beer whenever the time seemed right was part of the brewery scene; the men had their own little mugs, often within reach.

Foerster ownership ended in 1914, and Henry W. Hoch acquired the property. The Hoch Brewing Company, however, lasted only a few

Foerster workers in front of the brewery in 1912. Michael J. Sullivan, the boy at the far right, had the job of supplying everybody with beer. At age eighty-five, he provided the photograph through his son-in-law Robert Kompsie, a former Stroh employee.

The former Foerster brewery in 1916, after it was renamed the Hoch brewery.

Christopher Vogt posing with a new Dodge truck, probably in the winter of 1934. The inscription on the keystone is "L. Z. Foerster 1887." COURTESY YPSILANTI HISTORICAL MUSEUM.

years, and the brewery stood idle during Prohibition. Louis Z. Foerster died in 1921 at age eighty-five.

VOGT BEER

The former Foerster Brewery was revived after Prohibition. It was known briefly as the Liberty Brewing Company, and between 1934 and 1941 as the Ypsilanti Brewing Company with Christopher Vogt as the owner. Vogt purchased machinery and a couple of trucks. He first called his beer Old Ypsilanti and later placed his own name on the label. Sales after two years of operation totaled 16,300 barrels. The Ypsilanti brewery struggled against competition from Detroit and Ann Arbor until 1941, when Vogt sold it to a group of Detroit investors who changed the name to Dawes. The name was probably chosen to lend Dawes Premium Draft the aura of a Canadian import. The product never had a chance to establish itself against wartime restrictions, if indeed there was a market, and the small brewery closed in 1943.

Much of the equipment was purchased by the Altes Brewing Company in Detroit, but the refrigeration was retained. A locker plant used the building, and later an upholstering shop, and some space was turned into apartments. The building ultimately was razed for industrial redevelopment.

MEMORABILIA

Only old bottles and Vogt labels are usually seen. An old outdoor sign for mounting on a tavern wall and lithographed "Grove Brewery," with a partial figure of Gambrinus holding a foaming mug, is in the Don Limpert collection.

MANAGEMENT

1902: Louis Z. Foerster, president and treasurer; Louis K. Foerster, vice president; Jacob L. Foerster, secretary and superintendent.

1916: Henry W. Hoch, president; James J. Hoch, secretary-treasurer and general manager.

1942: Frank Skelnik, president; William J. Betzwieser, vice president and brewmaster; George J. Schneider, secretary-treasurer and advertising manager.

APPENDIX A:
DETROIT BREWERIES

Breweries are listed alphabetically by their first owner, followed in chronological order by any subsequent business names or owners. These are also listed alphabetically, with the reader being referred to the original name. Breweries that appear in bold print are described in detail in the text, under their last and almost always their most important name. In the few cases where the last name was used only briefly, an asterisk indicates the name under which the brewery is described.

The original listing of Detroit breweries appeared in Manfred Friedrich and Donald Bull, *The Register of United States Breweries 1876–1976* (Trumbull, CT, 1976). This book was greatly expanded in Donald Bull, Manfred Friedrich, and Robert Gottschalk, *American Breweries* (Trumbull, CT, 1983). A second enlarged edition, *American Breweries II* by Dale P. Van Wieren (West Point, PA), was published in 1995 and includes extensive research conducted by the author of *Brewed in Detroit*. Additional information from the research by Bruce Heckman for a comprehensive listing of embossed Detroit beer bottles has been included.

A lapse of seven years occurred between the first Detroit directory of 1837 and its successor. Information on continuing brewing operations during the 1830s and 1840s has not been researched. Also, many small brewers did not advertise and were not listed in directories, or were listed only sporadically, during the 1850s and 1860s. No doubt there were families who operated saloons in their homes, where beer was brewed and served, whose names will never be known.

Albert Brewing Company. *See* Jacob Darmstaetter

Altes Brewing Company. *See* Frantz Brogniez

American Brewery. *See* Vollger and Ochsenhirt

American Brewing Company. *See* Exposition Brewing Company

Ameis & Schroeder. Clinton and St. Aubin, 1861
  Ameis, Nickolas. Clinton between Dubois and St. Aubin, 1862–1863

Ams, Frederick. 214 Russell at High, 1859–1866

Armada Corporation. *See* Conrad Pfeiffer

Arndt, Henry. Wight near Adair, 1862–1866; 745–760 Gratiot between Chene and Campau, 1867–1884
  Zigave, Charles. Brewery, 754 Gratiot; home and saloon, 221 Atwater; 1884–1890
  Toelle Brewing Company. Charles F. Toelle, proprietor, 1890–1891
  Honer, Emil. Honer's Brewery, 1891–1896

Royal Brewing Company, 1896–1897

Auto City Brewing Company. 8214 McDougall at Denton, Hamtramck, 1911–1919, 1933–1942

Avery, Elisha S. Detroit Brewery, First between Larned and Congress, 1845.
  Carew (Joshua L.) & Avery. Pale, amber and brown ale; 1846–1848. See Collins.
  Carew, Joshua L. 1849–1863; Seventh, 1865.

Bache, W. S. Company. 240 Salliotte, Ecorse, 1935–1937

Bavarian Brewing Company. See Anton Michenfelder

Beal (William) and Richardson (Samuel). 40 Woodbridge, between Bates and Randolph, 1864–1868
  Richardson, Samuel. Ales, 1869–1870

Beard, Jesse. Beard Brewery, Monroe Avenue, 1845.

Beider, Paul. 189 Gratiot, 1882–1884, later sold brewery supplies.

Bellow, Orlando. 228–230 East Lafayette, 1864–1869. See Collins

Berlin Weiss Beer Brewing Company. 86 Croghan, 1890–1893

Bilz, Frank, also Peter Stouder. 232 Russell at Sherman, 1874–1876
Stouder & Bilz. Brewery and summer garden, 1875–1876
Dittmer, Fred & Company. Wolverine Brewery, 1877–1884
Fred Dittmer Brewing Company, 1884–1888
Millenbach Brewing Company. Matthew Millenbach, 1888–1890
*Phoenix Brewing Company, 1890–1897
Endriss Brewing Company. Charles Endriss's son Herman, 1899–1904

Bloss, George. See Christian Mann

Bonninghausen (William) & Son. 274 Russell and Waterloo, s.e. 1864–1865
Bonninghausen, Hugo and William, 1866–1869 (William later bottler for Martz)

Bowker & Blackmur. See John Mason

Brogniez, Frantz. Mack and Hurlbut, 1897
Tivoli Brewing Company. 1549–1575 Mack, 1897–1919; 10205 Mack (renumbered), 1933–1948
Altes Brewing Company, 1948–1954
National Brewing Company of Michigan. Branch of National Brewing Company, Baltimore, MD, 1954–1967
National Brewing Company, 1967–1973. Acquired by G. Heileman, La Crosse, WI, and closed

Brown, Rufus & Company, N.E. corner Seventh and Abbott, 1860–1864.
Bowker (Peter) & Harris (William), 1865–1868. *See also* Bowker *under* Mason
Davis (Alonzo C.) & Newberry (Henry W.). Western Brewery, 1869–1882
East India Brewing Company. 630 Woodbridge, 1883–1885
*Union Brewing Company. 621 West Fort, 1886–1890
See also Union Brewing Company

Buehringer, John. 34 Marion, 1864–1865; 114 Marion, 1866–1871. Former cooper

Busch, Frederick. Weiss beer, 65 Macomb, 1877–1878

C&K Brewing Company. 11630 Klinger, Hamtramck, 1933–1935
Wagner Brewing Company, 1935–1937

Cadillac Brewing Company. *See* Union Brewing Company

Carew, Joshua L. *See* Elisha Avery

Carner, George W. *See* Roger Fitzpatrick

Champion Brewing Company. *See* George Hauck

Chicago Brewery. *See* Jacob Darmstaetter

Cincinnati Brewery. *See* August Goebel

City Brewing Company. *See* Anton Kuhl

City Brewery. Thomas J. Owen, proprietor. Congress and First, 1837

Clemens Brothers. 115 Chestnut, 1880–1882; 34–36 Jay, 1882–1885
Clemens, John. 115 Chestnut, 1886–1891
Clemens, Joseph F., Excelsior Brewery. 34 Jay, 1886–1888
Clemens, J. F. & Company, 1888–1893
East Side Brewing Company. J. F. Clemens, president and manager, 1893–1904
See also Robert Marsh

John Collins, Collins Brewery. 47 Abbott at Second, 1860–1861
Theodore Williams, 1861–1863. Agent for Carne's ale, 1866
Elisha Avery, 1864
Orlando Bellows, 1864–1866

Columbia Brewing Company. *See* Michael Darmstaetter

Continental Brewery. *See* Frank Martz

Darmstaetter, Jacob. 412 Howard, 1865–1886
Darmstaetter & Bro. Chicago Brewery, 1886–1893
West Side Brewery Company, 1893–1902
West Side Brewery Company, Ltd., 1902–1919
Mundus Brewing Company. 1736–1770 Howard (renumbered), 1933–1935
Albert Brewing Company, 1935–1938

Darmstaetter, Michael. 211 Catherine, 1852–1856

Darmstaeter, William. 92 Catherine, 1865–1885; malthouse only, 1885–1890
Columbia Brewing Company. Rudolf, Arthur, and William Darmstaetter, Jr., 1890–1917

Dash (Dasch), John. 67 Adams, 1860–1868. Also John Jr.; Dash, T. H., 1860.
Dash, Jacob, 1868–1869

Davis, Alonso C. *See* Rufus Brown

Detroit Brewery. *See* John Carew

Detroit Brewing Company. *See* Frank Martz

Deville, John and Nickolas. 228 Russell, 1862–1882

Dittmer, Fred. *See* Frank Bilz

Dorner, Jacob. Northeast corner St. Lawrence and Prospect, 1864–1866

Dullea, Dennis. Northwest corner Baker and Seventh, 1872–1875

Duncan (William C.) & Richman (George C.). Woodbridge and Third, 1850–1851

Duncan, William C. 186–190 Woodbridge, opp. M.C.R.R. depot, 1852–1862

Duncan's Central Brewery. 232 Woodbridge, between Third and Fourth, 1862–1865

George Langdon & Company, 1865–1872

Duncan's Central Brewery, Williams (Nathan G.) & Company, proprietors, 1872–1882

Williams, Nathan G. Maltster, 1882

Duncan, W. S. & Company. William S. and Ellison E. Duncan, malthouse, 1882–1885

East India Brewing Company. *See* Rufus Brown

East Side Brewing Company. *See* Clemens Brothers

E&B Brewing Company. *See* John Koch

Eldridge, Charles. Brewer at National Hotel, 1845

Elspass, Theodore. 36 St. Aubin, 1894

Ekhardt & Becker. *See* John Koch

Emerson, Davis & Moore. Proprietors Detroit Brewery, Woodbridge, 1837

Endriss, Charles. Southeast corner Maple at 350–352 Rivard, 1865–1889

Endriss Brewing Company, branch of Goebel Brewing Company, Ltd. 38 Maple, 1889–1904

Endriss Brewing Company. Sherman at 230–232 Russell, 1898–1899

Excelsior Brewery. *See* Joseph Clemens

Exposition Brewery. Chase and Mechanic, Delray, 1890–1901

American Brewing Company. Foot of Carey, 1901–1919

American Products Company, 1919–1933

American Beverage Company, 1933–1934

American Brewing Company of Michigan, 1935–1938

Fahsnacht, Daniel. Southwest corner Antoine and Napoleon, 1874–1879

Farmer's Brewery. *See* Owen & Scott

Farrell, Charles. Woodbridge between Thirteenth and Fourteenth, 1875

Farkel, Louis. Jay and St. Aubin, 1877–1878

Fitzpatrick, Roger. Hamtramck Brewery. Larned and First, 1845–1851

Carne, George W., 1851–1855; Atwater

and St. Aubin, 1856–1866; burned 1866; Woodbridge between Randolph and Bates, 1866–1869

Fort Gratiot Brewery. *See* Christian Mann

Fort Dearborn Brewing Company. Incorporated but not constructed, 1934–1938

Frey, Frederick. *See* Robert Marsh

Fuller, A. 310 Thirteen 1/2, 1877–1878

Germania Brewing Company. *See* Frederick Grieser

Goebel, August & Company. Cincinnati Brewery, 54–56 Maple, 1873–1889

Goebel Brewing Company, Ltd. 351 Rivard at Maple, 1889–1919

Goebel Brewing Company, Inc. Maple and Rivard, 1934–1936

Goebel Brewing Company, 1936–1964. Acquired by Stroh and razed

Grieser, Frederick. 294 Sherman, 1871–1873

Grieser, Eliza, 1874–1880

Grieser, Eliza. Germania Brewery, 1880–1884

Germania Brewing Company, 1884–1900

Grosshans, Frederick. Detroit between St. Aubin and Dequindre, 1862–1867

Grosshans, Jacob F. Russell and Napoleon, 1868–1873

Hafele (also Haefele), Otto F. 274 Russell, 1899–1902

Hammond, S. G. First between Larned and Congress, 1862–1863

Hamtramck Brewery. *See* Roger Fitzpatrick

Harris, William. *See* Rufus Brown

Hauck, George. 400–408 Wilkins, 1873–1877

Hauck, George & Company, 1877–1879

Hauck & Bauer (Christian), 1879–1882

Hauck & Kaiser (Peter), 1882–1883

Hauck Brewing Company, 1883–1892

Reuter (Edward O.) & Kaiser, 1892–1895

Kaiser & Schmidt (George). Champion Brewery, 1895–1916

Champion Brewery Company, 1916–1919

Schmidt Products Company, 1920–1933

The Schmidt Brewing Company. 1995 Wilkins (renumbered), 1933–1952

Hawley, Richard, also Hawley & Company. Woodbridge near Woodward, 1845; Bates between Woodbridge and Jefferson, 1846–1858

Henri, Alexander. High and St. Aubin, 1867–1868

Henry, John. Ann between Sixth and Seventh, 1863

Henser or Heuser, Joseph. Gratiot near Mt. Elliott, 1874–1876

Hermann, Mathias. Northwest corner Clinton and Elmwood, 1864–1877

Home Brewing Company. *See* Vollger & Ochsenhirt

Honer, Emil; also Honer's brewery. *See* Henry Arndt.

Independent Brewing Company. Michigan Central R.R. at Spring wells, 1907–1919; Central Ave. Near W. Warren, 1934–1936. Construction incomplete. Acquired by Pros't, 1936

Johnson, Edward. *See* Bowker & Blackmur

Kaiser, Adam. 270 Clinton, 1866–1871

Kaiser & Schmidt. *See* George Hauck

Kimze, Karl. 73 Thompson, 1864

King, C. Beaubien and Harriet, brewery and saloon, 1860–1861

Kling, Philip & Company. Peninsular Brewery, with Michael Martz and Henry Weber. Jefferson near Belle Isle bridge, 1863–1871, probably since 1856

Kling, Philip & Company. Peninsular Brewery, 1424 Jefferson, 1871–1884

Philip Kling Brewing Company, 1884–1919

Philip Kling Products Company, 1919–1920. Reopened in Flint, 1934

Koch, John. Ulmer Brewery, 224 Russell, 1871–1883

Koch, John. Michigan Brewery, 1883

Ekhardt & Becker. Michigan Brewery, 1883–1891

Ekhardt & Becker Brewing Company. 475–481 Orleans at Winder, 1891–1919; 1530–1575 Winder at Orleans, 1934–1944

E&B Brewing Company, Inc. 2437 Orleans (renumbered), 1944–1962

***Koppitz-Melchers Brewing Company.** 1115–1136 Gratiot, 1891–1919

Koppitz-Melchers, Inc. 151 Dubois at Atwater, 1934–1947

Goebel Brewing Company, Plant No. 2, 1947–1958

Kraft Brewing Company. *See* Von Brewing Company

Krueger, August. Rivard and High, 1862

Kuhl, Anton. Brewery and saloon, 3 Clinton, 1868–1870; 425 Clinton, 1870–1873

Kuhl, Anna, 1874–1884

City Brewing Company. 425–475 Clinton, 1884–1887

Westphalia Brewing Company, 1887–1895

Kunze, Carl. 48 Harrington at Beaubien, 1862–1863; 74 Thompson, 1864–1869

Kurtz, Joseph A. 25 Macomb, corner of Brush. Weiss beer, 1877–1884

Zynda, John, 1886–1891

Zynda, John & Bros. White Eagle Brewery, 4232 Riopelle, 1891–1919

Zynda Brewing Company, 1933–1948

Langdon & Company. *See* William C. Duncan

Langston, Frederick (Jr.). 242 Rivard, 1894–1895

Leonhartt, Christopher. 121 High, 1862

Lion Brewing Company. *See* Bernhard Stroh

Mackay, John. D. Fifth and Beech, 1864–1874; 748 Twelfth at Howard, 1874–1877

Moloney, Schneider & Company, 1877–1879

Moloney, William E. Vienna Brewery, 1879–1891

Vienna Brewing Company, 1891–1896

Moloney Brewing Company, 1896–1898

Mann, Christian. 278 Russell, 1872–1877; Gratiot between Mt. Elliott and Bellevue, 1878–1880

Mann, C. & Company, Ft. Gratiot Brewery. 2000 Gratiot, 1880

Walz, Daniel, 1880–1882

Walz, Minnie (Mrs. Daniel), 1882–1884

Bloss, George, 1884–1890; 1340–1352 Gratiot, 1891–1897

Mann (Jacob) & Endriss (Gottlieb F.). 20 Maple, 1866–1868

Mann, Jacob. 28–30 Maple at Rivard, 1869–1889

Jacob Mann Brewing Company (branch of Goebel Brewing Company, Ltd.), 1889–1891

Marsh, Robert F. 91–93 Catherine, 1862–1865

Marsh, R. & Son (Robert F. and Robert J.). 115 Chestnut, 1865–1877

Seeger, George. 1877–1880

*Clemens Bros., 1880–1884

Naecker & Clemens, 1884–1888

John Clemens, 1888–1891

Kellar & Schultz (Frederick), 1891–1893

Schultz & Frey (Frederick), 1893–1896

Frey, Frederick W., 1896–1907

Martz, Frank & Company. Continental Brewery, Bronson and Orleans, 1868–1874

Martz, F. & Bros., 1874–1877

Martz Brothers, 1877–1886

Detroit Brewing Company. 490 Orleans
at Adelaide, 1886–1919; 2530–2536
Orleans (renumbered), 1933–1949
Mason, John. Michigan and Sixth,
1853–1858
Bowker (Peter J.) & Blackmur (John
W.). Mason's Brewery, Michigan and
171 Sixth, 1862–1866
Johnson, Edward (also Edward Jr.),
1870–1876
Johnson, Edward Jr., 1876–1888
McGrath, Thomas. 511 Seventh,
1874–1880; 498 Grand River, 1880–
1893
St Louis Brewing Company, 1893–1899
McRoy, Daniel. Fifth and Abbott,
1865–1869
Michenfelder, Anton. Sherman and
Rivard, 1867–1868
Michenfelder, Anton. Bavarian Brew-
ery, 71 Sherman at Rivard, 1874–1882
A. Michenfelder & Company. Bavarian
Brewery, 1882–1884
Bavarian Brewing Company,
1884–1889]
Branch of Goebel Brewing Company,
Ltd., 1889–1890
Michigan Brewing Company.
1262–1296 Military, 1913–1919
Michigan Brewery. *See* John Koch
Millenbach Brewing Company. *See* Frank
Bilz
Miller, Henry. 131–137 St. Antoine at 355
or 358 Jefferson, 1856–1878; 1015 Jef-
ferson, 1878–1879. Miller's Pleasure
Garden, Elmwood and Jefferson, since
1863
Milwaukee Brewery. *See* William Voigt
Minard, Charles W. 547 Michigan,
1861–1864. Charles W., Jr., 1865–1875
Moloney, William. *See* John MacKay
Mundus Brewing Company. *See* Jacob
Darmstaetter
Mutual Brewing Company. *See* Julian
Strelinger
Naecker & Clemens. *See* Robert Marsh
Nagel, Philip. 249–251 Mullett, 1887–1891
Nagel, Philip, Estate, 1891–1893; also
Frank Nagel, 1892
Nagel, Philip Brewing Company,
1893–1899
National Brewing Company. *See* Frantz
Brogniez
National Brewing Company of Michigan.
See Frantz Brogniez
National Brewery. *See* Thomas Zoltowski
New York Brewery. *See* Frederick Reutter
Nothnagel, Frederick. 74 Twelfth,
1874–1877

Nothnagel & Son, 1877
Oakman Brewing Company. *See* William
Voigt
Ochsenhirt, Adam. *See* Vollger & Ochsen-
hirt
Old Holland Brewing Company.
563–565 Larned, 1935–1939
Owen & Scott. Farmer's Brewery, oppo-
site Mansion House, 1829–1831
Owen, Thomas. City Brewery, Congress
and First, 1837
Peninsular Brewery. *See* Philip Kling
Pfeiffer, Conrad. 908–940 Beaufait,
1890–1902
Pfeiffer Brewing Company. 912
Beaufait, 1902–1919; 3700
Beaufait (renumbered), 1934–1962
Associated Brewing Company,
1962–1972
Armada Corporation. Buhl Building,
1972–1973
Phohman, Adam or Andrew. 255 Mullett,
1862–1864; Clinton and St. Aubin,
1865–1869
Phiringer, John. 34 Marion, 1862–1863
Phoenix Brewing Company. *See* Frank
Bilz
Pros't Brewing Company. 9920 Knodell,
1933–1936
Voigt-Pros't Brewing Company,
1936–1938
See also William Voigt
Regal Brewing Company. 3220 Belle-
view, 1934–1937
Branch of E&B Brewing Company,
1937–1938
Reuter & Kaiser. *See* George Hauck
Reutter, Frederick. New York Brewery,
367 St. Antoine, 1868–1869. Frederick
Reutter ran a bottling operation at 395
St. Antoine, 1876–1909
Richardson, Samuel. *See* Beal and
Richardson
Royal Brewing Company. *See* Henry Arndt
Ruebelman, Elias. 184 Croghan,
1852–1856; 262 Russell at Clinton,
1860–1869
Ruoff, August. Brewery and saloon, 367
Gratiot, 1864–1884
A. Ruoff Brewing Company, 1884–1904
Sandhill Brewery. *See* Vitzhum & Com-
pany
Scheu, John. 351 Russell, 1876–1877,
lager; 507–515 Hastings, 1878–1911,
weiss beer
St. Louis Brewing Company. *See* Thomas
McGrath
Schmidt Brewing Company. *See* George
Hauck

Star Brewery. *See* John Steiner

Steiner, John. Star Brewery, 327 Marion at Orleans, 1875–1884

Fulda (Frederick) & Bommer (John). Winder and Orleans, 1885–1891

Merged with Ekhardt & Becker, 1891. *See also* John Koch

Sterrett & Hunter. 187 Croghan, small beer, 1876–1877

Stegmeyer, Francis (also Stickmeyer, Frank). 229–235 Hastings, 1865–1869

Stouder, Peter. *See* Frank Bilz

Strelinger, Julian. 910 Jefferson, 1865–1873; 113 Bates, 1874–1884; brewery at 139 Jay and St. Aubin, office 113 Bates, 1885–1890; 247–251 Mt. Elliott, 1891–1893

Mutual Brewing Company, 625 Hastings, 1893–1915

Stroh, Bernhard. 57 Catherine, 1850–1875

Lion Brewing Company. 331 Gratiot between Hastings and Rivard, 1875–1885

B. Stroh Brewing Company. 253–275 East Elizabeth, 1885–1902

The Stroh Brewery Company, 1892–1919

The Stroh Products Company, 1919–1933

The Stroh Brewery Company. 909 East Elizabeth (renumbered), 1933–1978; 1 Stroh Drive (renamed), 1978–1985. Operates breweries in other cities. Corporate headquarters, 100 River Place, 1981–1999

Tivoli Brewing Company. *See* Franz Brogniez

Toelle Brewing Company. *See* Henry Arndt

Tregent, P. (Patrick) & Company. North side Lafayette, between Griswold and Shelby, 1853–1854

Ulmer Brewery. *See* John Koch

Union Brewing Company. Mitchell near Gratiot, 1898–1919

Cadillac Brewing Company, 1934–1936

Union Brewing Company, 1936–1937

See also Rufus Brown

Vienna Brewing Company. *See* John McKay

Vitzhum & Company (C. Vitzhum and Henry Beck). Sandhill Brewery, Grand River, 1867–1868

Voelkel, Joseph. Gratiot and 42 Maple, 1862–1869

Voigt, William. 209–213 Grand River, 1866–1872

Voigt, E. W. Milwaukee Brewery, 1872–1888

Voigt Brewery Company, Ltd., 1888–1919

*Voigt, E. W. Brewing Company, 1934

Voigt-Pros't Brewing Company, 9737 Knodell, 1934–1937; 1 East Ten Mile, 1937

Oakman Brewing Company, 1937–1939

Vollger (Charles V.) & Ochsenhirt (Adam). 142–148 Sherman, 1871

Ochsenhirt, Adam. American Lager Beer Brewery, 1872–1878

Ochsenhirt & Freund. American Brewery, 1878–1882

Ochsenhirt, A. & Company, 1882–1890

Home Brewing Company, 1890–1897

Von Brewing Company. 1800 East Forest at Orleans, 1933–1935

Kraft Brewing Company, 1935–1937

Kraftig Brewing Company, 1937.

Wagner Brewing Company. *See* C&K Brewing Company

Waltensperger, C. F. 274 Russell, 1862–1863

Walz, Daniel. *See* Christian Mann

Wayne Products & Brewing Company. 3601 Hancock, 1933–1936

Wayne Brewing Company, 1936–1937

Wegener, Anthony. 393 Riopelle, primarily sodas, some weiss beer, 1888–1897

Werner, Henry. 217 Croghan at Russell, 1862–1869

Western Brewery. *See* Rufus Brown

Westphalia Brewing Company. *See* Anton Kuhl

West Side Brewery Company. *See* Jacob Darmstaetter

White Eagle Brewery. *See* John Kurtz

Williams, Nathan G. & Company. *See* C. W. Duncan

Williams, Theodore. *See* John Collins

Wolf, Paul. Michigan and Trowbridge, northwest corner, 1864

Wolverine Brewery. *See* Frank Bilz

Zigave, Charles. *See* Henry Arndt

Zoltowski, Thomas. 733 Hastings, 1891–1919. National Brewery, 1903–1913

Zynda, John. *See* John Kurtz

APPENDIX B:
DETROIT BEER BRANDS

(1) before 1919; *(2)* after 1933

LAGER

Alt Pilsener—Wayne *(2)*
Altes—Tivoli *(2)*
Altweiser—Auto City *(2)*
Bartosz—Auto City *(2)*
Black-Out—Koppitz *(2)*
Blue Label—Goebel *(1)*
Bohemian—Detroit *(1)*, Old
   Holland *(2)*, Stroh *(1, 2)*
Bornheim—Tivoli *(1)*
Boss—Voigt *(1)*
Champion— Schmidt *(1)*
Cream Top— American *(1,
   2)*
Crystal Pale—Zynda *(1)*
Dutchman—American *(2)*
Edelgold Export—Vienna
   (1)
Export Pilsener—Goebel
   (1)
Extra Pale Champagne—
   Wayne *(2)*
Famous—Schmidt *(1, 2)*
Favorite—Goebel *(1)*
Gilt Edge—Union *(1)*
Gold Label—C&K *(2)*,
   Goebel *(2)*
Gold Seal Export—Kling *(1)*
Gold Top—Detroit *(2)*
Golden Lager—Tivoli *(2)*
Hofburger—Wagner *(2)*
Ideal—Independent *(1)*
Imperial Pilsener—Stroh,
   draft only *(2)*
Kraftig—Kraft *(2)*
Light—Stroh *(2)*
Maduro—Voigt *(1)*
Martz Select—Detroit *(2)*
Master Bru—Walker *(2)*
Mundus—West Side *(1, 2)*
Night Club—Wayne *(2)*

Old Eagle—Zynda *(2)*
Old Fashion— Schmidt *(1)*
Old Krug—Goebel *(1)*
Old Style—Regal *(2)*
Pale Select—Koppitz *(1, 2)*
Pfaffenbrau—Stroh *(1)*
Pilsener—E & B *(1)*, Kling
   (1), Goebel *(1)*
Pros't—Kling *(1)*
Rheingold—Voigt *(1)*
Royal Amber—West Side *(2)*
Royal Crown—Walker *(2)*
Royal Special Lager—Regal
   (2)
Saazer—Millenbach *(1)*
Salvador—Ruoff *(1)*
Salvator—Stroh *(1)*
Select Export—Columbia *(1)*
Signature—Stroh *(2)*
Silver Star—Koppitz *(2)*
Sir Albert—West Side *(2)*
Skyball—Tivoli *(2)*
Stag—Detroit *(2)*
Steinie—E&B *(2)*
Tivoli—Stroh *(1)*
Ulmer—Koch *(1)*
Velvet—Phoenix *(1)*
Victory—Koppitz *(2)*
Waldbrau—Albert *(1)*
Würzburger—Goebel *(1)*,
   Pfeiffer *(1)*, Schmidt *(2)*,
   Stroh *(1)*
XXX Pale—Stroh *(1)*
XXX Special—Stroh *(1)*
Zyndapride—Zynda *(1)*

ALES, DARK TYPES, PORTERS, AND STOUTS

Ale—Goebel *(2)*
Bishop's Ale—Wayne *(2)*

Black Velvet Porter—Kop-
   pitz *(1)*
Boss Lager—Voigt *(1)*
Brown Stout—Duncan *(1)*,
   Stroh *(1)*
Canada Black Horse Ale—
   Auto City *(2)*
Cream Top Golden Ale—
   American *(2)*
Dublin Stout—Moloney,
   Union *(1)*
Empire Crown Ale—Old
   Holland *(2)*
Empire Half & Half—Old
   Holland *(2)*
Esquire Ale—Voigt *(1)*
Extra Pale Ale—Kling *(1)*
Golden Bud Ale—E&B *(2)*
Imperial Stout—Bache *(2)*
   Oldbru—Detroit *(2)*
Jolly Ale—E & B *(2)*
London Porter—Davis &
   Newberry *(1)*
Micawber Ale—West Side
   (2)
Nottingham Ale—Wagner
   (2)
Porter—Goebel *(1)*, Hawley
   (1), Kling *(1)*, West Side
   (1)
Premium Ale—Detroit *(2)*
St. Clair Ale—Voigt-Pros't
   (2)
Scotch Pale Ale—Union *(1)*
Sportsmans Ale—Tivoli *(2)*
Steam Ale—Duncan *(1)*
Stratford Stout—Bache
   (2)
XXX Ale—Regal *(2)*

319

APPENDIX C:
SALES VOLUMES OF DETROIT BREWERIES
IN THE 1870s*

Barrels of 31 Gallons

		1874	1875	1878	1879
Arndt, Henry	754 Gratiot	660	741	883	741
Darmstaetter, Jacob	412 Howard	1,908	1,335	1,347	1,617
Darmstaetter, William	92 Catherine	3,492	3,152	1,944	887
Davis & Newberry (a)	630 Woodbridge	4,398	3,386	2,723	2,226
Dittmer, Fred	Russell & Sherman	n.a.	n.a.	4,369	7,438
Endriss, Charles	350 Rivard	969	3,120	5,218	6,616
Fassnacht, Daniel	Antoine & Napoleon	467	428	279	—
Goebel, August & Co.	54 Maple	1,075	5,491	8,224	9,620
Grieser, Eliza	294 Sherman	1,237	1,355	153	238
Hauck, George	400 Wilkins	722	1,967	2,551	1,568
Johnson, Edward	Sixth & Michigan	2,551	1,568	565	456
Kling, Ph. & Co.	1424 E. Jefferson	18,953	19,181	13,326	14,053
Koch, John	244 Russell	2,133	2,231	3,694	4,248
Kuhl, Anna	425 Clinton	2,545	1,869	882	74
Kurtz, Joseph (b)	25 Macomb	—	—	473	320
Lion Brewing Co.(c)	319 Gratiot	7,116	4,274	5,581	9,499
Mann, Christian	278 Russell	696	1,162	1,441	1,341
Mann, Jacob	343 Rivard	4,211	3,633	5,220	5,006
Martz, F. & Bros. (d)	Orleans & Bronson	5,753	4,775	5,632	5,985
MacKay, John	Fifth & Beech	814	414	—	—
McGrath, Thomas	500 Grand River	1,475	1,345	1,367	2,658
Michenfelder, Anton	71 Sherman	4,403	4,724	5,270	5,103
Miller, Henry	1015 E. Jefferson	2,237	2,439	1,658	308
Moloney, William	12th & Howard	—	—	499	924
Ochsenhirt, Adam (e)	148 Sherman	2,280	1,639	1,917	2,268
Ruoff, August	333 Gratiot	3,847	3,351	4,508	4,741
Scheu, John	515 Hastings	—	1,713	21	66
Steiner, John	327 Marion	—	559	2,871	3,450
Voigt, E.W.	213 Grand River	7,587	n.a.	17,358	17,552
Williams & Co. (f)	232 Woodbridge	n.a.	n.a.	4,027	3,710

320

*From *Brewers Handbook for 1876,* Louis Schade, Washington, D.C., and Salem, F. W., Hartford, CT, 1880.
(a) Later Union Brewing Company; (b) Later John Zynda & Brother; (c) Later B. Stroh Brewing Company; (d) Later Detroit Brewing Company; (e) Later Home Brewing Company; (f) Successor to W.C. Duncan.

Appendix D:
Sales Volumes
of Detroit Breweries After Prohibition

Barrels of 31 gallons x 1,000

	Stroh	Pfeiffer	Goebel	Altes	E&B	Schmidt	Detroit	Koppitz	Zynda	Auto City
1934	439	206	177	154	—	229	184	—	48	70
1935	592	389	367	218	35	168	125	—	32	67
1936	732	255	311	341	167	174	127	—	24	75
1937	706	301	270	336	240	198	119	86	14	50
1938	560	379	224	271	164	213	97	70	11	35
1939	536	391	272	238	178	247	95	90	10	36
1940	497	398	335	247	168	248	95	98	9	27
1941	620	428	445	224	154	274	95	94	8	26
1942	621	494	471	291	154	270	102	94	11	5
1943	582	517	541	342	211	299	148	132	13	
1944	632	545	597	400	258	328	209	155	15	
1945	670	554	639	397	264	321	211	162	13	
1946	543	520	635	417	284	281	199	145		
1947	877	792	896	619	284	195	110	59		
1948	822	1,114	1,022	631	200	172	72			
1949	596	1,460	1,142	461	193	149	7(a)			
1950	514	1,652	1,066	356	185	105				
1951	510	1,367	1,023	232	108	44				
1952	671	1,318	1,036	220	170					
1953	1,145	1,465	1,303	314	250					
1954	1,450	1,087	1,216	320	221					
1955	2,153	889	1,009	347	184					
1956	2,709	792	806	290	150					
1957	2,584	676	812	209	136					
1958*	1,923	538	606	169	113					
1959	2,111	571	546	206	174					
1960	2,075	532	399	228	337					
1961	2,029	522	309	240	317					
1962	2,037	493	268	201	276(b)					
1963	2,045	677	216	199						
1964	2,201	651	155(c)	362(d)						
1965	2,402	345		393						
1966	2,418	272(e)		445						
1967	2,403			366						
1968	2,536			395						
1969	2,939			467						

(Continued)

	Stroh	Pfeiffer	Goebel	Altes	E&B	Schmidt	Detroit	Koppitz	Zynda	Auto City
1970	3,276			491						
1971	3,676			469						
1972	4,231			464						
1973	4,649			451						
1974*	4,364			30(f)						
1975	5,133									
1976	5,765									
1977	6,110									
1978	6,330									
1979	6,015									
1980	6,161									
1981	6,185									
1982	22,300(g)									
1983	24,300									
1984	23,900									
1985	23,400(h)									
1986	22,731									
1987	21,508									
1988	20,353									
1989	18,256									
1990	16,199	including contract beers								
1991	14,726	15,228								
1992	13,920	14,493								
1993	12,613	14,027								
1994	11,831	14,405								
1995	10,771	13,624								
1996	12,941	16,552(i)								
1997	15,870	19,689								
1998	13,593	16,249								
1999	3,975	4,297(j)								

(a) Plant closed in February; (b) E&B acquired by Pfeiffer; (c) Goebel bought by Stroh, plant closed and demolished; (d) Altes bought by National of Baltimore, shipments include National Bohemian; (e) Plant closed and production moved to Associated breweries; (f) Brewery closed and production moved to Baltimore; (g) Schaefer and Schlitz acquired; (h) Brewery closed and production moved to other Stroh breweries; (i) G. Heileman acquired July 1996; (j) Brewing buiness sold to Pabst and and Miller April 30, 1999.
*Strike year

Adjunct. Starch sources other than malt that are used for brewing to lighten "body" (mouth feel), especially for the typical U.S. lagers and beers that are shipped. Historically, rice was used in the United States, but since the 1930s, corn has replaced rice to a large extent, now used in the form of syrup and added to the brewkettle.

Ale. A malt beverage having been fermented with a top-fermenting yeast at a higher temperature (60 to 75 degrees Fahrenheit) than lager, usually with more fermentable sugar to create more alcohol, and with minimum aging. True ales are fermented with a top-fermenting yeast, but this is no longer considered practical by many brewers. *See* Yeast.

Barley. One of the small grains (*Hordeum*) suitable for malt, because the seed remains enclosed in the husk after threshing, protecting the grain during the malting process.

Barley, two-row. A barley species in which the two side kernels on each alternating node are undeveloped, giving rise to one row of central kernels on each side of the grain head. Technically, the lateral florets on each spikelet are vestigial. Two-rowed varieties are cultivated in Europe and in drier regions of the northwest.

Barley, six-row. A barley species in which both the central and the side kernels develop. Six-row varieties are cultivated in the Red River Valley in North Dakota, in Minnesota, and to a lesser extent in South Dakota. Six-row barley is the predominant source in malt used for U.S. beers.

Beer barrel (object). A vessel made from oak staves prior to World War II, having a flat top and bottom and bulging side, with an opening for filling at its widest circumference (bung hole), and a smaller opening at the top for emptying ("tapping"). Now often a straight-sided stainless vessel with a single top fitting suitable for automatic cleaning and filling. Usually of half-barrel size.

Beer barrel (volume). The official U.S. measure for beer volume, equivalent to 31 gallons, abbreviated *bbl*.

Bock beer. A darker, heavier beer produced from highly roasted malts, usually prepared for early spring consumption.

Brewhouse. The part of a brewery where wort is produced and boiled, usually the tallest building and considered to be the heart of the operation.

Brewkettle. The vessel in which wort is boiled with hops, historically fabricated out of copper, in recent decades out of stainless steel.

Cooper shop. The place where wooden barrels were made by coopers before metal barrels (now stainless steel) replaced wood after World War II.

Cooperage. Barrel supply.

Crown. The industry term for a bottle cap.

Crowner. A machine used in the bottling operation that seals filled bottles with crowns, now a very high-speed rotary operation.

Fermentation. The process of changing wort into beer by the metabolic action of yeast, in which sugar yields alcohol, carbon dioxide gas, and small amounts of fermentation by-products.

Fermenting cellar. Historically, underground tunnels where wort was fermented in wooden tanks or casks. Since the 1870s, the operation was moved mostly above ground, now often in very tall cylindrical tanks with conical bottoms.

Filler. A circular machine where bottles or cans are filled as the machine rotates. Filling occurs against carbon dioxide counterpressure to avoid foaming and air.

Government cellar. Beer tanks that are usually located below the bottling floor, containing beer that has been metered for tax purposes and is being readied for packaging.

Grant. A receiving vessel—historically, a long, round, horizontal tube open at the top—through which wort passes on its way to the brewkettle, located below the lauter tun and usually close to it.

Grits. Degermed ground corn of a uniform small granular size, which can be boiled with some malt and added to the malt mash as adjunct. Now largely replaced by corn syrup, which is added directly to the brewkettle.

Hops. Commercial cultivars of a climbing vine (*Humulus lupulus*), whose dried conelike flower clusters contain aromatic and bitter flavor compounds, used to flavor beer during boiling since the Middle Ages. Traditionally shipped compressed in large bales, hops are now frequently processed into pellets.

Kilning. The drying of germinated barley at increasing temperatures to preserve the malt and provide the characteristic malt flavor. Higher temperatures will result in caramel-type flavor and darker beer color. *See* Bock beer; Malt

Lager. The typical malt beverage developed in Germany, characterized by a cooler (50 to 65 degrees Fahrenheit) and slower (five to seven days) fermentation than for ale and usually a minimum aging period of two weeks. The historic storage period of several months to aid clarification has been replaced in modern times with a shorter and colder process, and with better filtration equipment. Modern lager beers are of the Bohemian type, pale and with a detectable hop bitterness.

Lambic. A Belgian beer type still brewed in a traditional manner, mostly in abbeys. Fermentation occurs with yeasts present in the fermenting room without addition of a yeast culture. Lambic beers are characterized by a very long aging period, high alcohol content, and a dry, estery, fruity flavor.

Lauter tun. A large, round, shallow vessel where wort is separated from the mash by draining through slotted bottom plates ("false bottom") into the brewkettle.

Malt. Barley that has been steeped–e.g., soaked in cold water–approximately thirty hours, sprouted or germinated four days under cool and moist conditions, and then dried (kilned) in air of increasingly warm temperature.

Mash. The heated mixture of ground malt and water which produces wort for fermentation.

Pilsener, Pilsner. Originally pale beer with a pronounced hop character as developed by the municipal brewery in Pilsen, Bohemia (Czech Republic), now used mostly to describe lager beer.

Racker. the machine where barrels are filled ("racked"), consisting of a raised horizontal tank with several racking "arms" for individual barrels. Manual racking has been replaced in recent decades by automatic keg washing and filling lines.

Seamer. A high-speed rotary machine that seals lids on cans.

Soaker. A very large machine for cleaning returnable bottles, which travel through zones of hot alkaline solutions, followed by several rinses with hot and cold water.

Stock house. *See* Storage cellar.

Storage cellar. Historically, similar to fermenting cellar, except that river or lake ice was used for cooling before the use of mechanical refrigeration. The term continues to be used a century after the operation moved above ground. Also Stock house.

Wort. The sugary liquid extracted from a mash, consisting primarily of maltose.

Yeast (brewing strains). A unicellular organism (*Saccharomyces*) that reproduces by budding and is used to ferment wort into beer. Top-fermenting strains are used for traditional ales; after the fermentation is completed, the yeast floats to the surface, where it is skimmed off. Typical lager beer is fermented with bottom-fermenting strains. The yeast settles to the bottom ("flocculates") in tanks that often have conical bottoms.

TERMS RELATED TO COLLECTIBLES

Corner sign. A curved metal sign supplied by breweries to taverns before Prohibition, to be mounted at the entrance or the building's corners.

Lithograph. A colored print produced by the method of printing individual colors sequentially from a large polished limestone, a cumbersome process but the only method known to produce vivid colored art in quantity before the invention of rotary presses.

Reverse-on-glass ("R-O-G"). Glass signs created between about 1850 and 1940 which were painted in reverse and mounted with the clear back pane facing the viewer.

Shell. A thin and usually short glass, commonly etched with a brewery's name, brand, and logo, which may also depict the brewery. Originally supplied by breweries to taverns before Prohibition, now very collectible.

Slug plate. A circular, interchangeable glass insert in a bottle mold that carries the embossing of the brewery's name and location, used in bottle manufacture about 1885–1900.

Stock, as in Stock tray. A generic metal or paper advertising already in the manufacturer's stock, which could be sold to various clients by adding the proper corporate and brand names. Typical brewery stock designs showed women, women's faces, a stag, or certain scenes. Stock items were obviously much less expensive to purchase than ordering a custom design.

Tin-over-cardboard ("T-O-C"). Metal signs, usually rectangular and often embossed, where the printed sheet metal ("tin") was crimped over a cardboard backing and equipped with a cord or chain for hanging. Commonly used in the 1930s.

Tip tray. A small, usually four-inch-diameter, tray with product advertising, believed to have been used to present the bill in restaurants or bars.

REFERENCES

Much of the detailed information about the breweries of Detroit comes from the directories of the City of Detroit in the Burton Historical Collection, Detroit Public Library, and from five books: C. M. Burton, *The City of Detroit, Michigan 1701–1922,* (Detroit-Chicago, S. J. Clark Publishing Co., 1922); *Detroit of Today: The City of the Straights* (Detroit-Chicago: Phoenix Publishing Co., 1893); Richard Edwards, *Industries of Michigan: City of Detroit* (New York Historical Publishing Co., 1880); J. W. F. Leonard, *The Industries of Detroit* (Detroit: J. M. Elstner & Co., 1887); and *One Hundred Years of Brewing* (Chicago and New York: H. S. Rich & Co., 1903). These are cited below by author, title, and page number.

Carlson's Brewery Research of Walker, Minnesota, abstracted entries for Detroit breweries from *The Brewer's Journal* and *Western Brewer* on events between about 1890 and 1910.

Important sources in the archive of the Stroh Brewery Company were a booklet published for the ninth annual convention of the Master Brewers Association, held in Detroit in 1897; the annual reports of the Investment Statistics Company, Detroit, particularly for 1934–1938; annual "Blue Books" published by *Modern Brewery Age* for information on brands and staff, beginning with 1941; and various brewing industry magazines. Term papers on Detroit breweries written for Professor Gordon Grosscup, Anthropology Department, Wayne State University, were also reviewed. Richard L. Sweet's *Directory of Canadian Breweries* (2nd. Ed., Saskatoon, Sask., 1996) was the source of information on the early breweries on the Canadian side of the Detroit River. An article by Mary Hunt in the December 1979 *Ann Arbor Observer,* "Brewed in Ann Arbor," and early Ann Arbor city directories were very helpful.

CHAPTER 2

Cleveland Herald, May 14, 1829. Cited in Baron, Stanley, *Brewed in America: A History of Beer and Ale in the United States.* Boston: Little Brown & Co., 1962.

Detroit Daily Advertiser, Nov. 21, 1861: 1.

Detroit Free Press, March 6, 1889: 8; March 7, 1889: 5; May 13, 1889.

Essex County Emigrant & Western District Advertiser, Dec. 1, 1831.

Free Press and Advocate, Sept. 7, 22, and 29, and weekly in October, 1831.

Milwaukee Sentinel, Nov. 28, 1892: 1, 2.

CHAPTER 3

"Bernhard Stroh's New Brewery," *Detroit Tribune,* Aug. 20, 1867, p. 1.

"Betting the Barn at Stroh," *Fortune,* May 31, 1982, p. 118.

Cauer, Caroline. *400 Jahre Kirn.* Bad Kreuznach: Harrach, 1980.

"Coors Wins Last Call," *Detroit Free Press,* Sept. 26, 1989, p. 1.

Detroit Free Press, June 11, 1891, p. 1; May 3, 1958, p. 1; April 29, 1964, p. 4A; June 8, 1983, p. 12.

"Guinness to Buy Largest Brewer in Spain," *New York Times,* Nov. 22, 1990, p. F1.

"Last Hurrah for Stroh's Crews," *Detroit Free Press,* May 26, 1985, p. 1H.

"A New Brewery," *Detroit Advertiser & Tribune,* May 14, 1867, p. 4.

One Hundred Years of Brewing, p. 251.

"The Stroh Brewery Company in Detroit, Michigan," *Brewers Digest,* August 1968, pp. 28–51.

"Stroh to Buy Heileman Brewing, Ending Hicks, Muse Beer Bath," *Wall Street Journal,* March 1, 1996, p. B4.

CHAPTER 4
Duncan

American Biographical History of Eminent and Self-made Men. Part 1. Cincinnati: Western Biographical Publishing Co., 1878.

Detroit Free Press, Dec. 19, 1877; Aug. 5, 1960.

Evening Post (Windsor), Nov. 26, 1897, p. 3.

Ross, Robert, and George Catlin. *Landmarks of Detroit.* Detroit: The Evening News Association, 1898.

Hawley

American Biographical History of Eminent and Self-made Men. Part 1. Cincinnati: Western Biographical Publishing Co, 1878. p. 68.

Baron, Stanley. *Brewed in America.* Boston: Little Brown and Co., 1962, p. 170. (Early Hawley history.)

Detroit Free Press, Nov. 12, 1910. (Obituary of H. W. Rickel, leasing of malthouse.)

Johnson

Edwards, *Industries of Michigan,* p. 285.

Moloney

Burton, *City of Detroit, Michigan,* p. 37.

Detroit News, Aug. 23, 1893, p. 7.

Edwards, *Industries of Michigan,* p. 279.

Leonard, *Industries of Detroit,* p. 255.

Western Brewer 24 (1899): 383, 398.

St. Louis

Detroit of Today, p. 221.

Western Brewer 18 (1894): 431 (sale of firm); 24 (1899): 349 (lawsuit).

Union

Edwards, *Industries of Michigan,* p. 288.

One Hundred Years of Brewing, p. 512.

Ross, Robert, and George Catlin. *Landmarks of Detroit.* Detroit: The Evening News Association, 1898.

CHAPTER 5

Bavarian

Detroit Free Press, May 13, 1889, p. 2. (Plant sold to English syndicate.)

Columbia

Brewers Journal 41 (1916): 80. (Walker chosen brewmaster.)

One Hundred Years of Brewing, p. 340.

Endriss

Detroit Free Press, May 15, 1889, p. 4. (Plans for closing.)

Edwards, *Industries of Michigan,* p. 213.

Leonard, *Industries of Detroit,* p. 225.

Western Brewer 23 (1898): 1400. (New incorporation.)

Germania

Brewers Journal 23 (1899): 480.

Western Brewer 23 (1898): 1582.

Ochsenhirt/Home

Brewers Journal 26 (1902): 317. (Plant closing.)

Edwards, *Industries of Michigan,* p. 186.

Koch

Edwards, *Industries of Michigan,* p. 147.

Mann

Detroit Free Press, May 15, 1889: 4.

Edwards, *Industries of Michigan,* p. 147.

Dittmer/Phoenix

Brewers Journal 17 (1893): 208 (sale of brewery); 18 (1894): 210 (fire).

Detroit Free Press, July 22, 1914. (Obituary)

Edwards, *Industries of Michigan,* p. 131.

Leonard, *Industries of Detroit,* p. 174.

Ruoff

Brewers Journal 29 (1905): 546.

Detroit Free Press, Dec. 26, 1915. (Obituary.)

Detroit News, Jan. 22, 1935.
Edwards, *Industries of Michigan,* p. 154.

CHAPTER 6
Auto City

American Brewers Review 25 (1911): 109, 410. (Plant construction.)
Brewers Journal 35 (Dec. 1911): 88. (Incorporation.)
Brewery Age, Sept. 1933, p. 90 (plant description, stock offering); April 1938, p. 60 (obituary).
Detroit Times Sunday, Sept. 8, 1935: 11. (New brewhouse.)

Wayne

American Brewer, Jan. 1934, p. 48 (new brewery); July 1934: 48 (more capacity).
Brewery Age, Jan. 1935, 72. (Champagne Type Extra Pale.)

Zoltowski

One Hundred Years of Brewing, p. 510.

Zynda

Brewers Journal 19 (1895): 393; 26 (1902): 472.
Burton, *City of Detroit, Michigan,* vol. 5, p. 1050.
Detroit News Dec. 13, 1913, p. 1 (breach of promise suit); Dec. 30, 1927, p. 36 (obituary).
Gherkiere, J. Term paper, Dec. 1970.
Zynda, Frank. Interview with author. Detroit, Michigan, 1994.

CHAPTER 7
Union

American Brewer, Mar. 1935, p. 50.
Brewers Journal 22 (1898): 530 (new brewery); 23 (1899) 69, 226 (officers).
Modern Brewery Age, Feb. 1934, p. 70.
Western Brewer 50 (1918): 181. (Name change, near beer.)

East Side

Brewers Journal 17 (1893): 256, 344; 28 (1904): 315; 30 (1906): 486.
Detroit Free Press, Feb. 18, 1929, p. 19. (Obituary.)

Independent

American Brewer, June 1934, p. 48 (packing company); Mar. 1935, p. 50.
Brewers Journal 30 (1906): 486 (new officers), 583 (new brewery).
Brewers News, Jan. 5, 1933: 5. (Judgment by Master of Chancery.)
Brewery Age, Sept. 1933, p. 90 (new company); July 1934, p. 75 (plans for new plant).

Mutual Brewing

Brewers Journal 18 (1894): 248.
One Hundred Years of Brewing, p. 510.

CHAPTER 8
Bache

Brewery Age Buyers Guide, 1936. (Management.)

Fort Dearborn

American Brewer, July 1934, p. 46. (Board members.)
Brewery Age, Sept. 1933, p. 90 (organization by E. R. Stroh); May 1934, p. 67 (site acquired, offices opened); Aug. 1936, p. 72 (reorganization).
Modern Brewery, Nov. 1933, p. 10.

Kraftig

Brewery Age, July 1936, p. 74; Aug. 1936, p. 72.

Michigan

Brewers Journal 36 (1912): 337; 37 (1913): 185, 188; 40 (1916): 298; 41 (1917): 295.
Detroit Free Press advertisements, Dec. 30, 1912; July 1 and 15, 1913.

Old Holland

Brewery Age, Dec. 1935, p. 78; July 1936, p. 75.

Regal

Brewery Age, July 1934, p. 66; Aug. 1934, p. 74.
Brewery Age Buyers Guide, 1936.
Investment Statistics Co. *Annual Report.* Detroit, 1937, 1938.

Wagner

Brewery Age, Feb. 1936, p. 73; May 1936, p. 31.
Modern Brewery Sept. 1935, p. 30.

Walker

Brewers Journal, 41 (1916): 80.
Detroit Free Press, Feb. 12, 1953.
Rickabus, Mrs. Gertrude. Correspondence and interview with author. Mio, Michigan, 1993.

CHAPTER 9
West Side

American Brewer, March 1935, p. 50 (new board of directors); April 1935, p. 52 (new ad campaign); Aug. 1935, p. 60 (stockholder suit).
Brewery Age, Feb. 1934, pp. 79–80 (history and current developments); June 1934, p. 82; Aug. 1936, p. 60 (election of McCormick); Jan. 1938, p. 64 (trustee appointed); April 1938, p. 82 (obituary of Oswald Kulewatz); June 1938, p. 76 (reorganization plan).
Burton, *City of Detroit, Michigan,* vol. 4, pp. 463, 906. (Biographies of Armin and Herman Darmstaetter.)
Detroit Free Press, June 3, 1898, p. 5. (Obituary of Jacob Darmstaetter); Oct. 4, 1936 (obituary of A. T. Montreuil).
Detroit of Today, p. 205. (Family biography.)
Leonard, *Industries of Detroit,* 252. (Description of brewery.)
The Month at Mundus, Carl J. Darmstaetter, ed. Vol. 1 (1933–1934). Courtesy Charles Walter. (Business developments at Mundus.)
Schachtner, Frank X. Oral and written recollections, 1981.
Williams, Nellie G. Term paper.

American

Brewery Age, Sept. 1933, p. 90.
Brewers Journal 26 (1902): 516.
Burton, *City of Detroit, Michigan,* vol. 4, p. 764.
One Hundred Years of Brewing, p. 510.
Wasily, Gregory. Term paper.

Kling

American Brewer, Feb. 1938, p. 21. (Reopening in Flint.)
Brewers Journal 17 (1893): 303 (fire); 33 (1909): 169 (racking capacity).
Burton, *City of Detroit,* Michigan, vol. 4, p. 563. (Biography.)
Detroit Free Press, Jan. 28, 1936.
Detroit News, Dec. 4, 1921. (Brewery demolished, interview with K. Kling.)
Detroit of Today, p. 188.
Edwards, *Industries of Michigan,* p. 110.

Voigt

American Brewer, July 1934, p. 46.
Brewers Journal 17 (1893): 428 (depressed state of business); 18 (1894): 523 (deficit); 24 (1900): 160, 220 (sale to E. W. Voigt).
Brewery Age, June 1934, p. 83.
Burton, *City of Detroit, Michigan,* vol. 3, pp. 30–34.
Burton Library Scrapbook 5A, 1871. (Edward buys brewery from father.)
Findlay, Steve. *[Royal Oak] Daily Tribune,* Dec. 4, 1892, p. 8.
Detroit Free Press, Nov. 10, 1878, p. 5.
Illustrated Detroit. Detroit: Harry Hook, 1891.
Kiessel, Willian C. Private correspondence with author. Bearsville, New York.
One Hundred Years of Brewing, p. 426.
Western Brewer 15 (1890): 2276; 16 (1891): 2342.

CHAPTER 10
Detroit

Brewers Journal, 17 (1893): 248, 428
Detroit of Today, p. 116.
Edwards, *Industries of Michigan,* p. 154.
One Hundred Years of Brewing, p. 429
Western Brewer 23 (1898): 1411–13.

E&B

American Brewer, Jan. 1936, p. 74. (Obituary of A. Ekhardt, Jr.)
Brewers Journal 19 (1895): 291. (Purchase of Westphalia.)
Brewery Age, March 1938, pp. 69–70.
Eastern Market News, Aug. 1980, p. 1. (Purchase by J. L. Hirt & Co.)
Investment Statistics Co. *Annual Report.* Detroit, 1938.
Leonard, *Industries of Detroit,* p. 203.

Koppitz

Brewers Digest, Feb. 1941, p. 50. (Hicks appointed, 1940 sales.)
Brewers Journal 23 (1899): 274 (officers), 534 (Preston); 28 (1904): 213 (officers).
Detroit Free Press, Oct. 4, 1936, p. 10. (Old firm in new setting.)
Illustrated Detroit. Detroit: Harry Hook, 1891.
Marquis, Albert Nelson, ed. *The Book of Detroiters.* Chicago: A. N. Marquis & Co., 1908, 1914.
Master Brewers Association of America, convention book, 1935, p. 40.
Modern Brewer, May 1936, pp. 30–33 (history and new officers); April 1937, pp. 37–64 (detailed description of new brewery).
Modern Brewery Age, Aug. 1942, p. 57 (new officers); June 1944, p. 68; Aug. 1947, p. 88 (Hicks returns to agency).
One Hundred Years of Brewing, p. 510.
Reed, Francine M. Interview with Kenneth Koppitz, Dec. 12, 1968. Term paper prepared for Anthropology Department, Wayne State University.

Tivoli

Biographie Nationale de Belgique 44, part 1. Brussels, 1985, pp. 118–121.
Brewery Age, March 1935, p. 28.
Brogniez, Raymond. Correspondence with author, May 20, 1995.
Burton, *City of Detroit Michigan,* vol. 4, p. 515.
One Hundred Years of Brewing, p. 512.
Western Brewer 23 (1898): 1231–1233.

Schmidt

American Brewer, Jan. 1934, p. 48.
Brewers Journal 25 (1900): 67; 26 (1901): 22.
Brewery Age, March 1938, p. 68.
Investment Statistics Co. *Annual Report.* Detroit, 1937.
Edwards, *Industries of Michigan,* 250.

CHAPTER 11

Brewers Journal, June 1941, pp. 2–12.
Brewery Age, Sept. 1933, p. 90; Feb. 1938, p. 59.
Detroit Times, Jan. 10, 1954.
Edwards, *Industries of Michigan*, 243.
Master Brewers Association, 1897 Convention Booklet, p. 29.
Michigan Manufacturing and Financial Record, Aug. 4, 1947, p. 6.
Moon, Philip, interview with author, 1993.
One Hundred Years of Brewing, p. 510.

CHAPTER 12

Brewers Journal 19 (1895): 532 (construction); 26 (1902): 270 (incorporators).
Burton, *City of Detroit, Michigan,* vol. 3, p. 384 (Biography.)
Detroit Free Press, Nov. 23, 1976. (Obituary of Alfred Epstein.)
Epstein, Herbert. Interview with author, 1993.
One Hundred Years of Brewing, p. 510.
Pfeiffer Brewing Co., annual reports, 1934–1967. Collection of James Joswiak.

CHAPTER 13

Burns, Priscilla. Interview with author. Detroit, Mich., 1995.
Edwards, Ben. Interview with author. Detroit, Mich., 1995.

CHAPTER 14

American Brewer, July 1934, p. 46. (Enlarged capacity.)
Burton Library Scrapbook 61: April 21, 1913, p. 141. (Harry sells interest to Armin.)
Detroit Journal, Nov. 12, 1910. (Obituary of Henry Rickel.)
Leonard, *Industries of Detroit*, p. 205. (Early Rickel history.)

CHAPTER 15

Hooper

Envelope with rubber stamping mailed Aug. 28, 1862. Stroh Archive.

Northern

History of Washtenaw County, Michigan. Chicago: Charles C. Chapman Co., 1881, p. 943.
Stevens, Wystan. *Report for the Ann Arbor Historical Commission,* 1972.

Ann Arbor

History of Washtenaw County, Michigan. Chicago: Charles C. Chapman Co., 1881, p. 943.
Hunt, Mary. "Beer the Way Ann Arbor Liked It!" *Ann Arbor News,* March 16, 1975.
Salem, F. W. *Beer—Its History and Its Economic Value as a National Beverage.* Hartford, Conn.:
   F. W. Salem & Co., 1880.

Brewpubs and Microbreweries

Detroit Free Press, May 24, 1995.

CHAPTER 16

Miller

Burley and Platt. *Lake Shore Gazeteer and Business Directory*, 1868–1869. Buffalo: The Sage,
   Sons & Co., 1868.
Map of Mt. Clemens (original in Michigan State Archives, Lansing), 1859.

Biewer

Eldridge, Robert P. *Past and Present of Macomb County,* 1905, pp. 204, 207.
M. A. Leeson & Co. *History of Macomb County*, 1882, p. 566.
Macomb County directory, 1896–1897.

Mount Clemens

Brewers Journal 30 (1905): 207. (Oberstadt to become manager.)
Brewery Age, July 1934, p. 67; Aug. 1936, p. 72; April 1938, p. 64.
Detroit Free Press, June 25, 1995, J6: 1. (Belgian workers.)
Freimann, Leonard. Compilation in Mt. Clemens Public Library.
Macomb County directories.

CHAPTER 17

Dawson

Michigan Gazeteer and Business Directory, 1856–57, 1860–61.
Pontiac and Flint directory, 1870–1871.

Carharrt

Pontiac and Flint directory, 1870–1871.

Pontiac

One Hundred Years of Brewing, p. 512.
Pontiac city directories, 1904, 1907, 1912, 1915.

Wolverine

Brewery Age, April 1934, p. 70. (Stock offering, capacity, officers.)
Pontiac city directories, 1935–1941.
Pontiac Daily Press, Dec. 16, 1933 (draft beer to be released); April 4, 1934; May 26, 1934 (bottling plant completed, officers); Nov. 16, 1936 (description of buildings); July 30, 1938 (financial data, reduced loss). Clippings from the collection of Paul Rothrock.

CHAPTER 18

A comprehensive article on the British-American and Walkerville Brewing companies and the Windsor Brewery of J. J. Guittard appeared in *The Evening Record,* Nov. 26, 1897, p. 3 ("Essex County's Three Breweries").

Windsor

Sweet, *Directory of Canadian Breweries,* p. 93.

Hofer

Benoit, Milton. Interview. *Windsor Star,* May 11, 1985.
Gervais, C. H. *The Rumrunners.* Thornhill, Ontario: Firefly Books, Ltd., 1980.
Sweet, *Directory of Canadian Breweries,* p. 79.

Riverside

Rosenbusch family oral history.
Sweet, *Directory of Canadian Breweries,* p. 77.

Tecumseh

Stock promotion for Old Comrades Brewing Co., Ltd. Collection of Lawrence Sherk.
Sweet, *Directory of Canadian Breweries,* p. 83.
Windsor Daily Star, April 24, 1954, sec. 3, p. 14; Nov. 26, 1956, sec. 5, p. 5; Sept. 27, 1963, 5.

Carling

Evening Record, Dec. 17, 1904, p. 8 (detailed history); April 24, 1954, sec. 3, p. 14 (recent history of Irion and Taylor period).

Walkerville

Sweet, *Directory of Canadian Breweries,* p. 90.
Windsor Daily Star, March 12, 1928, p. 3; Nov. 26, 1956, p. 5 (plant closing).

CHAPTER 19

Marx

American Brewer, Aug. 1934, p. 57; Jan. 1935, p. 58.
Wyandotte Herald, Jan. 14, 1910. Wyandotte Historical Museum.
Wyandotte Historical Museum. Collection of newspaper clippings, March 1933 to May 1941.

Eureka

Wyandotte Herald, Aug. 22, 1890; Aug. 22, 1930.
Wyandotte city directories, 1898, 1901–1902.

CHAPTER 20

Grob

History of Washtenaw County, Michigan. Chicago: Charles C. Chapman Co., 1881, p. 1207.
Ypsilanti city directories, 1873–1874.

Eagle, Swayne's

History of Washtenaw County, Michigan. Chicago: Charles C. Chapman Co., 1881, p. 1141.

Foerster

Ann Arbor and Ypsilanti Directory. 1883.
History of Washtenaw County, Michigan. Chicago: Charles C. Chapman Co., 1881, p. 1141.
Investment Statistics Co. *Annual Report.* Detroit, 1937.
Mills, Glen V. *Ann Arbor and Ypsilanti Directory.* Ann Arbor: The Inland Press, 1893, p. 318.
One Hundred Years of Brewing, p. 428.
Ypsilanti Press, June 5, 1962.
Salem, F. W. *Beer—Its History and Its Economic Value as a National Beverage.* Hartford, CT: F. W. Salem & Co., 1880, p. 219.
Sullivan, Michael J. Personal recollections. 1986.

BIBLIOGRAPHY

BOOKS

American Biographical History of Eminent and Self-Made Men. Part 1. Cincinnati: Western Biographical Publishing Co, 1878.

Baron, Stanley. *Brewed in America: A History of Beer and Ale in the United States.* Boston: Little Brown and Co., 1962.

Beakes, Samuel W. *Past and Present of Washtenaw County Michigan.* Chicago: S. J. Clarke Publishing Co., 1906.

Bull, Donald, Manfred Friedrich, and Robert Gottschalk. *American Breweries.* Trumbull, CT: Bullworks, 1984.

Burton, C. M. *The City of Detroit, Michigan 1701–1922.* Detroit-Chicago: S. J. Clark Publishing Co., 1922.

Detroit of Today: The City of the Straits. Detroit-Chicago: Phoenix Publishing Co., 1893.

Edwards, Richard. *Industries of Michigan: City of Detroit.* New York Historical Publishing Co., 1880.

Eldredge, Robert F. *Past and Present of Macomb County.* Chicago: S. J. Clarke Publishing Co., 1905.

Gervais, C. H. *The Rumrunners.* Thornhill, Ontario: Firefly Books, Ltd., 1980.

History of Washtenaw County, Michigan. Chicago: Charles C. Chapman Co., 1881.

Illustrated Detroit. Detroit: Harry Hook, 1893.

Leonard, J. W. *The Industries of Detroit.* Detroit: J. M. Elstner & Co., 1887.

Loomis, *Michigan Biographical Index.* Vol. 4. 1946.

Marquis, Albert Nelson, ed. *The Book of Detroiters.* Chicago: A. N. Marquis & Co., 1908, 1914.

Mason, Philip P. *Rumrunning and the Roaring Twenties: Prohibition on the Michigan-Ontario Waterway.* Detroit: Wayne State University Press, 1995.

Master Brewers Convention Program, Detroit 1897.

Miller, Carl H. *Breweries of Cleveland.* Cleveland: Schnitzelbank Press, 1998.

Modern Brewery Age Blue Book. Stamford, CT: Modern Brewery Age Publishing Co., 1941–1990.

One Hundred Years Of Brewing. Chicago and New York: H. S. Rich & Co., 1903.

Salem, F. W. *Beer—Its History and Its Economic Value as a National Beverage.* Hartford, CT: F. W. Salem & Co., 1880.

Shade, Louis. *The Brewer's Handbook for 1876.* Washington, D.C.

Sweet, Richard L. *The Directory of Canadian Breweries.* 2nd ed. Saskatoon, Sask.: self-published, 1996.

Tovey's Official Brewer's and Maltster's Directory, 1884.

Youngstrand, C. O., ed. *Our Michigan Friends "As We See 'Em."* Detroit: Newspaper Cartoonists' Association of Michigan, William Graham Printing Co., 1905.

PERIODICALS

Michigan Brewery Record. Detroit: Investment Statistics Company, 1934–1938.

Beer Production by Michigan Breweries. Lansing: Michigan Liquor Control Commission, 1933–1977.

American Brewer

Brewers Journal

Michigan Volksblatt

Modern Brewer

Modern Brewery Age

Western Brewer